Into One Body . . . by the Cross

Into One Body
. . . by the Cross

VOLUME TWO

Karl A. Olsson

ABBREVIATIONS

BOS	*By One Spirit*
CW	*The Covenant Weekly*
FF	*A Family of Faith*
YB	*Covenant Yearbook*

ISBN 0-910-452-64-4
Copyright © 1986 by Covenant Press
3200 West Foster Avenue
Chicago, Illinois 60625
312-478-4676

Design and layout: Mary M. Helfrich
Production assistants: Jane K. Swanson-Nystrom, Janet Meyers,
Gregory Sager, Jane Nordeen

THE CORPORATE SEAL

At the first Annual Meeting of the Covenant in Princeton, Illinois, following the organizational meeting of February 1885, the concluding action was the adoption of a corporate seal with an appropriate design. Because the design of the seal so well expresses the spirit of The Evangelical Covenant Church today, a few words of narrative and interpretation have been thought helpful.

In the official minutes for the closing session of September 30, 1885, there is the following entry: "The decision was made to produce a corporate seal of the following specifications: the name of the Covenant; the seal of a recumbent lamb and two joined hands, because the Covenant owes its continued existence to a true union in Jesus and is founded upon the crucified and risen Savior; and a motto, 'Conjuncti in Christo' [united or joined in Christ]."

Two significant details of the seal are not included in the description. The first is the resting of the lamb on a copy of the Scriptures, as representing the Word and its fulfillment. The second is the placement of a resurrection cross between the lamb's feet. In some medieval representations of the Lamb of God the triumphant cross appears in a banner or pennon carried by the lamb.

The Covenant seal has been used as the cover design of this book and reinforces the title which is taken from Ephesians 2:15,16, and reads "that he might create in himself one new man in place of the two, so making peace, and might reconcile us both to God in *one body through the cross* . . ." (italics mine).

Karl A. Olsson

Acknowledgments

In completing this task I have been aware of all those persons, both living and dead, who have contributed to its substance and spirit and to whom I owe a debt of great thankfulness.

They include an impressive cadre of in-house historians: C.M. Young-quist, Josephine Princell, Axel Mellander, John G. Princell, E.A. Skogs-bergh, C.J. Nyvall, David Nyvall, Hjalmar Sundquist, C.V. Bowman, Carl A. Backstrom, E. Gustav Johnson, Eric G. Hawkinson, Earl C. Dahlstrom, L. Arden Almquist, Zenos Hawkinson, Earnest S. Larson, Oscar E. Olson, Glenn P. Anderson, J. Irving Erickson, and Phillip J. Anderson. They also include a number of students who in graduate papers and essays have significantly supplemented our knowledge of the Covenant.

Let me add to that honor roll of Covenant archivists: John Peterson, E. Gustav Johnson, A.M. Freedholm, Eric G. Hawkinson, and Sigurd F. Westberg, whose work in gathering, sorting, cataloguing, translating, and systematically storing the growing volume of historical data of the Covenant has given evidence of great devotion and unflagging energy. Behind these efforts of the loyal servants of the church must be seen the quality work of the Covenant Historical Commission, which has provided the vision, the strategy, and the funds for this crucial development. Reinforcing the work of the Commission on Covenant History has been the interest of the entire denomination focused in the devoted personal leadership of its presidents: T.W. Anderson, Clarence A. Nelson, and Milton B. Engebretson.

My work could not have been completed without the involvement and support of James R. Hawkinson, executive secretary of publications, and especially Jane K. Swanson-Nystrom and Naomi Wood, whose work in fine-tuning the manuscript and readying it for the final printing has been most meaningful.

Indispensable has been the contribution of two persons, very close to me personally and professionally: my daughter, and for several years highly valued secretary, Sarah McCarthy, and my good companion, advisor, faith exemplar, and wife for now fifty-one years, Sally.

Foreword

Assigned by the editorial committee for the Covenant's Centennial (1885-1985) to write this book, Dr. Olsson here completes the story begun in Volume One (Covenant Press, 1985). As Milton B. Engebretson, president of The Evangelical Covenant Church, wrote in his foreword to that volume, the whole of this Centennial history "is a much needed view of the struggle and pain experienced in producing the mystique that embodies the freedom espoused and enjoyed by the Covenant Church today."

Here our emergence as a part of Christ's body, the Church, is carried forward from the mid-1930's, where Volume One left off. This particular book, therefore, catalogues the second 50 years of our history, roughly equivalent to the Americanization of the Covenant and its development to the present in the new soils of the United States and Canada.

Because history is of a piece, and because it all belongs ultimately to God, readers of both these volumes will benefit from Dr. Olsson's consistent attempts at relating our religious history to the broader world in which, at any given point, it was emerging.

Thoughtful students of the history will also do well to ponder with Dr. Olsson the future that is even now breaking in upon us. To know what our forebears believed and intended is neither to deny our right to be nor to free us of responsibility for those coming after. Every present moment needs rooting in eternal realities if it is to participate meaningfully in God's future for his Church and his world.

May he, therefore, crown every sincere effort to look with Dr. Olsson backward and forward, that Christ's body may be built up and his name glorified among us.

James R. Hawkinson
Executive Secretary of Covenant Publications

CONTENTS
VOLUME TWO

Introduction

Some twenty years ago, a learned and judicious churchman of a sister denomination reviewed *By One Spirit*, the recently published history of The Evangelical Covenant Church. His comment, after reading the book, was made in the form of a question, gently ironic, "By what spirit?"

Conrad Bergendoff's real or feigned puzzlement was not unrelated to the comparative calm of the history of his own denomination, the Augustana Synod, which in 1962 was merged with other Lutheran bodies to form the Lutheran Church in America. Since the Augustana Synod was established in 1860, it had experienced a century of independence before allowing itself to be mortised into the larger structure.

When the histories of the two denominations, i.e., the Augustana Synod and the Covenant Church are placed side by side, the contrast between them is obvious and, despite striking similarities of tradition and mood, somewhat painful. The communion of Swedish Lutheran churches, which began in the 1850s, became after a decade of struggle more and more doctrinally Lutheran, and after 1867, a stable and valued member of the Lutheran Council. The forebears of the Covenant Church, became in the period 1875-1885 less Lutheran and less and less any one thing; in its organizational process the Covenant Church set sail on the turbulent confessional waters, as I have noted elsewhere, without human astrolabe, sextant, or compass. It chose to be guided only by the eternal stars of the scriptural galaxy.

In reviewing a hundred years of Covenant history under the banner of Psalm 119:63 "I am a companion of all them that fear thee, and of them that keep thy precepts" (AV), it becomes clear that the ever-blooming promise of the denomination has been this amplitude of community that seems to offer almost total freedom of thought and action within the boundaries of Scripture. It is equally clear, on the other hand, that the amplitude has posed a vexing perennial problem. Doctrinal spaciousness has not infrequently bordered on anarchy. A constant struggle has been required in order to establish and maintain a denominational identity.

In this the Covenant Church has not been unlike the national envelope in which it originated and grew. American democracy, although zealously embraced by most of our citizens, has never been defined in terms of a precise political doctrine. American democracy also has a Bible—albeit secular—that is, a composite of the ideas and insights culled from the Judaeo-Christian Scriptures, from Plato and Aristotle, Cicero, Thomas Hobbes, John Locke, Montesquieu, Thomas Paine, Thomas Jefferson, and a list of other distinguished presidents, judges, lawyers, orators, poets, philosophers, novelists, and playwrights. But democracy is experienced and felt rather than rationally known, and is less determined by precise, codified statutes than by an intuitive certainty and transmitted within a community of shared experience and agreed-upon human values.

This analogy may be helpful if we do not seek to make its application too precise and if we draw from it only what is intended. My point with it is only to emphasize that, like American democracy, Covenant piety has emerged in a conscious communal setting where propositional truths and even traditional norms, though meaningful, have carried less weight than the process of living together as a family of faith and applying principle to life through shared reflection and day-to-day decisions.

Political faith has helped to shape the American community; scriptural faith has shaped the Covenant Church. But the analogy does not allow us to confuse the faiths. American faith at its best chooses not to absolutize its principles. Covenant faith is based on the strong belief that the Holy Scriptures, the Old and the New Testaments, are the "Word of God and the only perfect rule for faith, doctrine, and conduct."

What this means for the Covenant Church is that its aims, and to a large extent its methods, are determined by the Scriptures. God's design, as it emerges in the Scriptures, is to fashion the body of Christ through the cross and through the healing, reconciling, and unifying power of the Holy Spirit. Hence the ultimate nature of this church body in history (i.e. the Covenant Church) cannot be dissociated from God's purpose.

By contrast American democracy, although informed by many of the values that the Church cherishes, cannot draw its ultimate design or even its guidelines form the Judaeo-Christian Scriptures. By a series of decisions made throughout its history as well as by a process of default the United States has chosed to dissociate itself formally from any specific religious value system. This does not mean that many, perhaps the majority of Americans, do not subscribe to Judaeo-Christian values. Indeed these values may emerge as implied norms in our making and interpreting of law. But formally America is not and indeed cannot be a Christian nation.

But the Covenant Church, like many of its sister denominations, is a Christian church based on biblical faith. A hundred years ago it made a historic decision to risk doctrinal freedom within scriptural faith. This might be said to be the substance of its constitution. Throughout its history the Covenant Church has no doubt been tempted, in the midst of the embarrassment of its doctrinal freedom, to change the constitution and establish more precise theological norms. Some of the faithful have wanted to return to the Lutheran confessions of its origins. Others have argued for an evangelical stance as reflected in the confessional statements of the National Association of Evangelicals or of a number of cognate denominations.

Now undoubtedly there may be greater hearts ease and tranquility in such prescriptions than in the jangled tunes with which theological diversity assaults our ears. Someday we may have to conclude that the Swedish Lutherans and not the Rosenian Mission Friends were right when in 1867 they cast their vote for a more rigid Lutheranism. I need not remind my readers that the power to make or to resist such a decision is not mine.

However, this book will be written from the perspective that the hundred years of history under the guidelines of Psalm 119:63 and the present constitution have been preponderantly good and should be celebrated as to the greater glory of God, *Ad majorem gloriam Dei.*

Hence, I see my task in this book as finding the values in all the influences that have shaped us whether these values have emerged at the center or periphery of our life together. In carrying out this task I shall seek to recognize the unity of faith *in* and *of* our diversity during the past century and to allow that diverse history under the guidance of the Holy Spirit to suggest effective guidelines for our decisions during the next century if such an opportunity is vouchsafed the denomination.

In performing this task I claim no ultimate objectivity. Like everyone else who is part of the process, I am a biased observer of it. But despite this, I would pray for the gifts of truth and fairness so that I may work prudently among motives and avoid presenting those who agree with me in fairer colors than those who choose to disagree. In all of this I believe that it is God who cooperates for good with those who love him and are called according to his purpose.

PART FOUR

An Americanized
Church
1936-1946

CHAPTER TWENTY-NINE

On the Road to War

The "mid-channel" of the Covenant paralleled some major developments in the larger world. It is possible to speak of a coincidence of peaks or valleys. The Depression had now reached its low point, at least in the United States. Financially things were not yet significantly better, but a hope had been kindled that they might be moving out of the trough. The country's agricultural woes, epitomized in foreclosures, "dust bowls," and abandoned farms (now starkly exposed in the photography and reporting of the new "news magazines" like *Life* and *Look*), were beginning to give way to variant themes. These new themes were certainly not less gloomy, but they were emerging at some distance and this may have made them more endurable. Isolation was less and less a viable option, but the military and political impact of Russia, Japan, Germany, and Italy had not yet become real to the majority of Americans. Much of what was later seen as the grim scenario of the Axis powers was being dismissed at this time (the 1930s) in the United States as rumor or propaganda. The public mood, especially in America's heartland where most Covenanters were concentrated, favored isolation rather than intervention.

This was certainly true of the Covenant as a people. Among them there seemed no theological necessity for pacifism. As indicated earlier, the Covenant never saw itself as a sect in relation to the secular powers. Unlike some of the groups, identified by Troeltsch's typology as the historic "sect" types—such as the Quakers, the Dunkers, and the Mennonites—the families of Pietistic faith lived in an unresolved relationship to the state, never conforming totally but never either clearly "opposition-al," except in circumstances where the state was so demonic that no alternative seemed possible, for example, in Hitler's Germany.

Even Waldenström, who had fought so bravely against the State Church of Sweden and had shown little deference for its bishops and theological professors, was far from a sectarian in his attitudes towards questions of national defense. During the early years of World War I he assumed, if not a hawkish, at least a strongly patriotic stance. And he took the occasion to express himself publicly, even in pamphlet form, against twenty-seven members of the Riksdag belonging to the Swedish free churches, whose liberal sympathies led them to assume a more pacifistic position. Waldenström saw such manifest opposition to national defense as not only questionable politics but an actual sin that needed to be confessed and forgiven. These pronouncements on the part of the venerable spiritual leader had a disastrous effect on the unity of the executive board of the Covenant of Sweden to which several of the persons attacked by Waldenström belonged, and a wider and more permanent division in the ranks was barely avoided.

Despite Waldenström's sentiment, however, the peace movement among Swedish Christians expanded during the concluding years of the war, and in 1917 the annual meeting of the Svenska Missionsförbundet expressed strong sentiments *against* international military conflict and *for* immediate and constructive efforts in the interest of a durable peace. The executive board of the Svenska Missionsförbundet also petitioned the king to make proper allowances for those who conscientiously opposed the war.

Such actions did not, however, give the Covenant of Sweden the character of a "peace church." The same can be said about the American Covenant. Pacifistic convictions did come out of World War I, particularly among some of those who had served in the military, but membership in a Covenant church did not commit one to a particular social conviction in matters of race, labor relations, or political sympathies, and the same was true of the peace issue.

SOCIAL AWARENESS

In the interim between the two wars, however, the social awareness of the younger generation was significantly raised, and although personal evangelism and spiritual growth were still the major emphasis of the denomination, the ruinous financial depression of 1929-1937 did much to expand social consciousness, especially among high school and college youth.

The tendency to think socially and ethically was also stimulated by non-Covenant Christian leaders who had the ear of young people, even though some of them were seen by evangelicals as somewhat suspect. Among these foreground figures were Francis P. Miller, Francis J. McConnell, Harry Emerson Fosdick, Kirby Page, Sherwood Eddy, Daniel Poling, John R. Mott, E. Stanley Jones, John Mackay, Toyohiko Kagawa, Paul Scherer, Elton Trueblood, Oscar Blackwelder, C.F. Andrews, and Robert E. Speer, to name only a few. The impact of several of these leaders was largely in the area of applied Christianity, what was then called the "social gospel." Because the understanding among some conservative evangelicals was that concern for the social witnesses of the Scriptures precluded commitment to evangelism and missions, the interest of Covenant young people in leaders of this type was often severely criticized. I recall reviewing E. Stanley Jones's *Christ and Human Suffering* for a Covenant publication in the early thirties and being branded a "Modernist" for that modest effort.

The 1930s, nonetheless, saw an interesting melding of the "social" and the historic Gospel of God's mighty acts in Jesus Christ. The world depression and the saber rattling of the Axis powers had begun to weaken the easy optimism of the 1920s, and the biblical faith of the Reformers and Pauline Christianity were being given a fresh hearing. Three titles drawn from my earliest pastoral library illustrate the process of change: *The Christian Message for the World Today*, 1934, with essays by E. Stanley Jones, John A. Mackay, and Francis P. Miller; *The Church Against the World*, 1935, by H. Richard Niebuhr, Wilhelm Pauck, and Francis P. Miller; and *An Interpretation of Christian Ethics*, 1935, by Reinhold Niebuhr. For me the crucial chapter in the last of these was "The Christian Conception of Sin."

Generalizations are tricky and unreliable. Nonetheless, both my personal impressions from this time and the historical studies that have been made in the last half century suggest that the decade of the thirties saw both a deepening and widening of Christian faith and discipleship.

The faith was deepened through its recovery of the major biblical themes. Christianity was seen as more than idealism with a scenario of amiability. It was given its due as a profound, disturbingly realistic, but ultimately compassionate diagnosis of the sins of individuals and societies—especially the evils of self-deception and self-destruction—and as a source of saving truth and grace for persons in terms of redemption and healing, and for societies in terms of a graciousness expressed in justice, equity, and comity.

This renewed faith, without any loss of social concern, was given expression in several ways. In the fall of 1937 a series of preaching missions were held in major cities throughout America. It was my privilege to attend the sessions in Chicago at which the preachers, among others, were Oscar Blackwelder of Washington, D.C., Bishop Harold Spencer of Kansas City, John A. Mackay of Princeton, and missionary E. Stanley Jones, who served as a catalyst of the process. It is not easy to communicate the excitement and new hopefulness that the Mission conveyed from its opening moment in the historic Chicago Temple. The theme was "Entrusted with the Gospel," the text 1 Thessalonians 2:4, "As we were allowed of God to be put in trust with the gospel, even so we speak; not as pleasing men, but God, which trieth our hearts" (AV).

Blackwelder was the first speaker and he referred in a simple but dramatic way to the first fluttering banners of the faith which the apostle carried into a solidly pagan world, a world both hostile and potentially receptive to the good news of salvation. The situation, the task, the resistance, and the hope are identical today, said Blackwelder.

The Mission was given a generally sympathetic hearing, especially in its emphasis on a revival of interest in faith and mission. But when, at a large luncheon for Chicago businessmen, E. Stanley Jones pleaded for modification of capitalism in the direction of greater sensitivity toward laboring people, he met strong opposition, particularly from the laity. They had expected an old-fashioned call to repentance and faith and were greeted by an appeal for widened social concern. The same response typified the Sunday afternoon rally. On that occasion Jones spoke on Mark 9:7, "And there was a cloud overshadowed them, and a voice came out of the cloud, saying, 'This is my beloved Son: listen to him.'" Jones pleaded with the massed congregation for an openness to Christ's call in all areas of life, individual as well as social. His climax was a call for active involvement in the peace effort, an endeavor to which he personally gave himself until the attack on Pearl Harbor in December, 1941.

It would be fair to say that in this situation a growing number of Covenant people, especially the young, became increasingly aware of the social dimension of the Gospel. For a time this awareness extended also to the issue of war. In the mid thirties the Covenant probably came as close to pacifism as it ever had in its history. The high point in antiwar sentiment came at the Annual Meeting, June 19-23, 1935, when the denomination celebrated fifty years of its history. At an evening service during the conference, Harold M. Carlson, pastor of the prestigious Bethesda Covenant Church in Rockford, Illinois, delivered an impassioned plea for peace. The statement was not unlike the epochal sermon a few years earlier by Harry Emerson Fosdick, "My Pledge to the Unknown Soldier," which he gave both at Riverside Church and on the

"National Radio Pulpit" (Sweet 1950, 428).

Because the Covenant is not a "peace church," much of the sentiment for peace was individually rather than corporately felt and acted upon. I remember that a number of Covenant young people then at the University of Minnesota joined in a peace parade under the leadership of Floyd B. Olson, the governor of the state. Because in times of crisis things become greatly simplified, it was then popular to attribute the drift toward war as the work of a coalition of British armament manufacturers bound in an unholy alliance with Krupps of Germany and some Japanese counterparts. My own contribution was a bad poem about "munition makers" which I fired off to *The Christian Century*. That publication for good reasons fired it back with a rejection slip, an act of both divine and human mercy.

But it was a time of irritating uncertainty. "America First" brought together people who had one common objective—to stay out of war. Some of the young people in a church I was serving were drawn toward something called "The League Against War and Fascism," until they discovered that the "League" was more against Fascism than war and that they had been flirting with a covert Communist-influenced organization. Meanwhile, the discussions, the debates, the public and private forensics continued. Arguments based on the disillusionment around World War I vied with those based on the obvious real peril of Hitler and Mussolini.

Meanwhile, the outbreak of the Civil War in Spain in 1936 added to the confusion. There was considerable moral backing for the Republican forces in their struggle with both domestic Falangists as well as foreign imports. For example, the Abraham Lincoln Brigade as well as other voluntary contingents had the sympathy of many democratically minded Americans, a sympathy given fictional form in Ernest Hemingway's *For Whom the Bell Tolls*. But the political and military alignments in Spain were far from simple in the period 1936-1939, and the support given to Spanish Republicans by the Stalinists of the Soviet Union was hardly reassuring to any but the most committed leftists among American liberals.

In the prewar years, Christian pacifists in America "almost to a man lined up on the side of non-intervention though they did not like to be considered isolationists." Thus an eminent church historian summarizes the mentality of the 1940s. "The logic of events, however, threw them into the arms of the isolationists of the *Chicago Tribune* type together with the Roosevelt haters, the anti-British, the pro-Nazi, the pro-Fascist, and numerous others, who for one reason or another wanted to keep America either from helping the Allies or from active participation in the war" (Sweet 1950, 430).

EXPANSION IN EUROPE AND ASIA

Events themselves, however, were to prove the ultimate determinant. And these moved rapidly across the face of the globe. By the end of the thirties the major powers, whose actions provoked the outbreak of World War II, had all moved into an expansionist phase. As early as 1927 Japan had determined to dominate Asia. The Mukden incident in 1931 and the establishment of the state of Manchukuo in 1932 eventuated in the trigger clash between Chinese and Japanese troops in Beijing in 1937 which started the Sino-Japanese War.

With the death of Lenin in 1924 and the succession in power of Joseph Stalin, Russian Communism entered a radically new phase. Lenin had envisaged an evolving world revolution through the establishment and growth of Communist cells in each nation and the development of the Comintern (Communist International). Congresses of the Comintern were consequently held at fairly regular intervals from 1919 to 1935. But during its life, largely because of the death of Lenin and the enormous thrust of Stalin, the Comintern gradually became dominated by the Soviet Union. Stalin saw the struggle between capitalism as exclusively a struggle between capitalistic countries and the U.S.S.R. And he saw himself as the effective leader of world communism through the development of the industrial, economic, and military power of the Soviet Union. This program was developed in several stages: a) the collectivization of the peasantry and the establishment of agricultural cooperatives and state farms; b) the expansion of heavy industry (coal, oil), the forming of industrial combinations, the exploitation of labor, and the growth of a technocratic elite; c) the concentration of political power in Stalin's hands by the establishment in 1929 of an autocratic dictatorship, and the completion of the Stalin constitution of 1936 which expanded the Union of Soviet Socialist Republics to eleven constituent republics (now fifteen); and d) a resulting elimination of all oppositional elements beginning with the banishment of Trotsky in 1929 and culminating in the ruthless and systematic purge (in 1936-1938) of all of Stalin's opponents of the 1920s (Kinder and Hilgemann 1978, 189).

Although in the early years the Soviet Union had been careful about violating national sovereignties, under Stalin such courtesy or diplomacy evaporated rapidly, as is evidenced by the Russian attack on Finland in 1940, the rape of the Baltic States at the conclusion of World War II, and the subsequent fate of Poland, Hungary, Czechoslovakia, Rumania, and Bulgaria.

So the Red Peril was real enough, even then, and no less ominous because the Soviet Union kept switching allegiances. But real or not, both German National Socialists and Italian Fascists found the danger of

Communism a powerful means of rallying national loyalty, inflaming the war spirit, and justifying expansionist tactics. In each instance the dream of empire was supported by a different "mythology" or "philosophy." The Nazis dreamt, or said they dreamt, of a pure Aryan stock represented by blond and buxom Wagnerian types and nourished by Germanic fantasies of *Übermenschen*—a master race composed of super persons or demigods, a race purified forever of the taint of the Semitic sub-race that had brought defeat and shame to the nation. The German people (*das Volk*) under the leadership of the leader (*Der Führer*) would assume their rightful place as the Third Reich—a super kingdom worthy to lead and to achieve life space (*Lebensraum*) by conquest, annexation, plebiscite, or subversion. Finally, by an almost metaphysical propriety, it would dominate the world.

In my library I can look at a copy of Hitler's *Mein Kampf* printed during the glory years and lifted by me in 1945 from a pile of discards (banners, insignia, SS helmets, medals) on a cobbled street in some obscure German village. The book looks hauntingly like a Bible with its black spine and its gold Germanic script. Even now it breathes an ersatz sanctity.

This is appropriate because National Socialism saw itself as returning to a pre-Jewish, pre-Christian Teutonic ideology unencumbered by any moral imperatives except those related to *Blut und Boden* (blood and soil). The race, the people, and the nation, seen not as a grouping of persons but as a feverishly industrious ant heap, claimed ultimate religious loyalty.

Adolph Hitler, the Moses, the Joshua, and in some measure the "Christ" figure of this weird myth, was born in unimpressive surroundings in Branau, Austria, and was educated unsuccessfully in Linz. He reached adulthood in Vienna and Munich just before World War I, supporting himself by a number of odd jobs and by his indifferent talent as an artist. He became a soldier in the German Army in 1914 and served until severely gassed in 1917 at which time he was invalided out of the military. But he carried with him into civilian life the inoculant of a powerful megalomania—the dream of Germanic greatness, a dream in which he himself would share.

He returned to Munich, in so many ways the breeding ground of his cosmic fantasies and not too far from Berchtesgaden, his Germanic Parnassus. There in 1919, still a nobody, he joined the D.A.P. (the German Workers Party), later called N.S.D.A.P. (the National Socialist German Workers Party), which became shortened to *Nazi*. He may have been a nobody, a noncommissioned officer of the subordinate ranks, but in 1921 he was elected party chairman. The "Munich Beerhall Putsch," which he helped to engineer in 1923, was unsuccessful in reaching its objective and Hitler spent a few months (of a shortened term) in prison. But like other folk heroes (the Apostle Paul, John Bunyan), Hitler used his time behind bars to instruct and inspire his followers. The result was the first part of *Mein Kampf* (*My Struggle*). With this under his belt he set about to make his party a dominant force in German politics (Kinder and Hilgemann 1978, 193-199).

At first Hitler was seen as a pretentious clown, particularly in the Western centers of power, and nothing much was expected of his shrieking rhetoric, the brown and black uniforms, the bunting, and the songs. But soon enough the comic opera became embarrassing and then offensive. Wasn't somebody going to stop him? What were the sensible giants doing with their massed armies and their powerful navies? Unfortunately, the answer was, "Not much." There was a lot of rhetoric and there were a few nervous and ineffectual gestures, but in the end the Great Paralysis became evident.

Ultimately all effective opposition to Hitler and the Nazis in Germany had eroded and early in 1933 with the complicity of the aging and confused von Hindenburg, Hitler became chancellor. From that point until the beginning of World War II with the Nazi invasion of Poland, things moved very rapidly. The National Socialists were now, under the *Reichsführer*, the ruling party of Germany, in fact, the only party. The program is familiar: theoretical and practical anti-Semitism based on the most distorted rewriting of anthropology and history; the gradual actualization of a plot to subordinate, subvert, annex, and conquer lands and people seen as an integral part of the Reich or as obstructing essential expansion. These provocations wedded to rapid militarization led to an inevitable confrontation with the democratic Western powers in 1936-1939 and hence with the United States, which despite its wan gestures in the direction of isolationism and noninvolvement, was weighted in the direction of engagement. Other factors that contributed to the flammability of the times were the German-Soviet nonaggression pact of 1939 (with its secret clauses about a shared dominance of Eastern Europe) and the Three Power Pact (Germany, Italy, and Japan) of 1940 which promised mutual assistance.

A fourth character in the drama—with an unfortunate suggestion of *pastiche* (this is how a dictator acts)—was Benito Mussolini, *Il Duce* (the leader). His anti-climactic, even ludicrous, demise in 1945 and the collapse of his vaunted forces may have led to an underestimation of his power to hurt. But he was never just a bad boy brandishing a toy pistol. Like his contemporary Adolph Hitler, Mussolini had served in World War I. Like Hitler, he wanted to see his country restored to its ancient glory; he dreamt of a revival of the *Impero Romano*. Though originally a Social Democrat, Mussolini was drawn by his patriotic impulses to a concept of government in which all entities of the state would be subsumed under a one party system and this party would be the P.N.F. (the National Fascist Party).

In Italy Fascism was more preoccupied with the remote historic past—the age of Roman power, grandeur, and elegance—than by the racial mythology prevalent among the Nazis. Another important difference in Mussolini's climb to power was a continuous utilization of the monarchic principle, the court, the officer's corps, and the Roman Catholic Church. In 1929 Mussolini was able to resolve a question that had troubled Italy for decades: how to deal with the political assumption and pretentions of the Vatican. That year he signed a treaty with the Vatican which made the pope the sovereign of "The City of the Vatican," a newly created state.

Thus although Fascism resembled Nazism in many ways, it seems not to have gone to the extreme of German National Socialism in such areas as anti-Semitism, the use of terror and mass arrests, and the repressive utilization of the secret police. But, as indicated, the Fascists dreamt of the restoration of lost territory. Mussolini and his disciples saw the Adriatic Sea as *Mare Nostro* (our sea) and proceeded (in the period 1922-1939) with a program of conquest which secured the Dodecanese Islands (off the southwest coast of Turkey), Corfu, Fiume, Albania, and Abyssinia. The last of these were forced into the Fascist orbit by the Italian victories in 1935-1936 (Kinder and Hilgemann 1978, 159, 178, 179, 202f).

A MIDDLE TERM

It was at this point that the world political situation suddenly became politically relevant for me. Toward the end of 1935 we saw in the Chicago newspapers that a volunteer Swedish ambulance unit that was serving the beleaguered Ethiopian army, although with evident Red Cross markings, had been attacked and bombed by Italian warplanes. Several members of the ambulance unit were reported killed or at least seriously wounded. Among these was Anders Joelsson, my first cousin. Later the report proved exaggerated and although the unit did suffer some casualties, my cousin was not injured. But that night before I knew the full story, I had trouble sleeping. I went over my own position on the conflict that was beginning to tear the world apart. Toward morning I went into my study and wrote a page and a half of blank verse in Swedish in tribute to my cousin. I later typed the poem on a piece of yellow paper which spoke to me of the lurid dawn. I recall the poorly typed black words—the ribbon was fresh—stark against the chrome paper. It was a personal manifesto for me and it indicated a dramatic change in my feelings about the world and about war.

Several years were to pass before I had the chance to volunteer for military service, but my resolve to make a personal contribution toward the neutralization of the tyrannical powers, then beginning to dominate the world, never wavered. Nor have I had any occasion, in the years that followed, to regret the time I then devoted to military service.

In this resolve I was supported by a number of relatives and friends who were similarly "converted." I was particularly helped by the writings of Reinhold Niebuhr and Sherwood Eddy. They enabled me to find a middle term between love and hate, pacifism and militarism, passivity and violence. This middle term was justice. I did not confuse justice with love and I did not look to justice for any ultimate redemption, but I did see it as a means of order in a disordered and destructive world.

That middle term even helped me make sense of Romans 13:1, "Let every person be subject to the governing authorities. For there is no authority except from God, and those that exist have been instituted by God." I well understood that the authority under which Paul lived and worked may well have been the Emperor Nero, and if so, then his logic is driven to its utmost point. But Paul is not here vouching for anything in Nero except his responsibility to govern. In dealing with a person in authority we may wish that he or she be a better person or that he or she not be a bad person, but the fact of authority is, if we follow Paul, dependent on neither. We are called to obedience even under a tyrant. For ultimately we obey not the tyrant but God who is the ground of the majesty of law.

In any event, my decision to participate actively in the war was in no way unique. Thousands of young people from The Evangelical Covenant Church responded similarly. Others left the decision on their military involvement to the government or, more particularly, to their local draft boards. The way into the service obviously did not determine the loyalty or distinction with which anyone served.

AMERICANIZATION

Although the Covenant had struggled for many years with the difficulty of a persistent ethnic image and had theoretically accommodated itself to being an American church, its de facto posture in 1941 was still Swedish. Until quite recently and in many communities the Covenant church has been known as the "Swede" church. Forty years ago this was so much more general that it tended initially to set apart Covenant young people in the service from their more Americanized contemporaries.

In response to the slowing rate of immigration, strenuous efforts had been made since World War I to redress the imbalance in Swedes and non-Swedes. Nathaniel Franklin was elected to the office as Sunday school secretary in 1919 and assumed office in 1920. He introduced a graded lesson system that was calibrated to the needs of different ages. Before this, everyone had used the same curriculum. The assumption underlying that procedure was that the essential service of the church was to evangelize and that everybody became a Christian in the same way. With the graded system, the crying need for Americanization became more evident and with that the need for understanding the child as a child, and for addressing the needs of each age differently.

With the gradual shift to English, the door was opened for more realistic and effective Sunday school recruitment. Sunday schools were started in communities adjacent to the established churches and began their work by renting available space or using public school buildings. In some instances Sunday school chapels were built and these became satellite centers not only for Sunday school and daily vacation Bible school ministries but for the beginnings of interest communities in largely Americanized settings. In some instances the children of these attached centers were brought into the pattern of confirmation and the process of becoming church members. But in terms of church growth, the permanent results were disappointing. Some of the "mother" churches were reluctant to give up the care and the control of the chapels and some suspicion seems to have lingered that a loss of identity would follow too rapid Americanization.

A consequence of this reluctance was that to begin with, at least, relatively few of the Sunday school chapels went on to become independent congregations, and few of the interest communities of children and youth gathered at these satellite centers were ever integrated with Covenant church life. In 1930 David Nyvall could mourn that total membership in the Covenant had increased by only 10,000 from 1909 to 1927 (that is, during the presidency of E.G. Hjerpe) and half-humorously described the results as "statics" rather than "statistics" (Nyvall and Olsson 1954, 81).

Worse yet, the growth in the number of local congregations in the period 1910-1930 was even more modest. Nyvall speaks of twenty new churches, "most of them small and insignificant." Actually, in the period 1910-1930, forty churches were organized. But of these only fourteen were added in the decade 1921-1930.

We are indebted to Philip Anderson's *A Precious Heritage*, 1984, for important research in the area of church extension in the Northwest Conference. Anderson emphasizes the administrative and evangelistic efforts of Jacob Elving in the years 1933-1950 which resulted in the addition of twenty-three new congregations to the conference. In this period the Covenant as a whole added ninety-one new churches, which means that more than 25 percent of church growth as measured by new work took place in the Northwest Conference.

With this statistical improvement, growing numbers of young people joining the armed forces of the United States in the period 1940-1945 were aware of a Covenant identity. Some of this was due to numbers alone. In World War I nearly 4,200 Covenanters served. In World War II the total was 12,765. Since the Covenant of 1917 had approximately 27,000 members and the Covenant of 1940 less than 50,000, the proportionate increase in those with a Covenant association is significant.

But more significant than a mere quantitative increase in the numbers of Covenanters in service was the quality of impact made on them prior to joining the service. In contrast to the World War I Covenanters, those serving in World War II had had many opportunities for contact with the denomination's life and faith. The Covenanters of a later generation were able to bring with them into the expanded world a much greater sense of belongingness and of spiritual identity than their predecessors. This had been made possible through worship in a language they understood, through an improved educational experience in Sunday school and daily vacation Bible school as well as in confirmation classes, youth camps, and National Covenant Youth Quadrennials, through enrollment at schools like Minnehaha Academy and North Park College, and through exposure to Covenant publications and training materials.

We have mentioned Covenant Youth Quadrennials. These were particularly important to the denomination's young people, for the thought content of these conferences as well as the personal contacts with other youth encouraged by them were to provide significant bonding for Covenanters in uniform.

The first two Quadrennials were held at Lake Geneva, Wisconsin, and Lake Koronis, Minnesota, in the years 1933 and 1937. They resulted from the vision and administrative efforts of Nathaniel Franklin, who in addition to serving as Sunday school secretary also had responsibilities as director of Covenant young people's work.[1]

1. Franklin and his gifted associate Olga Lindborg had spearheaded the "graded lesson" emphasis within Christian education in the Covenant. They had also shared the task of interpreting Christian values for the children and young people of the denomination. Franklin and Lindborg discharged this duty in different ways. This was due not so much to a difference in values as to a difference in temperament. Franklin was imaginative and innovative, but was dominated by a calm and reflective spirit and a strong commitment to

The third Quadrennial was held on the campus of North Park College in recognition of the school's fiftieth anniversary. Previous Quadrennial speakers had been drawn from a domestic cadre of gifted, acceptable Covenant pastors and educators. However, in 1941 North Park College, whose representatives had been added to the arrangements committee for the meeting, suggested that the program for the Quadrennial fittingly recognize that fusion of faith and learning which the school represented. Hence the scenario became a potpourri of themes, some of which departed enough from the traditional offerings to entail a risk.

Nevertheless, despite its obvious bumpiness, the program did proclaim one unmistakable truth to the young people in attendance and to the absent ones who became apprised of the proceedings: the Covenant Church would try to deal forthrightly with some of the issues then confronting its youth as well as the constituency in general, and it would, without specific endorsement, arrange programs that dealt with topics of consequence to the community even though these might seem dangerously controversial.

structure and circumstance. Lindborg was equally creative but less sensitive perhaps to the rich variety of Covenant reactions and responses.

In 1929 on the heels of the distressing Annual Meeting at Omaha the year before, Olga Lindborg had plunged the Covenant into its second major controversy in two years by an article pleading for a recognition of motion pictures both as an exciting and useful technical invention and as a source of the dramatization of good literature. She mentioned as examples such innocent films as *Ben Hur, Pilgrim's Progress, The Sky Pilot, The Crusaders,* and *Les Miserables*. To a generation suckled at the television this seems innocent enough, but in 1929 to an immigrant people whose introduction to the movies had come through trivial nickelodeons, morally scandalizing actors and actresses, and a film colony which by reputation trampled every significant Christian value underfoot, Olga Lindborg's defense of the cinema seemed a vindication of Satan. Even stable and sensible people panicked and forced the troublesome genie back into its bottle (BOS, 546-549).

As we now know, the genie did not remain confined for long. While the Covenant argued hotly about the motion pictures and tried to distinguish between a technical invention and a source of questionable entertainment, a more potent spirit was being invoked. This spirit, when freed up to do its work, would make the whole question of movies academic. Its name was television and a sketch of it was already on the drawing boards. But the future was not yet the present and the problem of the movies would surface in 1941 with the holding of the third Quadrennial.

CHAPTER THIRTY

THE WAR: ITS IMPACT

The Annual Meeting of the Covenant in 1941, held on the campus of North Park College, June 12-15, decided by a vote of 85 to 53 to support a resolution opposing the entry of the United States into the war. There had been another resolution with similar intent in 1935 (*YB* 1935).

But despite this unquestionably earnest action, the tide for confrontation with the Axis powers was running powerfully during this last year of peace. In the period 1940-1941 Britain and the United States would lose almost nine million tons of shipping to German U-boats. Selective Service System (the draft) had become effective in 1940. In January, 1941, Franklin D. Roosevelt gave his Four Freedoms speech; in March, 1941 Congress passed the Lend Lease Act which empowered the president to supply war materials to "any country whose defense the president deems vital to the defense of the United States." This was virtually a blank check for the Allied cause. Meanwhile, Germany was massing troops on its eastern front. The Covenant Annual Meeting ended on June 15 that year. A week later, June 22, 1941, the Germans invaded Russia without a formal declaration of war (Kinder and Hilgemann 1978, 208-215).

Meanwhile in the Pacific, Japanese expansion, which had begun in Manchuria and China early in the 1930s, was extending southward. Through the agency of the Anti-Comintern Pact, the Three Power Pact (Germany, Italy, Japan), and a separate pact with the Soviet Union (completed in 1941), Japan was able to act almost at will. Efforts on the part of the United States and other powers to check Japan by the cancellation of trade agreements, an embargo on oil and scrap metals, and the blocking of accounts did have a weakening effect on Japan but did not permanently stay the advance. The fact is that the Western powers did not yet take the Japanese seriously. In the late thirties the feeling among some officers of the American fleet was that Japan posed no real threat. "An afternoon raid by our planes would wipe them out," said a ranking naval officer in the presence of some friends. And he was apparently expressing feelings that were then generally current.

The facts are familiar. In 1940 the Burma Road was blocked, the northern part of Indochina occupied, and in December, 1941 came the "infamy" of Pearl Harbor and the declaration of war against Japan. Germany and Italy followed suit by declaring war against the United States and its allies (Kinder and Hilgemann 1978, 175, 217).

Some elements of the American navy escaped the Pearl Harbor bombing, but the gigantic scissors sweep of Japan could not be stayed. It developed by massive thrusts on the left and right flanks and through the center. The central push resulted in the capture of the Philippines and the Dutch East Indies. The right flank operating on the continent of Asia captured Singapore and Hong Kong and isolated Nationalist China by occupying Burma. The left flank dominated Oceania from the Aleutians to Guadalcanal and the Coral Sea. Guam and Wake were taken and the Bismarck Archipelago, New Guinea, and the Solomon Islands were attacked. At the end of six months Japan dominated a vast territory with a population of 450 million and a hoard of fabulous natural resources, including raw rubber, quinine, tin, and rice.

In May and June of 1942, with the battles of the Coral Sea and Midway and in August with the Guadalcanal landings, the tide began to turn for the United States and its allies. In 1943 came the major island offensive under the leadership of General MacArthur. The following year a huge offensive in the central Pacific under Admiral Nimitz won back much of the lost territories, and in 1944-1945 the Philippines and Burma were wrested from Japan. Growing American air power gave strategic and tactical support to the advancing forces. By 1943 air superiority had been achieved. Pressure on Japanese cities and industries as well as military installations culminated in August, 1945, in the dropping of the atomic bomb on Hiroshima and Nagasaki. Japan capitulated on September 2, 1945.

The United States entry into the war in December, 1941, had an immediate effect on the attitudes and actions of its citizens. Support for the war effort became virtually total, although the involvement of Americans lacked much of the juvenile athletic spirit that surrounded the participation in World War I.

The declaration of war on the United States by Germany and Japan formalized existing American sympathies and alliances and placed the formidable financial resources and industrial capability of the West fully at the disposal of the Allies.

In 1942 the twenty-six nations at war with the Axis powers formed the Washington Pact (later to become the nucleus of the United Nations). That year a British counter-offensive in North Africa and the opening up of a second front by the Allies in Morocco and Algeria led to a total frustration of the Axis master plan in that part of the world. Thousands of German and Italian soldiers were made prisoners of war, among them the members of the vaunted Afrika Korps, Hitler's most formidable troops.

The defeat of the Axis powers in North Africa in 1943 freed the Allies for an advance through Sicily, Italy, and France, "the soft underbelly of Europe" as Churchill called it, and a joining up with the offensive planned for the Atlantic coast of France. The Soviet Union had now joined the Western alliance, and although its major concern until the early months of 1943 was ridding itself of the German invasion of its territory, there was increasing hope among the Western powers that Soviet troops could eventually put pressure on the Axis armies in the east.

The soft underbelly proved not so "soft" and the Germans provided stiff resistance for the Allies in Sicily and Italy until May of 1945, when they finally capitulated. Meanwhile, thousands of American army troops, sizable elements of the U.S. Air Force (then still called the Army Air Corps), and mountains of equipment and supplies had arrived in the British Isles in preparation for "Operation Overlord."

American bombers had teamed with the bombers of the Royal Air Force in night and day bombing since 1942 and by mid 1944 largely controlled the air over Germany. Damage to military targets and industrial sites was devastating and the ensuing saturation bombing and "firestorming" of cites (Cologne, Dresden, Hamburg) terrorized the civilian population and proved decisively that the distinction between military and civilian involvement in war was no longer tenable. This was "total" war.

But another fact also became evident. Despite the catastrophic damage caused by the bombings, only an invasion of the continent could bring about the unconditional surrender of the German armies. Hence, after extensive planning and training, "Operation Overlord" was launched on June 6, 1944—D-day. Landings were made in Normandy and, although the resistance of the German forces was fierce and deadly, Allied forces pushed on, capturing Cherbourg June 30, Caen July 9, St. Lo July 18, and Avranches July 25. A titanic battle of armor in the Falaise Gap on August 16 neutralized German panzer resistance and opened the way to

Paris, which was entered on August 25.

But progress into Germany proper was not easy or simple and it was not until the Ardennes counter-offensive (December 16, 1944, to January 16, 1945) had been dealt with and the Russians had begun to put on pressure in the east that the collapse of Germany began. The final surrender came in early May, 1945, preceded by only a few days by the suicide of Adolf Hitler in his Berlin bunker. The dream of a *reich* that would stand for a thousand years had proved no more substantial than a soap bubble.

In any case, this is not a history of a war or the notation of a victory but the chronicle of a people. What happened to Covenanters during five years of conflict and in the aftermath? Looked at from the perspective of four decades, it becomes evident that the impact of the war on the denominational constituency, organization, leadership, educational program, concept of missions, behavioral norms and cultural attitudes, ethnic identity, and ecumenical perspectives as well as on many other concerns was vast and enduring.

THE COVENANT AND THE MILITARY

We have summarized hastily the scenario of World War II from 1939 to 1945. We must now consider in greater detail how the war affected people, particularly that relatively small faith family known as the Covenant. While it is certainly true that the Covenant did not see itself as a peace sect that derived its identity from long years in the cause of peace, it is equally true that it was practically innocent in the area of military tradition and usage.

In high school and college Covenant young people may have become aware of the CMTC (Civilian Military Training Corps) or the ROTC (Reserve Officers' Training Corps). Some may even have served briefly in the quasi-military Civilian Conservation Corps, which was organized under the Roosevelt administration in 1933 to provide employment for thousands of young men idled by the Depression. But in the years prior to the World War II call-up, I personally knew very few Covenanters who attended military school, served regularly in a branch of the armed forces, were involved in their reserve components or the National Guard, or belonged to any other organization devoted to military preparedness. In our circles it was just not "the thing to do."

Even scouting was not above suspicion. I remember overhearing a fairly serious conversation between a Covenant father and my own father in the summer of 1926. We were driving from Pittsburgh to a Boy Scout camp in western Pennsylvania called Kiondoshawa. The Covenant father, who was about to entrust his older son to the mystique of scouting in the company of the two Olsson boys, was wondering en route if the scout camp with its pyramidal tents, khaki clad youths, and mild forms of regimentation did not mask a military purpose and program. It took some reassuring.

There being no palpable military history or tradition among Covenant people, the rush into registration, call-up, and eventual enlistment during 1940-1941 came as a rude shock, not least to most of the young people directly involved. The depersonalization of the induction process, the merciless grind of basic training, the loneliness of barracks life, the deliberate tactics of humiliation in relation to superiors, the endless preoccupation with the processes of policing and polishing as well as of destruction, the severance of direct contacts with human feelings which had prevailed among relatives and friends, and the concurrent contact with the thoughtless ideas and grubby language of people deprived of self-esteem (Rubert Brooke's "half men and their dirty songs and dreary")—to begin with all this must have been painful in the extreme. This was especially true of those young people whose contacts with the rougher and ruder elements of the community, before this, had been infrequent and often superficial.

Fortunately, things or people often prove less threatening than they seem initially, and many of the blustering, domineering types that are such a trial in boot camp or basic training turned out to be no more intimidating than the hollow bullies or braggarts back home. Indeed, what was most surprising in the experience of many service persons was the depth of understanding and compassion they discovered among their associates once the superficial coverings had been scraped off and the people in the unit had become, in the heat of crisis, "a band of brothers and sisters."

There was, of course, a tragic amount of spiritual desertion in the service. The Christian value systems brought from family and church were often eroded, less perhaps by the actual horrors of combat than by the soft pressures of boredom and shared leisure and the radical anonymity of remote places and exotic situations. Fortunately, there were powerful counteragents.

In the first place, the services themselves spared no effort or expense to provide the very best in spiritual programs and leadership. The chaplaincies of the services attracted clergy from the full range of denominations and demanded standards of training and experience well above the average in some civilian churches. These candidates for the chaplaincy service were provided with four weeks of preparatory training before assignment and were usually placed under the supervision of experienced chaplains during their first months of service.

Considering the fact that the vast majority of chaplains had had no previous contact wih military circumstances, they adapted rapidly to the new situation and performed superbly in carrying out the mission entrusted to them. In effect, they carried the work and worship of the churches into nearly every place where men and women were assigned for duty and were present with service personnel in the most boring, trying, and hazardous aspects of their daily life. The massive performance of the chaplains in this week-to-week ministry is roughly indicated in a report from the chief of army chaplains published in 1943:

> During each month of 1943 each chaplain, on an average, conducted or supervised 19.4 religious services with a total attendance of 1,160. He had 12.4 sacramental occasions (communions, baptisms) with 151 participants. He made 14.1 visits to hospitals and guardhouses, visiting 253 people. He had 4.1 functional occasions in civilian communities which reached 323 individuals and 118.6 functional occasions in his pastoral ministry to his men, reaching 998 during the month. This is a total of 168.6 functional occasions involving a total of 2,885 personal contacts (*Our Covenant* 1946, 64).

In addition to the ministry of chaplains the services also provided another valuable source of spiritual leadership—the work of the chaplain's assistants. This granted enlisted personnel with a special talent for or interest in ministry the opportunity to serve in a number of ways and to associate with a corps of people committed to worship and witness. Church educators, organists and other musicians, and young people with a future commitment to the church were thus given a chance to develop their skills in activities they found compatible and rewarding.

A third aspect of the chaplain's work should also be mentioned. Service personnel devoted months and even years to the process of preparation for combat; much of this time was spent in the immense training areas established by the separate services. Posts, camps, stations, and fields teemed with thousands of soldiers, sailors, fliers, and marines. Effective contacts with congregations in surrounding communities were not always possible, and the government wisely set in motion a vast program of building cantonment-type chapels on service installations in sufficient numbers to parallel the civilian situation. Here the same worship area with pews for several hundred participants, but with arrangeable chancels, served the liturgical needs of Protestant, Roman Catholic, and Jewish adherents. The chapels also provided offices for the chaplains of different faiths, and a minister or priest in uniform who returned to his office after supper was likely to find numbers of people waiting for his services.

Despite such devoted ministry, chaplains did not always fare well in opinion polls, some army cartoons, and especially postwar fiction. In 1951 I shared responsibility for an after-action report on the chaplaincy that sought to assess how the chaplain image was reflected in both factual reporting and fictional materials. There were some obvious journalistic biases; for example, in the press Catholic chaplains were generally depicted as more heroic and sacrificial than their Protestant counterparts. But a much more serious skewing of the facts took place in some fictional accounts. When chaplains were not deliberately ignored, they were not infrequently described as venal, opinionated, hypocritical, immoral, and perhaps, worst of all, self-seeking and cowardly.

Among the thousands of clergy of all faiths who served as chaplains, there was undoubtedly a percentage who saw that ministry as an opportunity for egotistical pleasure and self-aggrandizement. I had the personal misfortune of meeting some of them. But in the main the record would not differ much from the confidential materials in most denominational or diocesan personnel files.

The fact is that the public clergyperson is an inviting target for any writer looking for a butt. Fielding, Sterne, Austen, as well as Dante, Chaucer, and Boccaccio all play their dart games with priests and parsons. It seems to be the fate of those who are labelled "professional holy men."

A more sober and truthful view of the work of the chaplain was provided by Renwick C. Kennedy in an article in *The Christian Century*, June 5, 1946, in which he stressed the prodigious amount of ministry provided by the clergy in uniform during World War II and concluded by saying, "There was no revival of religion in the Army [but] this cannot be blamed on the chaplain."

Because I have been so deeply involved personally in the Army chaplaincy, I have taken the opportunity to seek an assessment from personnel of the three services of the ministry of chaplains encountered in World War II, the Korean War, and the war in Vietnam. Few of those I have talked to have substantiated the distorted fictional judgment referred to earlier that chaplains were mostly ineffective. Most service personnel have seen chaplains as average or better representatives of their particular faiths. The main criticism I have heard, particularly from those with evangelical preferences, is that service chaplains devote too little time to the major themes of biblical faith and too much time to the common sense, moral homilies we have learned to expect from some civilian pulpits.

Whatever the truth of this, the twenty-nine Covenant chaplains who served in World War II (and those who have been service chaplains since that time) have been valued representatives of the denomination in a ministry that is both complex and arduous. Kennedy's conclusion that no revival developed in the military during World War II may be valid, but we now know, on the basis of four decades of observation since the end of those major hostilities, that the presence, example, and witness of chaplains, among them the disproportionately numerous Covenant clergy, deeply affected the personnel served. There were no doubt other factors, as we shall see directly, but the number of young people who stood ready at war's end to perform service as ministers or missionaries or to devote themselves to humanitarian service in social ministries, medicine, and related fields cannot be unrelated to the presence of chaplains in their midst and the persons they directly affected.

As noted, a disproportionate number of Covenant chaplains were credentialed for service in World War II. Denominations were allocated one chaplain for 100,000 constituents, which, even with the most generous criteria, would have given the Covenant, then about half its present size, less than one representative. That it managed to place twenty-nine in service was due to the opportunity presented by the Congregationalists, who found themselves with more spaces than they could fill and generously allowed the Covenant their unused spaces. The General Commission on Chaplains and Armed Forces Personnel, an umbrella organization that served as the endorsing agency for smaller denominations and as coordinator for larger Protestant denominations, became a friend at court for the Covenant and helped immeasurably in the task of presenting the latter denomination to the wider family of churches.

THE COVENANT AND SERVICE PERSONNEL

Valuable as the chaplaincy was to prove both as a symbol of spiritual concern for the Covenant and as a contact point with the services, the efforts of the denomination and its churches in keeping in touch directly with service personnel was of immeasurable and continuing significance both for the people in uniform and for those involved in this rewarding ministry.

No sooner had war been declared than the denomination began taking steps to get a contact program under way. Without waiting for the action of the Annual Meeting, the Executive Board used its prerogative to accept a recommendation of the Board of Mission, made at the Midwinter Conference in Grand Crossing (Chicago, now Trinity) in February, 1942, to establish the Office of Chaplain-at-Large.

Bernard A. Hawkinson, a Covenant pastor who had seen some service in World War I, was given the responsibility to head this office and he began his ministry in June, 1942. Initially the staff and office arrangements were minimal. The Depression was easing, but still only the barest essentials could be funded. Despite these limitations, Hawkinson set to work in his small office with one part-time secretary. Ultimately the staff would be expanded to three full-time and two part-time secretaries, but that was when both money and support had caught up with the greatly magnified task.

The chaplain-at-large had a talent for organization and administration. To begin with he made contact with all Covenant churches (459 in 1942). He asked these churches to keep sending him available information about service personnel, and as the war progressed, he developed an index with 40,000 entries that dealt with the nearly 13,000 members of the Covenant family of faith involved in one of the services.

The information asked for was as follows: the name of the service person, home address, home church, relationship to church (member, committed Christian, interested participant) as well as the names and addresses of family members. Much of this information was then entered in the index and the service address (APO or FPO) was added.

Only a brief summary of the activities of the office can be indicated, but these included: a) furnishing a list of other Covenanters in the same camp, naval station, air field or APO, and this led to some important get-togethers; b) mailing printed tracts, pamphlets, sermons, and invitations to request *The Covenant Weekly*; c) mailing *The Covenant Home Altar* to every service person; d) inviting all service personnel with Covenant associations to write personally to the chaplain-at-large with the promise to publish these letters if the contents were not confidential (the result of this suggestion was that 600 letters from service personnel were published in *The Covenant Weekly* during the war years). In addition to general letters addressed to the entire mailing list, the chaplain's office sent a printed list of all Covenant churches to service personnel. About this action Chaplain Hawkinson was to write: "These little blue books have brought thousands of our young people to nearby friendly Covenant churches where they have found Christian fellowship and also entertainment in our homes. Both service people and churches have been strengthened because of these contacts. A stronger Covenant unity and solidarity has been fostered." In his report Chaplain Hawkinson also referred to still another activity of his office: "Pastors and service committees in churches near camps or naval stations were notified of Covenanters in their district who in turn were taken into hearts and homes."

All in all, the chaplain's office sent out one million pieces of mail, published two specifically Covenant pamphlets ("The Christian Soldier" and "Comrades of the Way"), and provided a carefully prepared study kit for Covenant pastors on ministry to returning service personnel.

In his summary of his service, which covered four years, Hawkinson mentions some perspectives and conclusions of interest to the denomination. Against a background of virtual scriptural illiteracy in the services which amounted to 85 percent of the total, Hawkinson speaks with understandable gratitude of the fact that of the 13,000 service persons with a Covenant relationship, 50 percent confessed a definite commitment to Christ and 35 percent held membership in a Covenant church. Another thing that pleased the chaplain was that many of his correspondents expressed a strong preference for the kind of religious service in which the Gospel was presented as a gracious means of salvation from sin. The large number of Covenanters who were placed as chaplains' assistants was also gratifying. Many of the service people who reported their experiences in personal letters also indicated that they had had a first-hand witness to the power of Christian missions throughout the world. Finally, Hawkinson was able to report that a score of more of the young people writing to him were committed to pastoral ministry or missions as a life career. He wrote prophetically of the future: "Because of their broadened horizons, youthful enthusiasm and aggressiveness, visions of postwar spiritual needs, and desire for practical results, our returned servicemen will afford a new leadership for future years if given an opportunity to serve" (*Our Covenant* 1946, 29-41).

Allusion has been made to the twenty-nine chaplains who served. Covenant responsibility for them was also given to Chaplain Hawkinson, and on the basis of the experience of those chaplains who were privileged to work with him, witness must be borne to his devotion to duty, his warm personal concern, and his administrative competence. The direct result of Hawkinson's work after the war was concluded was a continuing personal interest in the service chaplaincy on the part of Covenant pastors as well as a growing appreciation in other denominations of the quality of service rendered by those Covenant clergypersons who chose this form of Christian service.

THE IMPACT OF THE LOCAL CHURCHES

As is often the case, it is the higher echelons of administration that are given the headlines and the accolades. The same is true of our assessment of the contact with service personnel. But in actuality very little would have been accomplished in contact ministry if local churches had not continued to carry a disproportionate part of the load through their professional staffs, but even more through their committees for service personnel. The latter carried on their work without financial remuneration and with only the motivation of profound love and caring for those entering the service.

The work of these committees deserves a much more careful treatment than is possible in these pages, for the ongoing contact it assured with absent service people not only helped to maintain a precarious status quo, but in many instances brought a deepened love for the local congregation as well as for the Covenant at large.

I was personally the beneficiary of the service of these committees in double measure. I entered military service from Chicago and was a member of the North Park Covenant Church. This assured me regular mailings of the sprightly newsletter from that congregation and its service committee. Once away, I discovered how important it was for me that there had been a bridal shower or a volleyball game or a weenie roast on the lakefront involving my friends. Because I was serving the Edgewater Covenant Church in Chicago as interim pastor when I entered the service, I was also blessed by their caring, and ate the crumbled cookies from their loving hands. Even if there had been a way of sending cookies intact, I don't believe that a perfect shape would have conveyed the good will of the "pepparkakor" that had undergone a eucharistic breaking before reaching my APO. God rest them merry!

Another ministry in which the local church played a significant role was that of evangelism. Especially on the West Coast, where many ports of embarkation and staging areas had been established for troops being deployed in the Pacific theater, Covenant churches and pastors carried on a significant gospel ministry to thousands. This was particularly true in the Seattle area and the San Francisco-Oakland and San Diego districts. Many service people who affiliated with our congregations after the war spoke with warm appreciation of the invitation to living faith they were given by Covenant churches and homes, particularly in the centers of embarkation, before leaving for their hazardous assignments.

CHAPTER THIRTY-ONE

The War: Its Aftermath

There was a record player in the sparsely furnished lounge of BOQ #37 which, in the summer of 1943, kept playing, "There'll be bluebirds over the white cliffs of Dover" and "When the lights go on again all over the world." You took the almost daily letter with the Iron Mountain, Michigan postmark and the dear, unmistakable handwriting into your cubicle, stretched out on the taut wool of the U.S. blanket, and began to savor every line from a land of pine scent and playing children. You wondered if that stuff about bluebirds and the end of the blackout would ever be true.

But prophecy did come true, at least for most of us. Two years later, in an Alpine village in Austria, the lights did go on and we could go home.

Thanksgiving Day, 1945, we drove up to a family gathering in Wisconsin with the children leading us in the singing of "Over the river and through the woods to grandfather's house we go." A voice on the car radio talked about thankfulness and grief, the emptied chairs that would never be filled. But we still lived in a kind of numbness, too tired and too glad to think any other thought than, "It's over. Thank God, it *is* over."

Before and during the war there were dire prophecies about the demise of religion after the war. But even on the returning troop ships the mood was upbeat. A lot of people wanted to get home and celebrate family life and community life and on a Sunday morning troop to the "little brown church in the vale." The theologians and sociologists would later talk about "acculturated religion" and a "confusion of values" and deplore that this was not the "high religion" of biblical faith; but to millions family, home, and church were blissfully homogenized in the forties and fifties. The sorting out and the perceptive judgment would come later.

Thousands upon thousands of women caring for children in substandard housing near the military installations or men dreaming of a white Christmas in the South Pacific had hoped for a white house in a quiet village and had been buying war bonds and saving quarters for the day of their exodus. At that point there were no negative thoughts about "suburban sprawl," "little houses made of ticky-tacky," and the sad men in the "gray flannel suits." That also would come eons later.

At the head of the procession of returning service personnel was a cadre of young people who, under a variety of circumstances, had already committed their lives to "the Lord of the harvest" and the service of the world. They were aiming for seminaries and Bible institutes or for colleges and universities to lay the academic foundation of a devout life. They were planning to be pastors, missionaries, youth workers, social workers, doctors, nurses, teachers, translators, evangelists, or evangelistic singers and musicians. They were headed for the inner city, the steaming jungle, the inaccessible, difficult place to witness to the grace of him who had loved them and given himself for them.

THE COVENANT'S POSTWAR MISSION

The Evangelical Covenant Church, although small and still struggling with its ethnic identity, was not unaware of both the challenge and the problem of young people now suddenly beating at the doors. By 1948 enrollment at North Park Theological Seminary had doubled—from forty to eighty—and three years later it was 140. On the youth front there was a similar surge. The 1950 Quadrennial at Covenant Heights, near Estes Park in Colorado, was packed out with over 500 young people under the overall leadership of Erick I. Gustafson, who had been appointed director of young people's work in 1949. In 1951 Aaron Markuson was elected executive secretary of Christian education and teamed with Erick Gustafson in another highly successful Quadrennial, this one at Mission Springs in Scotts Valley, California. Out of these events came Covenant Youth of America, more as a movement than an organization.

There were essentially three things that prepared the Covenant for its postwar misson and readied it for the utilization of the youth reservoir made available to it:

1. The maturing of concepts and methods of churchmanship—the "how to" of effective leadership for a new time.

2. The shaping of a program consonant with the Covenant's spiritual objectives.
3. The increase in available funding and in the spirit of stewardship.

When the war ended, T.W. Anderson was fifty-six and thus at the height of his powers. Although an ordained minister, he was a layperson at heart and saw the Covenant more as a mission organization than as a church denomination. But he was an effective church leader and had the insight to identify, encourage, and recommend for appointment people of unquestioned skills and devotion. At this time the central administration of the Covenant had a minimal organization consisting of the president and the secretary of missions (in 1945 a secretary of home missions was added). There were eight boards: Foreign (or World) Missions, Ministerial, Home Missions, Christian Education (Youth Work), Higher Education, Benevolence, Publications, and Stewardship and Pensions. There were liaison members from the Executive Board sitting on the various administrative boards, and the administrators had direct informal access to the president, but the structure did not permit the close interaction that would have made all the major concerns of the denomination equally present to the chief administrator.

A similar gap existed between the headquarters of the Covenant and the various regional conferences. In fact, no valid rationale had been developed for the place and role of the conferences and the conference superintendents in the total picture.

Ultimately, many of these problems were to be solved by the new Constitution adopted in 1957, but in 1945 that was still twelve years away. The best that can be said about the churchmanship of the 1940s is that it benefited from the intuition and goodwill of the leaders but may have suffered somewhat from the amiability that persisted in many situations. We shall return to this topic.

CHANGE AND GROWTH

Meanwhile, a step in the right direction was the placing of Edgar Swanson, Sr., the secretary of stewardship and pensions, in the position of secretary of home missions in 1945, a position he retained until 1951. His election coincided with the flight of rural workers, particularly young workers, to the cities. The following two decades saw an enormous expansion of activity in the urban and suburban churches to accommodate these thousands. Expenditures nationally for new church building alone rose to 500 million dollars annually. Evangelistic and missionary effort formerly concentrated in rural areas was all at once an anachronism and was transferred to the cities to which America's rural population had been drawn, not only by burgeoning war industries but by the population drift of returning service veterans (Anderson 1984, 115-116).

The establishment of "Frontier Friends" in 1951 (it initiated its program in 1952) to assist local congregations with the financing of church construction;[1] the growth of the Home Missions budget (Covenant and conference) from $44,000 in 1932 to $400,000 twenty years later; the designation of a year of emphasis for church extension (1956-57); and the rapid growth of resources in the Church Extension and Covenant Development Funds, both of which lent money for church construction—all these provide evidence for the commitment of the Covenant at this time to the expansion of Home Missions.

Reference has already been made to the effectiveness of the Quadrennials in channeling young gifts and energies toward the ministry of the church. A parallel activity for high school youth was developed in the Covenant High Congresses (CHIC) begun in 1956. Back of such programs lies an effective regional conference program of high league camps which goes back to the 1930s.

The establishment of the Covenant Caravan program in 1960, which enlisted scores of Covenanters, also served to motivate and canalize dedicated energies into service in a number of local churches.

Another way in which the Covenant served the younger generation was through the training of hospital and retirement home personnel. Until 1960 the School of Nursing at Swedish Covenant Hospital in Chicago served a crucial function in educating young women for professional, compassionate, and faith-motivated service as nurses. When in 1960 North Park College, with which the hospital had been affiliated in its nursing program, decided to establish a collegiate nursing department, the formal connection was severed. But the hospital continues to provide training opportunities for the North Park program. The Board of Benevolence also gives increasing numbers of youth internship opportunities in its expanding system of retirement homes.

Another area of service that appealed to the young people of the 1940s was that of world missions. With the presence of such youth in greater number than for several decades, hopes for and expansion of all Covenant mission fronts increased as well. Ralph P. Hanson replaced the ailing Gust E. Johnson in 1944 as secretary of missions. Hanson had been a career missionary in Alaska and was an able and energetic leader of the department. During his first decade of service the annual foreign mis-

---

1. By 1960, $500,000 had been contributed by 13,000 individuals.

sions budget climbed from $167,000 to $445,000 and the number of missionaries from 61 to 159.

Immediately after the war there was reason for optimism on all the Covenant mission fields. Africa and China were back in communication and Alaska looked more promising with the planning of a new congregation and the hope of establishing a radio station in Nome.[2] But Communists supplanted the troublesome Japanese in China and by 1948 the murder of three Covenant missionaries—Dr. Alik Berg, Esther Nordlund, and Martha Anderson—in Hupeh Province at the hands of robber-Communists hastened the abandonment of the field.

But the Chinese themselves were not abandoned, for work was started as soon as possible in Taiwan. By January, 1949, a mission was underway in Japan. Missionary energies were shifted to Latin America in 1947, and after preparatory language studies, seven missionaries began work in Ecuador in 1948.

In the early part of the postwar period the missionary situation in Belgian Congo (now Zaire) seemed most promising, and I could write with guarded optimism in 1954:

> In this area [on the Ubangi River] the Free Church in the period 1922-1937 had established three head stations: Kala, Tandala, and Karawa. By 1931 the project had become burdensome to the resources of the denomination (the Free Church), and in 1936 the Covenant was approached in the interest of establishing a joint mission on the Ubangi field. This offer was accepted in 1937 and the Covenant took over the head station at Karawa. Since that time the denomination has made the Congo field its largest missionary enterprise. This is understandable in the light of developments in China and the recurring problems of the Latin American field.
>
> By 1940 a new head station had been established at Gbado; By 1948 work was under way at Bokada; in 1950 a head station was organized at Wasolo of the Abumambazi area. From the four missionaries who initiated our Congo work in 1937 the African staff has grown to 55, of which four are doctors, 11 nurses, and 40 evangelists, teachers, and practical workers. The Covenant Church in the Congo numbers 10,000 baptized members. There are presently 5,000 children and young people enrolled in the mission schools. In 1951-52, 22,000 patients were given medical care in the head station clinics or in the hospital at Karawa. . . .
>
> At present the Covenant Mission also works actively as a member of the Congo Protestant Council and has one of its missionaries on the staff of the Congo Christian Institute at Bolenge, a training school for native teachers founded by Disciples of Christ mission.
>
> One of the promising signs of maturity in the Congo is the interest among the native Christians in the organization of the indigenous church . . . (Nyvall and Olsson 1954, 162-163).

2. KICY began broadcasting on Easter Sunday, 1960.

In most respects the situation in 1954 was full of unrealized possibilities, but even then there were ominous warnings. I concluded my brief summary of the African situation by writing:

> The African field is not without its problems. Chief of these is the ferment raised by the growing awareness of native Africans that they are . . . poor tenants on their own land. Ninety per cent of the continent is under the control of European powers . . . the Mau Mau terror in the Kenya colony which lies east of our Congo field must be interpreted in the light of this growing awareness. The repressive Malan regime in South Africa has given fuel to the flame, and the Communists here, as in China, are quick to exploit a golden opportunity to embarrass and humiliate the colonial and capitalistic west (Nyvall and Olsson 1954, 163).

But in 1945 much of this was not yet evident and the Covenant stood ready to train and equip missionary candidates for Africa and other promising areas.

The feasibility of these plans and programs rested upon adequate funding, and the Covenant was fortunate in having a constituency which both wanted and could give to denominational causes. With the end of the devastating economic depression of the 1930s, the financial stimulus of the war effort, and the rebuilding of America which followed, more and more money became available. In 1941 a Fiftieth Anniversary Fund of $150,000 was raised for the construction of a much needed seminary building; in 1944 the Covenant raised a Sixtieth Anniversary Fund of $500,000 for church extension, pension endowment, the contemplated seminary building, a Covenant administration building, and a foreign mission expansion program; the Diamond Jubilee Fund planned for 1960 and designed to raise $1,750,000 was oversubscribed and brought in over $2,000,000.

A major role in forming the Covenant image and motivating the denominational enterprise was played by Covenant Publications, self-conscious and active since 1894 but living until 1960 (when *Missions-Wännen*, its active opponent, finally expired) under the pressures of "loyal opposition." In 1955 the effort to keep Swedish alive in the pages of *The Covenant Weekly* was finally abandoned with the appointment of Carl Philip Anderson as editor. Anderson broke new ground, both with the innovative paper he edited and with his concept of publishing, and during the next fifteen years the publications program served as a source of significant information and motivation for the Covenant.[3]

3. See Nyvall and Olsson 1954, pp. 133-137 and *FF*, pp. 94, 113.

But despite all this activity, the crucial issue for the Covenant in 1945 was higher education—the role to be played by the seminary and, closely related to this, the need for expanded general education for the youth of the church. We shall deal first with the issue of theological education and its impact on the denomination.

THE COVENANT AND ITS SEMINARY

The returning veterans who enrolled at North Park Seminary at war's end represented a variety of backgrounds and expectations. The college at North Park was still only a junior college and the seminary was not yet accredited by the AATS, the American Association of Theological Schools.[4] At this time credentials for ministerial service in the Covenant were still two years of college and three of seminary with one obligatory year of internship, although more demanding requirements were being contemplated. Hence, in the early postwar years it was possible to find oneself in a number of academic classifications:

1. A seminary student with two years of accredited work from North Park Junior College or some equivalent institution and contemplating a four-year theological course at North Park Seminary.
2. A student with a four-year degree from an accredited college or university and now enrolling for the four-year theological course at North Park Seminary.
3. A special student with enough academic work at the college and seminary level in another institution and now enrolling for the so-called diploma course at North Park Seminary.

Among students registering in the period 1945-1955 there were quite a few who came out of Covenant churches, and of this number several who had attended North Park College. It is well to remember that not all students enrolling at this time were veterans or those with some type of service deferment. But there was a goodly number of these and among them not so few who had had virtually no previous contact with the churches of the Covenant or with North Park. For the most part these students had become acquainted with the Covenant while on wartime visits to hospitable churches or through contacts with chaplains and young people from the denominational family.

Often these "first contact" churches were in the West Coast group

4. It is now the ATS, the Association of Theological Schools, since it also comprises Canada.

alluded to earlier. They represented a more conservative theological view than the congregations of the Midwest or East Coast and perhaps a more aggressive type of evangelistic outreach. This is not to say that there were not many churches in the Midwest and East Coast that worked along similar lines, but because of differing troop concentrations, they did not have the same opportunity to minister to young people from the services.

In any event, the service people who came to a living faith in Christ in the port churches or were encouraged by them to consider some particular form of Christian service were often left with an impression, wittingly or unwittingly, that the Covenant was a Fundamentalist denomination or grouping of churches which differed from others of a similar type mainly in its freedom from concern about doctrinal minutiae and its openness to a variety of the theological viewpoints within the biblicistic grouping. Hence the impression developed among these young people that the Covenant throughout—its leadership, institutions, and membership—conformed to this pattern. As far as I have been able to determine, this impression was rarely if ever corrected, despite the fact that the majority of teachers in the seminary, a large number of pastors of influential churches, a significant percentage of conference superintendents, and a not inconsiderable proportion of laypersons did not embrace this type of conservatism (i.e. Fundamentalism). I am not saying that they were not conservatives, that is believers in classical Christianity with a strong commitment to the faith as stated in the tenets of the Apostle's Creed and to the Scriptures as spelled out in the Covenant constitution. I am saying that they were not believers in any form of verbal inspiration that would have satisfied those who called themselves Fundamentalists. And yet, despite this, a number of seminarians enrolled with the expectation that the teachers of the school shared these biblicistic views.

That this was so became apparent when some of the students without previous knowledge of the Covenant entered the classrooms. Donald C. Frisk, who was to give thirty-five years to distinguished teaching in the theological department of the seminary, joined the faculty in 1945; I came to the campus in 1948. How we and other members of the faculty and administration were viewed by some of these students becomes clear in Donald T. Robinson's careful documentation of William C. Doughty's experience with the seminary and the denomination. In a taped interview with Robinson, Doughty says:

> Now it was at Moody that I met my wife, who was a Covenant girl, born and raised in the Covenant. We would attend the Lakeview Covenant Church in Chicago . . . then her pastor was Edwin Johnson of the

Oakland Covenant Church and he subsequently performed the cere-
mony for Mrs. Doughty [and myself] when we were married in 1941.
Because of my acquaintance with these churches, I became involved in
the Covenant church life. Fact is, I joined the Oakland Covenant
Church.

Now while I was at Moody and after I separated from the Presbyterian Church U.S.A., I made quite a study of the various denominations
and what they stood for, principles and so on, with a view to determining which one I thought I would want to cast my lot with; and from
what I learned of the Covenant, I felt that the Covenant denomination
was one that I wanted to be affiliated with, and I joined it.

At this point Robinson interposes a question to which Doughty then
responds. "Now what were your original assumptions, suppositions
[about] what the Covenant was?"

With my introduction [to] and acquaintance [with] the Covenant in those
first and early years, I believed that the Covenant was a fundamental,
very conservative denomination. Everybody I met and talked to
believed like I did. I was introduced basically to the men in the California conference and to the pastor and the preaching of the Lakeview (if I
remember the name correctly) Covenant Church. So that my early impressions of the Covenant was that it was fundamental, strongly conservative, following the doctrines, beliefs, and positions that basically I
think pretty much were taught at Moody Bible Institute [as the] biblical
position.

Doughty then outlines briefly his life and training until his enrollment
at the seminary. He says:

And I set myself aside, and I prayed and fasted and read the Word to
get God's leading, and I felt very definitely led to go to North Park
Seminary to qualify for the Covenant ministry. . . .

Now it was while I was at North Park and in the classes there, in the
theology class and some of the other classes, that I became aware that
there was another side to the Covenant, a more liberal side, and a side
which I identified as a leaning toward neo-orthodoxy. *This was really
the first time that I realized that the Covenant had two faces, two sides
to it. I realized that the slant and emphasis in the theological classes, for
instance, was definitely a promoting of the Barthian viewpoint of the
Scripture.* I can remember that I did go in and talk with Professor Frisk,
and I asked him why in his assignment of collateral reading there was so
much given in reading the neo-orthodox men, and why there were not
some assignments in reading given in the men who would take a fundamental position on the Scripture and the Word. And Professor Frisk said
that they felt that most of the men coming to the seminary, because of
their background, already had this position and viewpoint and that they
needed to be introduced to this other side. . . .

Robinson then asks what Doughty's relationship was to his fellow students and some of the other instructors, and Doughty responds:

> . . . I would say probably that my relationship to the instructors was perhaps a little closer than the relationship to the students for the simple reason that I did take time to go in to talk [to] for instance, Professor Frisk and Dr. Karl Olsson, and discuss these matters. . . . And even though I disagreed with Professor Frisk and disagreed with Professor Olsson on some of the positions that they took, the personal relationship with them was good—yes, yes, very good.

PART FIVE

Crisis in Churchmanship
1947-1966

CHAPTER THIRTY-TWO

Polarization

William Doughty's statement clarifies the situation that obtained after World War II in the Covenant and at the school, especially among entering students. Many of those without previous contact with the Covenant came with the expectation that the seminary—its students and faculty— would be conservative evangelicals, "fundamental" if not "Fundamentalists," and that although there might be minor deviations from this norm in lectures and discussions, there was a basic unanimity in all matters pertaining to biblical faith.

Doughty's statement also clarifies the corollary of this inference about the seminary, viz., that serious deviations (such as adherence to dialectical theology in the thought of Karl Barth) would simply not occur. If they did, it was appropriate that such deviations be noted and the proper denominational authority or agency be informed.

Closely related to this conviction was a view of the Bible that not only rejected every form of higher criticism—an understandable antipathy—but also found the garden variety of textual criticism unacceptable.

To recapitulate: students of Doughty's convictions, and there were quite a few of these, did not expect and would not accept, at least initially, a teaching that used the biblical text as a source of theological truth but was not based upon a belief in verbal inerrancy. Nor were they happy about being confronted with problems of authorship of biblical materials or matters such as seeing contradictions in accounts, omissions, or probable editing of the texts.

311

CONCERN IN THE CLASSROOM

Because of the lack of instructors in the seminary when I came to teach in 1948, I was asked to teach in some areas outside, or almost outside, my professional competence. For example, I had a deep commitment to New Testament studies and had some acquaintance with the literature, but I was not a trustworthy guide in translating and interpreting the original languages. I was hence forced to teach the biblical courses assigned to me as courses in English Bible. This has some advantages, for in my graduate studies I had become acquainted with methods of formal textual analysis and I was able to apply these methods to the biblical texts with, I hope, some advantage to the students.

But even a nonlinguistic approach required me to deal with simple questions of general introduction and authorship. I discovered that raising questions of dating and authorship, such as those affecting the Gospel of John and the Epistles, induced not a little anxiety in some of my students. They had expected a simple and direct defense of the traditional approach to these questions and were understandably disappointed. At first this both surprised and irritated me, for textual criticism of this type had been part of the *modus operandi* at the seminary from the very beginning. P.P. Waldenström, to some extent David Nyvall and Axel Mellander, and certainly Nils W. Lund had raised these very questions without any intention of bringing the authority of Scriptures into doubt. Even so negative a critic of the Covenant as Eric Brolund indicated in his book *Missionsvännerna* that this kind of biblical study had been acceptable to the fathers and had been done by the great Waldenström himself.

But now the issues generally accepted as debatable among Covenant evangelicals were no longer thought arguable among some of the students at the seminary. The authorship of Hebrews, 2 Peter, and the Apocalypse, the relationship of the Synoptic Gospels to the Gospel of John, and the real or ostensible difference in the writings of Paul and James—to name only a few—these issues had to be reintroduced and re-argued before a student forum which, in part at least, struck me as curiously reactive and defensive.

Meanwhile, in other classrooms in the seminary, Eric G. Hawkinson, who became dean in 1951, Donald C. Frisk, and Nils W. Lund were meeting similar opposition in other areas of study. Frisk's lectures and discussions were taken down in shorthand by a zealous student and were later (1958) published by William C. Doughty in a pamphlet "A Cause for Concern in the Covenant." We shall return to this topic directly. Hawkinson was also a "cause for concern" and was made the subject of intercession by a group of students. Lund was not immune, although his scholarly interest had shifted from critical topics to form critical studies, notably *chiasmus*.

UNDERLYING PROCESSES

Those of us on the faculty who were confronted with this type of resistance became aware only gradually of the theological and cultural processes that underlay it. I think some of us had assumed that the bitter battles of the thirties and forties both inside and outside the denomination were largely behind us and that the dialectical theology already alluded to would provide a basis for future unity. The Bible, biblical theology, and the doctrine of the church had certainly moved back to the center of Protestant concern. What was now needed was a process of negotiation and mutual accommodation in order to achieve shared objectives and a more harmonious future.

But those of us who nourished such hopes were clearly wrong.

On the basis of my special interest in the conflict between old-line Mission Friend piety and Darby dispensationalism, which influenced the founders of the "Free," I am now better able to understand what we were confronting in the fall of 1948 when, after considerable wrestling with the question of vocation, I began my seminary teaching at North Park. Earlier I have indicated my indebtedness to Clarence Bass and Ernest R. Sandeen in seeking to develop an integrated view of Darbyism and its variations on the American scene. I must also acknowledge my debt to them in their analysis of what happened to dispensationalism after 1930. A further and more recent perspective has been provided by Timothy P. Weber in his well-documented and perceptive book, *Living in the Shadow of the Second Coming, American Premillennialism 1875-1982.*

The transmutation of American Fundamentalism and the World Christian Fundamentals Association (WCFA) into the group called the National Association of Evangelicals which was founded in 1941 was, as Sandeen has pointed out, inevitable. By overidentifying itself with the antievolution crusade, which was less than successful, the WCFA not only lost respect but proved unfaithful to one of its basic tenets: no effort on the part of any human organization, however noble or even faithful to what it understands as a calling, can reverse the downward trend of human history. Sandeen writes:

> . . . The philosophy of William Jennings Bryan and the antievolution crusade was incompatible with the assumptions on which millenarianism was built. The millenarian did not believe that legislative action could produce pure morals or right thinking. He was convinced that only the Spirit of God could furnish the power by which these things could be

accomplished. And he was convinced even more deeply, moreover, that man's thinking and acting were on an irretrievable downgrade which man was powerless to reverse and which was, indeed, one of the clearest signs of the imminence of the second advent. When a millenarian like Riley said such things as "If Christ delay, the defeat of Modernism is certain," he was falling into the most serious kind of millenarian contradiction. There does not seem to be any way in which a consistent millenarian could have justified the attempt to force "creationism" upon the schools or, for that matter, "orthodoxy" upon the churches. To do so was to forsake one of the basic ingredients in the millenarian world view. Does this suggest why some conservative millenarians such as G. Campbell Morgan left the World's Christian Fundamentals Association when it had turned toward antievolutionary strategy, or why A.C. Dixon found he could not remain associated with the Baptist Bible Union?

The association of millenarian leaders with the antievolution crusade was a total failure in terms of its own goals. The teaching of evolution was not stopped. Within the context of millenarian history this tactic seems to represent a further example of the decadence of millenarianism during this century. During the nineteenth century, though not dominant, it had fought its theological battles on the same theoretical grounds as its opponents and received the respect a fair and honest opponent deserves. But during the twentieth century the group splintered over the attempt to interpret the scriptures according to their crucial theory of literal exegesis. At the same time, the party of opposition rapidly discarded the assumptions and methods that it had shared with the millenarians and moved toward the liberal and critical understanding of the Bible and a wholly different conception of the nature of society and history.

The Fundamentalist controversy cannot be explained entirely through the millenarian movement, although millenarianism did play a large and quite unappreciated role there; but the controversy does illustrate quite poignantly the decline if not the collapse of this valiant nineteenth-century minority view. Millenarian leadership in the twenties did not show the strength of character, deep grasp of and reverence for biblical truth, or intellectual acuity demonstrated by the late nineteenth-century leaders. The movement appears split and stricken, possibly because some of the men who became most popular could not direct their followers either as consistent conservatives or as moderate liberals (Sandeen 1970, 267-269).

Sandeen's assessment is undoubtedly correct. By the middle of the 1930s the signs of the demise of the WCFA were multiplying. We have an extremely important letter dated January 4, 1933, from Gustaf F. Johnson to Gust E. Johnson, the secretary of the Covenant, promising to do what he can for the settlement of the controversial issues in the Covenant and to avoid personal matters in his published letters that might lead to misunderstanding. Most of these "controversial" matters had to do with the Fundamentalist-Modernist controversy which had reached an official climax in 1928.

In this connection Gust F. Johnson includes an item which indicates that even among Covenanters formerly loyal to the WCFA there is a cooling of ardor:

> I am glad that Paul Rood has been called as Covenant evangelist.[1] I hope that that will sever him from the World's Fundamentalist Association because it is no secret to either Rood or you that I would rather see him whole-heartedly devoting his full time to our work rather than to that work as I am afraid that no great headway can be made thru [sic] the Fundamentalist Association any more (Covenant Archives).

It is certainly true that insofar as Fundamentalism contained a considerable measure of dispensationalism with a commitment to millenarianism and an attendant pessimism about human history, the 1940s saw the emergence of something broader, more pragmatic, and more historically optimistic. I use the word "broader" advisedly, for the change from WCFA to NAE with the de-emphasizing of Fundamentalism did not by itself broaden the view of inspiration, nor was this intended. A form of strict biblicism remained at the core of the organization as is evident from paragraph three of its constitution, adopted April 7-9, 1942:

> It shall be required that those holding membership shall subscribe to the following doctrines:
> 1) That we believe the Bible to be the inspired, the only infallible, authoritative Word of God. . . .

It is clear that even today the biblical issue has not been resolved among evangelicals within or outside the NAE. Nor is biblical authority the only burning question faced by the "evangelical empire." As Timothy P. Weber points out:

> Despite its current power and prestige, evangelicalism cannot present a united front to the rest of the world. Now acceptable and generally respected throughout the culture, evangelicals apparently are left with no one to fight except each other. They are seriously at odds over the doctrine of biblical inerrancy, the role of women in the church, the practice and meaning of charismatic gifts, strategies and methods of mass evangelism and social action, and the use of wealth and natural resources in a needy world (Weber 1983, 4).

But we have gotten ahead of our story. There can be no question that present-day evangelicals are struggling with some controversial issues

---

1. Paul W. Rood, pastor of the Beulah Tabernacle in Turlock, California, 1922-1933, had organized the Bryan Bible League in 1925 and was president of the WCFA. He was a graduate of North Park Theological Seminary and served several Covenant pastorates. He died in 1956.

and can in no wise be considered a "seamless robe." In this respect, however, they do not differ greatly from their predecessors. But with all their differences, evangelicals continue to embrace an intransigence around the Scriptures which provides a crucial rallying point. It has been expressed popularly in Billy Graham's frequently used phrase, "The Bible says." What this means, at least in all that I have read of Graham or heard him say, is not only that the Bible is God's Word—a tenet in which he is joined by millions including this writer—but that every word is equally God's Word and hence equally useful or meaningful. He does not live by this rule, for there are obviously many biblical texts that he does not and would not use at almost any price, but his statement gives a character of total and invariable sanctity to every word found between the covers of the Bible.

My father used to tell an immigrant anecdote about a man who when asked if he had a Bible, replied that the Bible was so precious to him that he always kept it on the bottom of his trunk; which recalls a student from this period in the seminary who, through conversion from the Roman Catholic faith, had come into our midst. The credence he had once given his church and its vast and complicated systems of sanctity he now reserved for the Bible as a book, and I mean the actual physical volume. In a good-natured conversation with him, which was intended to uncover the theological root of this devotion to the book, a faculty member once asked him if he was not giving the Bible the status of a fourth person of the Trinity—a sort of "paper pope." But the student did not understand the question or perhaps chose not to understand it.

This overly reverential and somewhat defensive attitude toward the Bible, which often prevented some of the lowliest questions from being addressed to it, became the rallying point of much of the new evangelicalism. It may help to explain the establishment of new seminaries dedicated to biblicism and to the revitalization of some of the old. It provided the underpinning for a new thrust in media—publications as well as radio and very soon, television. *Christianity Today* began publishing in 1957 and very soon had become the dominant voice of the new evangelicalism. Radio and television programs of a nondenominational kind gradually pushed church programs off the air. Another result of this devotion to the Bible was the emergence of ecumenical youth agencies such as Youth for Christ, Young Life, Campus Crusade, and the intellectually more rigorous Inter-Varsity. But the most significant manifestation of the intense devotion to the Bible was the phenomenon of Billy Graham (Abraham 1984).

A MATTER OF CERTITUDE

Before treating this topic in more detail, it may be well to delineate brief-ly what postwar biblicism meant and why it became so central a concern for the evangelicals I encountered on the campus during my first years as a seminary instructor 1948-1959. The major preoccupation of these stu-dents was the matter of certitude. In their conversion and "new birth" they had discovered the Bible and the Holy Spirit as prime causes of "change." Hence their certainty about Christian truth came not so much from a process of rational study and inference or of meditation as from a personal faith experience received in concert with the believing commu-nity. The Christian verities, they felt, had come to them in regeneration. Thus they had passed "from darkness to light." Thus they who were once blind had come to sight. The metaphors were many and varied but the certainty was the same. They might have echoed the words of St. An-thony flung into the teeth of the skepticism voiced by some at the Coun-cil of Nicaea, "But I have seen him." The argument is unassailable.

Since the emergence of modern scientific thinking in the Western world, truth and certitude have often become identified, perhaps over-identified, with correct inferences from data. Truth is what can be proved to be so by a probable or necessary inference. The surety thus attained has been identified in the minds of many believers with the certitude of Christian experience. The Bible has been asked to be scientifically true in the same way as certain natural laws are said to be true. In the 1925 dis-cussions between David Nyvall and Gustaf F. Johnson about the nature of biblical truth, which were printed in the denominational press (see chapters 25,28), Nyvall suggested that the creation account in Genesis should not be considered biology; although true, it was not that kind of truth. But many of his readers were not happy with the distinction.

Such an equation between Christian certitude and the surety we may derive from the connections between natural phenomena is sometimes made by evangelicals anxious to establish the reliability of the Bible. I once heard Billy Graham tell about a flight between Korea and Tokyo in which landing in Japan was complicated by fog. It required the utmost instrumental precision to consummate. In commenting on this event Graham argued that just as the landing in order to be safe had to be sci-entifically certain with no allowable approximations or mere probabili-ties of any kind, so the biblical truth cannot admit any element of uncer-tainty. For it also functions as a carefully calibrated instrument of guid-ance. This illustrates the fact that as the demand for precision in science and technology grows and grows, so does the expectation for an analo-gous precision in scriptural truth.

The Bible is now asked to be true in a way never expected of it in the earlier centuries. The concern for verbal exactitude suggests that we are in effect asking for the veridity of the micrometer and ultimately of a super-micrometer. But if we are willing to be open to the historic facts as we know them, it must be obvious that the Scriptures, although trust-worthy *in their own way*, do not attempt to offer us any such scientific reliability. I submit a simple example from a well-known episode: Paul's experience on the road to Damascus.

The truth of the event itself is not at stake. Paul does not mention it specifically in the epistles known to be his, but does provide the frame-work for it in 2 Corinthians 11:31-33 and Galatians 1:13-17. In Acts the event is reported three times: 9:1-9, 22:5-16, and 26:9-28.

These three accounts (which we shall call A, B, and C) tell the same story but do differ in some details. For example, in A a great light shines on Saul as he is on his way from Jerusalem to Damascus. He falls to the ground and hears a voice saying, "Saul, Saul, why do you persecute me?" (NEB). Saul replies, "Tell me, Lord, who you are." And the voice answers, "I am Jesus, whom you are persecuting. But get up and go into the city, and you will be told what you have to do." The text continues, "Meanwhile *the men who were traveling with him stood speechless; they heard the voice but could see no one.* Saul got up from the ground, but when he opened his eyes he could not see; so they led him by the hand and brought him into Damascus. He was blind for three days, and took no food or drink" (italics mine). The encounter with Ananias follows.

Version B (Acts 22:5-16) is given by Paul to the Jerusalem mob on the steps of the Roman military barracks. In this account Paul, in describing the events on the road to Damascus, says, *"My companions saw the light but did not hear the voice that spoke to me"* (italics mine).

In version C (Acts 26:9-28), which Paul presented before a company of dignitaries at Caesarea that included the Governor Porcius Festus as well as King Agrippa and his spouse, Bernice, there are some differences from accounts A and B. In this story Paul speaks of a light that falls on him *and* his companion, he indicates that all the companions and not only he fell to the ground with him and he finally mentions that the voice of Jesus spoke Hebrew. But perhaps the most significant difference is the way in which Saul is told of God's plans for him. In A and B Ananias is given these plans but in C it is Jesus himself who provides the Pauline scenario. In A Jesus delivers the plan for Paul to Ananias in a statement half the length of the one in C. In A there is no indication that Ananias delivers the message he has been given. In B he gives the message to Saul and gives instructions about the latter's baptism.

My intention with this brief and all too simple exegesis is not to discredit the passage or to reflect in any way upon the authority of the biblical word. Despite variations in the telling of the story which I cannot deny or explain away, the basic message is clear. My aim is rather to indicate what degree of verbal accuracy the early Church demanded of its texts in order to make them reliable testimony to the Gospel or to salvation history. We must conclude on the basis of what the texts tell us and the manner in which they are communicated that criteria such as verbal inerrancy could not have been demanded.

This circumstance does not dispense with the need for the greatest possible accuracy in the conveying of a text. If the New Testament tells us anything, it is that the witnesses gave a very high value to textual and historical veridity and consistency. According to Acts, the apostles were credentialed on the basis of their witness to the resurrection. What further qualified them for this witness was their presence with the disciples "all the while we had the Lord Jesus with us, coming and going, from John's ministry of baptism until the day he was taken up from us" (Acts 1:21-22, NEB). The witnessing is crucial and so is the reliability of the witnesses; even more so is the intention and the work of the Holy Spirit in informing the Church of the meaning of these things, in other words, in providing a primal hermeneutics of the saving truth.

PRIMARY RESPONSIBILITY

In dealing with some of the seminary students who, like William Doughty, came with incorrect expectations of us, we saw it as our primary responsibility to share with them an authentic faith in the Scriptures as the saving truth while at the same time, with a meekness appropriate to such high matter, apprising them of the important questions raised by present day textual and theological studies.

I was then, as I am now, an adherent of classical Christianity, an evangelical and a conservative although not a Fundamentalist. I have felt strong intellectual and spiritual affinities with some English Christian writers, including T.S. Eliot, Dorothy Sayers, Charles Williams, J.R.R. Tolkien, and C.S. Lewis, as well as members of their circle. I consider all of them "believers" although I am sure that there are many matters of faith on which we would not agree. But I venture to say that none of them are biblicists in the sense that they consider the Bible inerrant. The one who probably comes closest to this position is C.S. Lewis, but his stand on the Old Testament would probably make him suspect in many Fundamentalist circles.

I mention my intellectual sympathies with these writers because it helps to define the milieu in which we of the faculty participated. We were not reluctant conformists to a creedal norm who lived in fear of being perceived in a doctrinal error. We were enthusiastic believers who were committed to share a positive scriptural faith with our students. We had been given the freedom to disagree and we disagreed on many things. We had no theological guru. We were called neo-orthodox, but I remember no particular devotion to Barth, Brunner, Tillich, or Bultmann. We were not even in agreement on Waldenström. Some stood closer to Luther or Calvin than to any modern thinker. My preferences ran to Paul and Augustine, Francis and Bonaventura. As an interpreter I chose Etienne Gilson, the great French Catholic historian of philosophy. But we were first and last primal Christians, being nurtured on the Scriptures and in the family of faith.

Despite this, some of the students in the seminary could not accept us as bona fide witnesses. Because we, although committed to an inspired and authoritative Bible, did not adhere to their view of inspiration, they felt that we were not quite trustworthy. I do not accuse these students of a lack of charity or grace. Most of them probably lived in as close fellowship with the Lord as we, but in their eyes we seemed to suffer from a tragic flaw because we were at variance on the issue of inspiration.

CHAPTER THIRTY-THREE

Crisis in Churchmanship

The difficulties around verbal inspiration also complicated attitudes toward ecumenism, just then in an upsurge. The first meeting of the World Council of Churches had been held in the summer of 1948 in Amsterdam. Although many of the leaders of the WCC were theologically conservative, their very association with mainline churches of miscellaneous composition rendered them suspect to many American evangelicals, particularly the members of the National Association of Evangelicals whose credo permitted no such waffling.

Meanwhile the SMF (the Covenant Church of Sweden) decided to affiliate with the World Council of Churches, and this action elicited a positive response from some of the members of the North Park Seminary faculty whose sympathies and associations were already causing concern.

The massive demonstration of ecumenical strength seen at Amsterdam served further to activate the effort for effective union among American evangelicals. Although no longer calling themselves, as formerly, "Fundamentalists," the evangelicals who rallied to the NAE standards generally adhered to the doctrine of verbal inspiration and found it unseemly to associate with theologians and pastors whose view of the Scriptures, although conservative enough, did not meet the inflexible biblicistic standards.

As indicated, the National Association of Evangelicals was organized in 1941 and attracted many of the older conservatives who had been associated with the World Christian Fundamentals Association. Considerable numbers of younger evangelicals, with a varied background, also joined the ranks, as did conservative denominations and local churches with strong biblicist sympathies, since the NAE provided the option of both individual and corporate membership.

The Covenant Church of North America did not join the World Council, nor did it affiliate with the National Council of Churches, the successor organization to the Federal Council. Although some local congregations and pastors joined the NAE, the creedless stance of the Covenant prevented the latter from joining, even though a considerable number of its members and churches may have wanted to take this step. Another barrier to any contemplated union with the NAE was the opposition among many young pastors and laypersons in the Covenant toward anything that smacked of Fundamentalism, although with another name.

Such opposition undoubtedly intensified the polarization within the Covenant family that had persisted for several decades. An informal poll conducted among Covenant church members in 1964-1965, which elicited an amazing response, indicated roughly in what direction the Covenant wanted to go (*FF*, 118). Of those responding, 37 percent wanted no conciliar affiliation of any kind, although of the remainder, 25 percent favored the NAE and only 11 percent the NCC.

The period 1945-1965 was hence in some sense "the best of times and the worst of times" in the seminary and the denomination. It was best in the sense that ethnicity was finally giving way to the opportunity of serving the whole community; it was best because the seminary was better equipped than ever to do its work. Nathaniel Franklin had observed in 1943 that the Covenant had "invaded Alaska, China, and Africa, but it cannot yet be said that we have invaded America" (Anderson, 1984, 97). But World War II changed all that.

It was the worst of times because for these twenty years the Covenant hovered on the edge of real division. This was not a new thing—freedom invites polarization—but it was now more serious because less held the Covenant together and because it had not yet developed a churchmanship appropriate to its nature. Presidents E.G. Hjerpe (1910-1927) and C.V. Bowman (1927-1933) were fine churchmen, but they worked largely within the ethnic envelope.

CHANGING TIMES

Before turning to the issue of churchmanship we shall look briefly at what the statistical data tells us about this time. Seminary enrollment, without reference to the ethnic element, shows significant change in the period 1945 through 1984. We are indebted to Glenn Anderson's study of enrollment from 1925 to 1985 for the salient facts. After hovering in the

40 to 50 range in the period of 1925-1945, enrollment soared from 40 in 1946 to 140 in 1951. It did not maintain this high profile for long, but it never again went below 60 except in the year 1971 when it was 54. After this it climbed to 79, 93, 116, 133, and 147. Since that time enrollment has stayed in the 140 range except for 1980 when it reached 155. The latest available figure is for 1985, when 160 students were enrolled.

Evidence for the radical ethnic modification taking place in the period 1942-1976 is provided by a simple study of ordinands based on surnames. Even though a study of this kind suffers from obvious inaccuracies (since numbers of Scandinavian immigrants changed their names from Johnson and Anderson to Jones and Andrews or from Carlson to Carlton or Gustafson to George), available biographical data and considerable personal acquaintance serve to moderate these deviations. The trends that emerge are significant.

In 1945 and 1947 Covenant ordinands did not include a single non-Scandinavian name. In 1943, 1946, and 1948 the number of non-Scandinavian names did not exceed 8 percent; beginning in 1949 the number never again sank beneath 10 percent, with one exception. The trend was generally in the opposite direction. In 1949 the percentage of non-Scandinavians was 24, in 1952 it was 22, in 1956 22, in 1957 34, in 1958 32, in 1959 28. From 1961 to 1963 it stayed in at 18 to 20 percent. Then from 1964 through 1970 it held between 36 and 48 percent. In 1971, an anomalous year, it fell to 9 percent but in 1972 it was 26 percent, in 1973 30 percent, in 1974 26 percent, and in 1975 63 percent. In 1976 it was 50 percent.

A significant conclusion emerges. The ethnic uniformity of the Covenant Church would never be recovered. Because so much of the identity of the denomination had been related not only to language and idiom but to a shared history and shared traditions (a common struggle as immigrants and the children of immigrants, a rich collage of worship experiences from the stately chorales of the established church to the folk melodies and lyrics of two centuries of awakening, a free and democratic working out of confessional and doctrinal issues in dialogue and personal witness, and the gradual maturing of a mode of governance), the process of Americanization was very threatening. A "family feeling" had held together even the most disparate; now an erosion of that feeling had begun.

I recall a small but highly sensitive meeting on the North Park campus in the early 1960s in which the participants were evenly divided between old line "Covies" and the newer and younger group "who knew nothing of Joseph." The meeting ended, as was the custom, with the serving of coffee and a somewhat strained joviality. One of the senior members of the negotiation began sharing some traditional Swedish-American anecdotes with touches of dialect and a trace or two of arcane humor. His comments were politely heard but the experience was like laying a naked sword between the two groups.

Of course, things were not often that desperate. Numbers of non-Scandinavians accepted the remnants of the ethnic "family feeling" with good grace. They learned to live with the allusions, the memories, the innuendos, the culture traits. They were grateful for the freedom they found and which they sometimes misunderstood. The authentic devotion to Christ and the Gospel and the commitment to being born again and hence to evangelism they found reassuring. They liked the emphasis on experience rather than dogmatic formulations and on the Pietistic discipline that made behavior important. Here, thank God, everything was not adiaphorous and indifferent.

The "Covies," on the other hand, made serious efforts to be hospitable and accepting. At the periphery pastors and laypersons were perhaps too ingratiating and made too short work of explaining the Covenant "mystique." To become a member of the fellowship was almost like the turning of a hand. The door was wide enough to include all believers in Christ but so narrow that only believers were invited into fellowship. So ran the rubric beloved by T.W. Anderson, president of the Covenant from 1933 to 1959.

But the implications of this were not always seen. Through the wide door came many believing, devout souls who relished both faith and freedom but were wise enough not to presume. But through that door came also people for whom freedom was an opportunity to devise a new yoke of bondage. They saw the Covenant as an untended garden which desperately needed pruning and cultivation. They set about to do this task with an almost Cromwellian gusto, not realizing that although much in the Covenant called for improvement, not everything needed to be changed so as to conform to Dogma A or Polity B.

The first critical situation developed in the Canada Conference, where a small group of pastors not only rejected the doctrine of freedom cherished by the Covenant and guaranteed by the denominational constitution, but insisted that henceforth the Covenant accept as an essential dogma the view of the atonement held by them. In his report to the Annual Meeting of the Covenant in 1946, the superintendent of the Canada Conference, G.A. Quarnstrom, summarized the matter:

> Some of our pastors have received their training at nondenominational schools, and these brethren hold very strongly to the substitutionary theory of the atonement, and lay particular stress upon its penal aspect. They are demanding that our conference accept their view of the atone-

ment and incorporate it into a creed, and that only this view be taught at our school.[1] . . . Traditionally our Covenant has maintained the right of freedom of conscience in the interpretation of non-essential Christian doctrines. To impose a creed would therefore violate one of our basic principles. (*YB*, 1946, 96).

When the Canada Conference followed the reasoning of its board and superintendent and refused to yield on this point, eight dissident pastors resigned and surrendered their ordination certificates.

A NEED FOR DIRECTION

This crisis weakened an already struggling conference, but perhaps its major significance lay in what it revealed of the hazards of Covenant freedom. So long as the ethnic identity of the Covenant proclaimed its character and served to filter out theological intransigence, the major struggles were domestic with the dimensions of a family quarrel, but once the doors were opened on the national and international scene with its infinite variety of dogmas and -isms, freedom needed some supplemental strategies. Above all it needed a clearer and more decisive concept of churchmanship.

In studying previous developments in the Covenant we have discovered the crucial role played by the churchmanship of Covenant presidents and in some instances by conference superintendents. In his informed discussion of the Northwest Conference, *A Precious Heritage*, Philip Anderson clarifies the implications of the presence and absence of effective churchmanship in the shaping of that strategic administrative unit of the Covenant.

But if churchmanship was a clamant need when the Covenant was relatively secure within its ethnic envelope, direction of much greater depth and power was needed once the barriers dissolved. Unfortunately, such churchmanship was not always available in the period now under consideration, and situations that might have been prevented were allowed to develop into explicit crises.

There were several identifiable reasons for this:

1. An intrinsic amiability made it impossible to call a spade a spade with the result that too many persons both lay and clergy were invited to come into the Covenant without any understanding of its history or its freedom. The consequence of this was often a kind of presumption.

---

1. The Covenant Bible Institute of Canada, now Covenant Bible College.

Such presumption might have been avoided if the church and its leadership had acted with greater prudence. An old country maxim talks about "confronting the bull in the gate," but the Covenant was then so anxious to be liked and so hungry for people, both clergy and laity, that it made the conditions for admission much too lax. It was only when some of the new recruits revealed themselves to be chronic problem persons that the full dimension of the imprudence became evident (to wit, the Canada fiasco).

2. Implicit in this problem was a general reluctance to see the denomination as a source of control. Many of those invited into the Covenant had been told that the denomination was congregational and that virtually all control was vested in the local church. But even at a time when the Covenant was most deeply pervaded by the ecclesiology of the "Free," this had not been true. From the beginning there was a pastoral registry and hence a denominational source of ministerial identification and ultimately of recommendation and credentialing. Early it made provision for the selection, training, and discipline of its clergy. It accepted responsibility for a number of functions: home and foreign missions, benevolences, publications, and Sunday school and youth work. And it moved progressively toward its present system of making the regional conferences administrative units of the Covenant, a step finally completed in 1957. As early as 1932 George M. Stephenson had spoken of the Mission Covenant as a compromise between congregationalism and presbyterianism (Stephenson 1932, 288), but despite this scholarly judgment, many Covenant leaders perpetuated the definition of the Covenant as congregational.

3. But even if the Covenant had come closer to the congregational model than it did, control could have been held by the elected leadership with greater effectiveness than has sometimes been the case. Leadership always implies more potential for creative decision-making than is spelled out in a constitution and by-laws, especially the capacity to set an imaginative course for the future and to shake and move for the common good.

I remember that as a young man I was invited to take a modest administrative position at a midwestern university. When I went in to see the dean about the job, I recalled my military experience and asked for a Standing Operating Procedure. "We don't have a SOP," said the dean. "That's why we *hired* you."

The effective leader is careful about developing consensus, but once he or she gets the best thinking that is available, it remains his or her responsibility to make the decision. Harry Truman will be remembered as one of our best presidents. He lacked Roosevelt's rhetoric and flair but he knew when he had to make a decision, even a very risky one. In that respect he was reminiscent of Abraham Lincoln who, in E.A. Robinson's line, "bore rancor with a cryptic mirth, Laconic and Olympian." No one who has tried to be a leader will be unmoved by Truman's pithy maxims, now a part of our folklore: "If you can't stand the heat, get out of the kitchen," and "The buck stops here."

When such opportunities for leadership are not claimed by the person or persons in power because the legal underpinnings are lacking or a standing operating procedure has not been developed, or a garden variety of courage is absent, critical situations may continue unchecked.

The political theory that underlies the mixed form of the Covenant constitution (democratic and republican, congregational and presbyterian) may seem practically unworkable. But the very presence of an accepted leader opens the door for informal tactics that can conduce to a high level of creative order without becoming arbitrary or despotic.

P.P. Waldenström, who was the formal leader of the Covenant of Sweden from 1903 until his death in 1917, had a very poor political theory about the denomination he led. He insisted that it was not a church but merely a gathering of congregations in which nearly all functions except foreign and, to a limited extent, home missions were the sole responsibility of the local church. With a stubborn persistence, for example, he fought the denominational pensioning of pastors, despite the practical impossibility of this for small congregations and despite the fact that he himself enjoyed a liberal pension from the state. But his personal prestige was so great that many of these errors were, if not overlooked, at least swallowed by his constituency, and he died as he had lived, a virtually unchallenged colossus.

Such informal "popery" is probably an ultimate threat to good order and is certainly a frustration to collegial creativity, and I am not suggesting that leaders are generally competent to direct without duly constituted authority and the readiness to consult their associates. But a constitution can sometimes mask cowardice. Hence it needs to be stretched to the utmost. Leaders *can* exercise ad hoc powers solely on the basis of who they are and are in the process of becoming in situations which require decisiveness. In contemporary discussions such an assumed right is sometimes called "moral power." This kind of power can grow with time in office and can remain on track without constant resort to constituted procedure, an anxious scanning of the rubrics. The creative leader can enable movement in the generally right direction by awareness of the

common will and a search for consensus, by established personal relationships, by a mutual exchange of needful concessions, by a persuasive
presence, and, on occasion, by a direct appeal.

A classical example of the last was J.F. Kennedy's dealing with "Big
Steel" in the crisis of 1962. He used a process called "jaw-boning" (from
Judges 15:16-17) to get the cooperation of the steelmakers in holding
down prices. That process had not been totally absent but not either con-
spicuously evident in Covenant leadership.

CHAPTER THIRTY-FOUR

TESTING THE COVENANT IDEA

If the campus of North Park College and Theological Seminary was ever cloistered and sleepy, that image was rapidly dissipated after World War II. A new administration taking office in 1950, an expanding and more youthful faculty, and, as we have noted, a rapidly growing and Americanized student body altered irreversibly the character of the school. Add to this the presence of a new building constructed like a fortress, boasting classical roof tiles and a copper-plated cupola, and equipped with a beautiful Georgian chapel, spacious classrooms, the novelty of faculty offices, and vastly improved library facilities, and the picture is complete.

Clarence A. Nelson was no sooner installed in his new responsibilities than he began thinking of and planning for an improved educational stance within the denomination both on the campus and beyond. Work got under way very soon to build on already initiated faculty and administrative plans toward a fully accredited four-year college with its first graduating class receiving bachelor degrees at the end of the decade (i.e. 1960). This goal was actually attained and much credit must be given to President Nelson for his role in this achievement[1].

---

1. I must mention a long and pleasant railroad trip from Iron Mountain, Michigan, to Chicago in the late 1940s with President Algoth Ohlson when he unfolded for me his hopes for a four-year institution on the North Park campus. But I was then at the University of Chicago and so enamored of Robert Maynard Hutchins's vision of a college that I proceeded to argue with Algoth Ohlson's perfectly reasonable plans for the future. I could not have been more misguided in my reasoning, and fortunately I lived to see the day that Ohlson's and Nelson's vision prevailed.

Simultaneously together with Eric G. Hawkinson, who became dean of the seminary in 1949, Clarence Nelson gave leadership to the upgrading of the seminary into a fully accredited, degree granting institution with the first class of Bachelors of Divinity slated to receive their degrees in 1963. At the beginning of the academic year 1953-1954 all candidates for graduation were obliged to present a bona fide bachelor's degree from a recognized college or its academic equivalent before being admitted to candidacy. Here also the best hopes were actualized.

THE SURVEY COMMISSION

But Nelson was also anxious to raise the Covenant's consciousness for the need of motivation, direction, and training of its young people. My recollection is that it was he whose vision and determination led in 1952 to the establishment of a task force called the Survey Commission which ultimately, under the chairmanship of Leslie R. Ostberg, produced the new constitution for the Covenant which was adopted in 1957. One of the three basic committees of the Survey Commission was that of youth and education; here Nelson had an opportunity to present some of his deepest convictions about a ministry to youth both in the context of the church community and of the Covenant's educational programs. The Survey Commission also devoted itself to two other primary concerns that formed the agendas of a finance committee and an organization committee. Of the twenty-two members of the commission eight were between the ages of thirty-two and forty-three, an indication that the denomination wished to benefit from the insight of a younger generation. But in spite of the fact that the 1950s were becoming aware of the potentials of female leadership, not a single woman graced the commission. That concern would emerge much later.[2]

The Survey Commission, which achieved a rare level of creative vision and work as well as of harmonious cooperation, brought to an end much of the ambivalence surrounding the Covenant's identity as a bona fide denomination. From its beginning, because of the presence of non-denominational and antidenominational influences (Waldenström, Skogsbergh, the "Free"), the Covenant had moved toward structure and responsible churchmanship only with the greatest caution. But the prolif-

---

2. In the summer of 1955 I was asked to conduct a seminar for women at a Covenant Bible camp. I based the seminar on the difference between the first-century family and community and those of the present. In the first century women lived and worked largely under the protection and leadership of men, and it is these attitudes that color the biblical view of women. In our world we have a much more open society, and women, even Christian women, need to learn to live in greater freedom and responsibility. I am not sure I was understood. I am very sure that my conclusions were not shared.

eration of ministries, the mounting complexity of the task, and the erosion of ethnic unity made a more sensitive calibration of accountability and control a growing need.

This meant that central administration could no longer carry out its task without closer contact with the diverse minisitries of the denomination. Not only did the departments of Home and Foreign (World) Missions need to be in constant interaction with the president and the secretary; the same need existed for Higher Education, Christian Education, Benevolence, and Publications as well as Stewardship and Pensions.

The new constitution instituted a most radical change in the structure of central administration. In the early years central administration had consisted of the president of the Covenant and the secretary. The president, in addition to other duties, had served as *missionsföreståndare*, that is as superintendent of missions. The secretary, in addition to being secretary of missions, had the function of recorder and correspondent as well as executive officer to the president. But in 1945 Edgar Swanson, Sr., who had served since 1941 as secretary of stewardship and pensions in order to lighten the burdens of central administration, became secretary of home missions.

With the new constitution central administration devolved upon a president, a secretary, and a treasurer (selected from among their number by the Covenant trustees). World and Home Mission joined North Park College and Theological Seminary, Christian Education, Publications, and Benevolence as well as Stewardship and Pensions, and in 1967, Ministerial Standing as administrative boards. The executives of these boards together with the president and the secretary became the Council of Administrators which served as an advisory body to the president and the Executive Board. Initially there was no executive secretary for the Board of the Ministry. Such a position was created in 1967 with the first incumbent being Earl M. VanDerVeer. The latter served loyally until 1984 and did significant pioneer work for the new secretariat.

A Board of Evangelism was created in 1977 and was served inititally by Randolph J. Klassen, whose ministry continued until 1981. He was succeeded by James E. Persson, who served for one year at which time the new Board of Church Growth and Evangelism replaced the Board of Home Mission and Board of Evangelism. Robert C. Larson became the executive secretary of the new board.

In 1978 the Annual Meeting authorized the establishment of a Board of Women's Work. This would allow the historic and highly significant activities of Covenant Women to be integrated with the top level administration of the Covenant. In 1982 the name was changed to Board of Covenant Women.

Another most significant change was the transformation of regional conferences from subordinate missionary associations having a tenuous connection with central administration to administrative units of the Covenant. This means that they occupy an administrative middle place between central administration—Covenant Headquarters—and the local congregation. In the minds of some this was a most disquieting development, for it suggested that conferences were on the way to become bishoprics and conference superintendents about to assume the status of bishops. The fear sounds ecclesiological but it was really an anxiety of too much control. The Covenant has not gotten much closer to bishops, but it has probably added some administrative machinery.

In any event, as we shall see directly, the new constitution seemed to some a step in the wrong direction. So did the addition of seminary teachers whose youthfulness and graduate training and whose theological sympathies seemed to ally them too solidly with the suspected faculties and liberal tendencies of eastern and midwestern seminaries. Harvard, Yale, Union, the Divinity School of the University of Chicago, Garrett, et al. were suspect.

Another component in the tension just then gripping the Covenant and the school was the development and growth in influence of conservative and neo-evangelical seminaries like Fuller, Trinity (after its relocation on the outskirts of Chicago), Gordon-Conwell, Northwestern Schools (now College) in Minneapolis, and Dallas. This did not conduce to harmony or unity at North Park Seminary, for the expectation was that the Covenant school would be like these "evangelical" schools. In fact, as we have already indicated, the assumption among many, if not most, of the non-Covenant people having contact with the Covenant and in some instances matriculating at the seminary was that the Covenant was solidly biblicist, that is Fundamentalist, in its view of Scriptures.

SEMINARY INQUIRY

This, as we have indicated earlier, was certainly the impression carried to North Park by William Doughty in 1948. That impression was not significantly changed by his contacts with Covenanters whom he met in his five years of parish ministry and motivated a 1954 inquiry directed by the Bethany Covenant Church of Mt. Vernon, Washington—a church Doughty was then serving—to Harold A. Anderson, chairman of the Board of Directors of North Park.

The writers of the letter indicate that their intention with the communication was not "to create ill will or schism" or to embarrass the teachers of the seminary but merely to make an inquiry about them. The church did not desire to arouse controversy or to engage in it "on these matters" nor to question these men on their own viewpoints. "We only desire," continues the letter, "a forthright declaration by these men as to what they believe" (Robinson 1978, 7).[3]

The writing of this letter was apparently prompted by the permanent appointment of Dr. Earl C. Dahlstrom to the seminary faculty and the three-year teaching appointment of Henry A. Gustafson, a doctoral candidate in New Testament at the Divinity School of the University of Chicago.

In reading the record it becomes apparent that procedural uncertainty plagued denominational leaders from first to last in the Doughty case. The request for information was referred by Harold A. Anderson to the president of the seminary, Clarence A. Nelson. Nelson, in turn, did not attempt to answer the questions presented by the Mount Vernon church, but instead provided brief biographies of Dahlstrom and Gustafson and averred that they stood within "the historic evangelical position of the Covenant." Nelson also suggested that Doughty speak personally with the two men at the Covenant Annual Meeting scheduled for Rockford, Illinois, the week of June 23-27, 1954.

These meetings did take place, but Doughty did not make the results public until 1958. We shall return later to the significance of these conversations.

The Mount Vernon letter had presented nine questions to the chairman of the North Park Board. These questions have been summarized for us by Donald T. Robinson, the chronicler of the Doughty case, in one pregnant query, "Are Earl Dahlstrom and Henry Gustafson Fundamentalists?" But the specific questions provide a dimension not unimportant for our query. Hence they will be found in their entirety in Appendix F.

These questions are pervasively "either-or," the assumption being that the respondent will opt for one or the other of the possibilities. But it would certainly be possible to formulate answers that approach faith statements less categorically, or, as Gustafson says, less "propositionally" and still remain in the evangelical tradition.

Doughty's procedure throughout the four years of the controversy is nonetheless clearly illuminated by this his first move on the chessboard. He defined the evangelical position in terms of that scientific certainty to which we have referred earlier. If the Bible does not provide him with that kind of laboratory surety or sureness, it cannot be a source of ultimate truth for him.

3. Donald T. Robinson's in-depth study is a valuable compilation of Doughty materials (correspondence, tapes, etc.) but it looks at the materials only from Doughty's point of view. My presentation has been helped by that aspect of the study.

Insofar as the Covenant's understanding of "evangelical" was not clearly distinguished from that of the "Fundamentalists" before Doughty's admission to the seminary, and insofar as he was not helped to see that Covenant freedom, within the boundaries of its faith in the authority of the Holy Scriptures, allows both Fundamentalists and non-Fundamentalists to live and work side by side for the Gospel, the denomination and its representatives were in the wrong.

And in the measure that Doughty chose to ignore the freedom in which the Covenant had then lived for almost seventy-five years and insisted with a number of his co-adherents that "evangelical" could have only one meaning—the Fundamentalist one as outlined in his questions—he was equally in the wrong.

An example of Doughty's insistence that the Covenant and all its institutions should be evangelical and Fundamentalist, in his understanding of these terms, is his encounter with Clarence A. Nelson in December, 1956, relative to the presence on the North Park campus of Professor Wilhelm Pauck of Union Theological Seminary. On the campus Pauck had participated in a popular cultural program called "Tuesday Evenings at North Park" which had first been instituted in 1934. Pauck delivered a lecture in a series entitled "American Christianity Today."

Doughty felt that Pauck's relationship to Union Theological Seminary, a "stronghold of religious Modernism" and a "heretical institution," made it highly improper for him to appear on the North Park campus and "will certainly not enhance the evangelical standing of our school" (Robinson, 11-12).

In his rejoinder Nelson accuses Doughty of inferring "guilt by association" and claims that such a policy is not operative on the campus. If it were, said Nelson, North Park audiences would be deprived of the opportunity to hear and meet firsthand "many of the outstanding leaders of American thought and culture."

Nelson then proceeds to clarify this aspect of North Park's educational philosophy:

> North Park does not endorse everything that a speaker says or does simply because he appears on our rostrum. The fact that Dr. Pauck spoke here does not make us Modernists, as you infer, any more than having Torrey Johnson, Bob Cook, and our late Paul Rood speak here makes us Fundamentalists. All of these men have spoken at one time or another at North Park, but we still retain our identity both before and after their visits. I expect we will continue to be ourselves in the future (Covenant Archives).

Doughty was far from satisfied with Nelson's defense of the school's philosophy, arguing that the scriptural policy throughout is separatist and exclusive, rather than inclusive as the school and its president seemed to suggest (Robinson, 13-15).

CONTROVERSIAL PAMPHLETS

Another area of deep concern for Doughty was the publication of some—in his opinion—questionable youth materials, especially a pamphlet "How the Bible Came to Be." According to Doughty, the pamphlet's treatment of the Genesis account of creation, the dual author- ship of Isaiah, and the late date for the writing of Daniel were evidence of "higher criticism" and of modernistic views on the part of the writers.

Doughty aired these concerns with some pastors in the North Pacific Ministerial Association. Later, as secretary of the North Pacific Confer- ence, he was asked by the executive board to send a letter to the confer- ence pastors asking them to review "Unit II Faith" materials published by the Youth Department, particularly the pamphlet "How the Bible Came to Be" before coming to the annual meeting of the conference and "be prepared to discuss it and take voted action concerning it" (Robinson, 17).

On April 7, 1955, Doughty sent the letter he had been asked to write to the pastors in the conference. The letter said in part:

> Specifically we refer to the packet "Unit II Faith," and to the pamphlet entitled "How the Bible Came to Be." This pamphlet dates the composi- tion of the Book of Deuteronomy as probably around 681 B.C. and the other books of the Pentateuch in the ninth and eighth centuries. It dates the writing of the book of Daniel after 200.

Doughty concluded his letter with the statement: "This pamphlet involves a radical departure from the conservative position of the Cov- enant by our Youth Department" (Robinson, 18).

Doughty also sent copies of his letter to selected people in the Califor- nia Conference, among them Wilbur Westerdahl (then serving as chair- man of the Youth Board) and Arvid Carlson. On April 13, 1955, Aaron Markuson, executive secretary of the Youth Department, sent a letter to all Covenant ministers asking that the controversial pamphlet be with- drawn from the kit of materials on "Faith."

Meanwhile Westerdahl responded to Doughty's letter by sending let- ters to Doughty and to Erick Gustafson in the Covenant Youth Depart- ment in which he spoke of the pamphlet as "a departure . . . from our historical agreement with conservative Christianity and biblical interpre- tation." He saw this departure as a threat to unity and harmony in the Covenant. But he also recommended that the matter be handled with dis- cretion between parties and not be allowed to encourage theological cleavages (Robinson, 19-20).

The stance of the Youth Department was, nonetheless, not allowed to rest there, for in subsequent correspondence by Doughty and others the department was seen as the sounding board for the fostering of "behind the scenes liberalism" for the advocacy of the Revised Standard Version of the Bible and certain programs of the social gospel, and of unwittingly letting itself be used to promote propaganda (presumably for a wider network of churches and agencies).

But an irremediable rift took place after another packet of materials was mailed by the Youth Department. It contained a piece called "The Exile and Restoration of the Nation" in which the writer presented the point of view of Deutero-Isaiah, that is, of a dual authorship of this prophetic book. Doughty objected strongly to this article and claimed that any view challenging the unitary authorship of Isaiah was modernistic and thus heretical.

Markuson's rejoinder ended the exchange of letters. He claimed that the position on Isaiah's authorship was not, so far as the Covenant was concerned, a matter of faith. So long as the book was considered to be divinely inspired, the number of authors was indifferent. "There is no reason to believe," he wrote, "that it makes any difference to God if he used one person or ten to bring his message to men."

Markuson concluded his letter by saying:

> Frankly, I do not have a strong conviction one way or another on the authorship of Isaiah. All that I know is that there are good Christian brethren holding different theories about it. As long as they agree that the book is inspired by God to bring his message to man, I am not going to say they must conform to any idea I have. If that is contrary to Covenant policy, I do not know the Covenant, and the Ministerial Board had better handle the matter (Covenant Archives).

Doughty's concluding word in this controversy was printed in his pamphlet "A Cause for Concern in the Covenant," published in 1958. There Doughty accuses Markuson of yielding to pressure from the North Pacific and the California Ministerial Association in the matter of the controversial pamphlet, "How the Bible Came to Be." As we noted, that pamphlet was withdrawn. Whereas, Doughty claims with some acerbity, his objections to the theory of the dual authorship of Isaiah went unheeded.

"What," he writes, "is the explanation for this contradictory action? The explanation is quite clear to this writer. The first was by action [on the part of official groups]. The second was by a lone individual. It is apparent to this writer that the Youth Department only yields to pressure" (Robinson, 32).

Still another of Doughty's "concerns" was the area of denominational trends. He addressd these in three categories: the new constitution (1957), *The Covenant Weekly* (now *The Covenant Companion*), and *The North Pacific Conference News*.[4]

CONCERN FOR AUTONOMY

The work of the Survey Commission in producing a new constitution that was presented at the Annual Meeting of 1956 and given final acceptance in 1957 became a source of anxiety for Doughty as early as 1955 when the first draft was published. He worried about the abrogation of the principle of local church autonomy, he feared the "concentration of great power in the administrative and headquarters departments," and he deplored such provisions as would make the "failure to support Covenant policy an act of ministerial disloyalty."

He had earlier expressed his admiration for "the freedom the Covenant gave their ministers on the secondary doctrinal issues," for example, "the interpretation of the Lord's Supper, how you perform baptisms, and the interpretations of prophesy."

"But" he continues, "I understand this freedom to be within the context of a very conservative, evangelical framework" (Robinson, 34-35).

In a sermon preached in a homiletics class at North Park Seminary, Doughty spoke very positively about the freedom enjoyed in the Covenant. He told his interviewer, Donald T. Robinson:

> I expressed this in one of my sermons. . . . I felt that the Covenant, because of its allowing different viewpoints on the secondary doctrines, was in a position to really be a leader in healing divisions. Christians having been at loggerheads and divided over the secondary issues . . . I really felt that the Covenant had a constructive contribution to make to the American church scene in this (Robinson, 34-35).

Doughty's concern for congregational autonomy was not merely theoretically motivated. He expresses his fear clearly in two letters to Carl Philip Anderson, then editor of *The Covenant Weekly*, the first written October 27, 1955, the second April 18, 1957.

---

4. At the time that *The Covenant Weekly* no longer published Doughty's strictures against Covenant policies, Doughty began to editorialize in *The North Pacific Conference News*, of which he was the editor. But after a short time he was asked by that conference board not to editorialize further in the *News*. Doughty claims that this action was taken in spite of wide popular support for his writings.

In the first he writes:

> The obvious purpose [of the new constitution] is to put teeth into the
> Covenant government so that uncooperative pastors and churches other-
> wise known as "lone star" pastors and churches can be brought into line
> (CW 11-11-55, 6).

It is evident that he felt threatened by a denominational process that
may limit his freedom as well as the freedom of his churches to oppose
the leadership of the Covenant on crucial issues. That such issues—that
is, troublesome to Doughty—were more and more evident in the Covenant becomes clear in his second letter to Carl Philip Anderson, which
he wrote just a few weeks before the final note on the new constitution.
In this letter he lifts up a succession of concerns:

1. Compromise and theological inclusivism in the seminary.
2. A lack of a true New Testament attitude at the seminary. (Doughty
   sees the New Testament spirit as imbuing faculty and students with
   convictions about the "heresies of liberalism and neo-orthodoxy."
   Such a spirit is absent.)
3. The lack of a New Testament attitude in North Park College evident
   in inviting persons of liberal persuasion to speak on campus.
4. The practice of Covenant Press to promote publications by liberal
   writers (Robinson, 36-37).

In conclusion Doughty pleads for a "native born Covenanter of such
stature and standing as to command respect and attention,[5] to lead us in
aggressive protest and corrective action concerning the above outlined
situation" (Robinson, 36-37).

UNPUBLISHED LETTERS

Doughty's second letter was not printed in the *Weekly*. When he asked
Carl Philip Anderson why it was withheld, he was told that T.W. Anderson and he (Carl Philip Anderson) had determined that printing it would
do more harm than good. The editor of the *Weekly* charged Doughty
with having written a letter without specific criticisms and which lacked
a positive attitude that would foster "good will and a spirit of unity
among our people" (Robinson, 38).

---

5. What Doughty means by this reference to a "native born Covenanter" I am unable
to determine. Did he have a particular person in mind or was he thinking of a group of pastors and laypersons who espoused his own type of conservativism?

At about the same time as Doughty's second letter (spring, 1957) the Mount Vernon pastor sent T.W. Anderson an appraisal of the Survey Commission's report. In this appraisal Doughty charges the Executive Board with being "controlled" by a group (Robinson, 39).

President Anderson's reply to Doughty (May 24, 1957) was prompt and courteous but not without some understandable impatience:

> You manifest, however, a suspicion of the Covenant leadership that is unfortunate, What basis do you have for your distrust?
>
> I think a key to your evaluation is the phrase, "whatever group controls the Executive Board." What do you mean? I have been a member of this board for a quarter of a century and have never seen any group even try to control the board, much less succeed in doing that. That is equally true of our administrative boards, in all of which I am an ex-officio member. I have invariably found these men and women open-minded, frank and sympathetic, guided by Christian integrity and devotion to Christ and the Covenant. . . .
>
> I think . . . that this attitude of yours colors much of your criticism. I do not see how you can be happy in such an atmosphere of chronic suspicion (Covenant Archives).

The difficulties that had developed in Doughty's relationship to Covenant leaders, particularly T.W. Anderson and Carl Philip Anderson, are somewhat clarified in the next exchange of letters. It makes abundantly clear that Doughty never fully understood the denomination with which he had become associated. The exchange was prompted by an article written by G.F. Hedstrand, a former editor of the *Weekly*, appeared in a series called "People I Have Known." The particular piece that disturbed Doughty dealt with Nils W. Lund, professor of Bible at the seminary who had died in 1954. Hedstrand called this piece "Fighter for Free Speech." Lund had been involved in a long controversy with some Covenant pastors in the 1920s and 30s on the issue of how the Bible should be interpreted. In that controversy Lund had argued against the position of the Fundamentalists and dispensationalists, especially against the doctrine of "verbal inspiration," which claims that the Bible is free of error in the original writings (see chapters 24,26).

In his letter to *The Covenant Weekly*, written February 15, 1958, Doughty quotes Hedstrand as saying, "Lund was a realist. He used the head God had given him, and it held a good mind. He could not accept verbal inspiration and [he] showed how impossible a theory of inspiration was in his lecture in Omaha in 1928."

Doughty writes:

> The doctrine of verbal inspiration is not a theory, but is clear teaching of Scripture based upon sound exegesis of those passages that deal with the inspiration and nature of the sacred writings. The term "verbal inspiration" is not to be equated with the "dictation theory" and it refers not so much to methodology as to the nature of the Scriptures in their written and original form.

He concludes by saying that the statement in the Covenant constitution relative to the Scriptures as the Word of God means:

> That for every Covenanter the Bible is the only perfect rule for determining the truth concerning the doctrine of inspiration. The uniform testimony of the Bible concerning itself is to the effect that Holy Spirit inspiration included not only the thinking processes of the writers but also descended to their words spoken and written (Robinson, 42).

As we might expect, this Doughty letter met the same fate as some of the earlier ones. T.W. Anderson and Carl Philip Anderson decided against publishing it. The reason given for not printing it was not that it contained negative criticism of the Covenant, but rather that it presented erroneous information and assumptions about Hedstrand's article, Lund's understanding of the doctrine of inspiration, and the Covenant's position on scriptural inspiration (Robinson, 42).

In his letter to Doughty stating why the letter in question would not be published Carl Philip Anderson made some clarifying statements about the Covenant's historical stand on inspiration which if they could have been understood and accepted by Doughty, may have precluded the protracted, painful, and in many ways destructive controversy which was to continue for at least another decade. On March 5, 1958, Anderson wrote:

> While your letter might be considered relevant from one point and though it states your convictions clearly, we feel that no purpose whatsoever would be served by printing it. Hedstrand's article about Lund in his series "People I Have Known" was not written for the purpose of refuting the verbal inspiration theory but to review the life and work of a man who made a significant contribution to our educational work. Your letter suggests that in rejecting the theory of verbal inspiration Lund actually rejected the concept of inspiration itself, and this, of course, is not the case. Had Hedstrand's article defined Lund's thinking on the matter of inspiration, I feel your letter would be entirely in order; under the present circumstances, however, I feel it would simply create misunderstandings and subject the seminary to further unnecessary criticism (Robinson, 42).

Anderson then spelled out what he assumed that Doughty already knew, viz. that the Covenant is a noncreedal church and does not commit itself specifically to one doctrine of inspiration or another:

> As you certainly must know, the Covenant itself neither accepts nor rejects the theory of verbal inspiration. As stated in our constitution, "the Covenant Church believes in the Holy Scriptures, the Old and the New Testaments, as the Word of God and the only rule for faith, doctrine, and conduct.
> Anyone who can subscribe to this confession should be able to feel at home in the Covenant fellowship even through no common agreement among the members of the church exists on such a matter as verbal inspiration. You apparently fail to understand that the controversy the Covenant experienced some thirty years ago and which reached its climax at Omaha in 1928 was not a "fight to the finish" between those who chose at that time to be identified as Fundamentalists and those whom they accused of being Modernists. The real good that came out of the controversy and the Omaha conference was the recognition by the denomination of the fact that there was a middle way for the Covenant to follow and that there is room within the Covenant for diverse points of view when men share a common faith in Jesus Christ and are willing to grant each other freedom of thought and expression (Robinson, 42-44).

AN EDITORIAL STAND

After Doughty had been refused by the president of the Covenant and the editor of the *Weekly* to publish his opinions freely in the denominational organ, he turned to the pages of the regional paper, *The North Pacific Conference News*, of which he was then the editor, and began to give editorial opinion on some of the matters of special concern to him.

His first article was entitled "The Least Common Denominator." It dealt with the minimal faith statement of the National Council of Churches and with the perils of sacrificing doctrine for the sake of unity (Robinson, 45). The result of such editorializing was a number of protests to conference authorities. In spite of this opposition, Doughty published a second editorializing article in the September 1957 issue, this one with the title "The Covenant and the Middle Way." In it he voiced his concern about the manner in which the Covenant tried to accommodate itself to both Fundamentalism and Modernism and he used as examples the school and the *Weekly*. He concluded with a warning note: "This drift, if continued, will lead to an unhealthy theological inclusivism. Such inclusivism leads to compromise, compromise leads to capitulation, and capitulation leads to captivity" (Robinson, 46).

What emerges in these statements of Doughty is a consistent refusal to walk the Covenant way so sensitively described by Carl Philip Anderson. In effect, Doughty ignored these historic developments and set as his goal the remaking of the Covenant into a Fundamentalist church where the criterion for admission was adherence to an extremely conservative dogmatic. In doing so he chose to ignore established and venerable guidelines which had been blessed for decades and to disregard the relatively modest authority exercised by the denominational conference leadership. He cherished freedom but only the freedom acceptable to him and defined by him.

When his utterances in the *Weekly* were deemed unpublishable, he used *The North Pacific Conference News* to trumpet his views despite the fact that his editorial deportment was a violation of a consistently irenic spirit of that paper. When the conference board asked him courteously not to editorialize in the October issue of the *Conference News*, he ignored the request, and proceeded to do just that, merely appending the statement to his article, "The above article is published without permission of the Official Board and speaks only for the editor" (Robinson, 47).

But what he sees and what he intends can be most clearly stated by himself. He writes in *The Conference News* for October, 1957:

> . . . Your editor does think it would be a shame to have such a controlled press that editorializing would be completely squelched or that comments only favorable to the denomination and its program can be printed. There is a place for editorial comment on policies and issues both at the denominational and broader church level, and it is a healthy situation when things that are wrong or questionable can be raised for examination and discussion" (Robinson, 48).

But in this instance Doughty really misses the point. Only if he were both publisher and editor would he have the freedom that he arrogates for himself. No editor, however powerful, has the right to set policy for his paper. That is the publisher's prerogative. In this instance the publisher was not Doughty but the North Pacific Conference Board. It was their right to decide whether or not they wanted editorializing in the paper. And it was Doughty's responsibility to follow the guidelines and to abide by the implicit contract to which he had agreed when he became editor. That he did not do so gave further evidence that he may have wanted to legislate for the Covenant but that he was often unwilling to live by a law with which, for whatever reason, he did not agree. And "that," in Robert Frost's imperishable line, "has made all the difference."

CHAPTER THIRTY-FIVE

Affirmation of Freedom

An eminent theoretical psychologist once likened Freud's psychodynamics to a system of gas under pressure. Which means, I suppose, that episodes occur at the weakest points in the line. The last six months of Doughty's tenure in the Covenant were not unlike this metaphor. Something was always happening or perhaps made to happen at the weakest point in the line.

Frustrated in his effort to get Covenant Publications to carry his strictures against the Youth Department, the school, and Covenant Publications, Doughty sought for expression in *The North Pacific Conference News*. But here also he was stymied when the board decided that the paper would no longer carry editorials. A third step in his effort to be heard was to seek a response with some political consequence from the local church. In this he was more successful, at least immediately.

On October 21, 1957, he told his church that he could no longer recommend financial support for the Covenant Youth Department, North Park College and Theological Seminary, and Covenant Publications. Bethany Covenant Church supported him in this and gave him a vote of confidence.

On November 16, 1957, the North Pacific Conference Board called a meeting to deal with the problem of the *News* and Doughty's role as an editor. T.W. Anderson, president of the Covenant, was then in the Pacific Northwest on another errand and was asked to sit in with the Board on the Doughty issue. In a letter to a friend Doughty describes his encounter with Anderson:

> I had to face him. He asked me several questions, all of which were
> designed to back me into a corner, apparently. However, there was little
> he could do for the simple reason that I had facts on my side. I
> answered respectfully, forthrightly, and frankly, and I feel I maintained
> my position (Robinson, 53).

In a letter to another friend about the same encounter Doughty indicated that he believed the crux of the problem (in the Covenant) was that
people couldn't stand to have the Covenant criticized. He concludes his
letter, "I thank God that he has delivered me from the fear of man"
(Robinson, 53).

At the annual business meeting of the Bethany Covenant Church on
January 7, 1958, which presumably gave approval to the 1958 budget,
Doughty reiterated his conviction that North Park Seminary, the Covenant Youth Department, and Covenant Publications should not be supported by the church. In the ensuing discussion Doughty was asked who
in the faculty did not have his support.

Up to this point Doughty had been careful about not naming names,
but under some pressure from a small minority in the church that had
remained loyal to Covenant causes, Doughty gave way and named Karl
A. Olsson, Donald C. Frisk, and Henry Gustafson as those particularly
guilty. It was an unfortunate question and an equally unfortunate
answer. In an unauthorized letter later sent to North Park, it was alleged
that Doughty accused Olsson of teaching evolution, Frisk of being neo-
orthodox, and Gustafson of getting his education at a liberal school.

Even more mystifying is the congregation's readiness to let this happen
even though it was later to accuse the Covenant of the violation and
abrogation of the rights of the pastor.

What seems lacking in this process is an awareness of churchmanship,
which in its simplest form means knowing what to do and having the
courage to do it within the framework of Christian decorum and good
will.

Following this meeting—after a three-week interval—the proceedings,
including the names of the accused, were reported by letter to Louis J.
Person at North Park College. This was an unofficial communication
from a member of Bethany Covenant Church not authorized by the
church and without the church's knowledge. Information about the letter, again without the knowledge of the Bethany Covenant Church, was
then sent to Carl H. Peterson, the superintendent of the North Pacific
Conference, who in turn shared the contents with Earl M. VanDerVeer,
chairman of the conference.

It was only at this point that Bethany Covenant Church became aware
of developments. Carl H. Peterson and Earl M. VanDerVeer decided to

make contact with the church and suggested that the seminary professors and Youth Department personnel involved in the allegations be brought together with the church. This suggestion was also communicated to President Clarence A. Nelson of North Park. Nelson did not respond favorably to this suggestion. His counterproposal was that Peterson and the North Pacific Conference Board meet with the Bethany church board and that Doughty be referred to the meeting of the Covenant Ministerial Board (later the Board of Ministerial Standing, and now the Board of the Ministry) at its imminent meeting in Denver, Colorado.[1]

The dynamic in the situation now becomes more evident. Until now Doughty had been playing the role of a plaintiff presenting a bill of particulars, but it is clear that Clarence Nelson did not want to continue on this track. He did not see the Covenant accountable to the Mount Vernon church and least of all to William Doughty. The North Pacific Conference may have had some direct juridical responsibilities for both the Mt. Vernon church and Doughty, but the Covenant did not play this role. The Covenant would deal with Doughty through the Ministerial Board and the Covenant would deal with Bethany Covenant Church through the North Pacific Conference. This battle for position continued until the issue was resolved.

It is already obvious that in pursuing the process the local church, the pastor, the conference, and the Covenant dropped some stitches. I have alluded to the unofficial letter to North Park and the steps that followed. There was to be more. The Covenant and its boards did not seek facts from Bethany Covenant; it did not apprise Doughty of his situation; it did not formally summon him to the Denver meeting. The North Pacific Conference made no recommendation to the Covenant Ministerial Board through its own ministerial board and the latter board did not provide any statement of charges.

In the confusion that followed, Doughty did not always proceed with much more clarity than Covenant leadership, although this should probably not have been expected. Much of his irritation stemmed from the fact that North Park had no right to give the unofficial January correspondence from a member of Bethany Covenant Church to the Ministerial Board without apprising him and the church.

Even a second letter in the case followed the same route. It went from Louis Person to Eric Hawkinson and from Hawkinson to the Ministerial Board. But it also resulted in a letter from Hawkinson to Doughty. At

---

1. Doughty did not receive a formal summons to this meeting and did not appear during the meeting. A member of the board telephoned Doughty and asked him to the Denver meeting, but he refused on the grounds that the method was improper.

this time Hawkinson was dean of the seminary and as such an ex officio member of the Ministerial Board, but he told Doughty that his letter of response to him was personal and not official. He also claimed that the controversial communication from the Mt. Vernon church to Louis Person was not the major cause for inviting Doughty to meet with the board in Denver.

It is clear that Hawkinson here made a valiant and characteristic effort to defuse a situation that threatened to get out of hand, but Doughty seemed to be asking for more and not less formality.

THE BOARD'S DECISION

On March 3, 1958, a very important quarterly meeting was held by the Mt. Vernon church. In attendance, in addition to the membership of the church, was a delegation from the North Pacific Conference and Virgil D. Wickman, secretary of the Covenant Board of Ministerial Standing. The delegation consisted of Carl Peterson and Earl VanDerVeer, to whom allusion has already been made, Selmer Jacobson and Theodore Nyquist. At this time Wickman, acting for the Covenant Board of Ministerial Standing, delivered a mandate to Doughty that inasmuch as he had refused the board's invitation to meet at Denver and inasmuch as other steps of adjudication were under way, he was now to maintain a strict silence about the matter. He was to "refrain from all oral or written, public or private personal judgments." He was also informed that he was summoned to appear before the Board of Ministerial Standing in Miami, Florida, in June.

The decisions of the Board of Ministerial Standing as they were delivered to Doughty were not destined to improve attitudes towards the Covenant in the Bethany Covenant Church of Mt. Vernon; rather they tended to solidify support for Doughty in the church.

In the interest of improving relations with the church in Mt. Vernon, T.W. Anderson wrote a letter to its chairman, Robert Elde. The letter was written on March 12, 1958, and in it Anderson offered the service of the Pastoral Relations Commission to the Bethany Covenant Church for the purpose of conversing about the issues surrounding the Doughty matter. "We want to further the God-given interests of the church, the pastor, the Conference, and the Covenant," wrote the president (Robinson, 79). This offer was refused by the church as being unnecessary, but the real motives may have been deeper. The church offered as a counterproposal a visit by T.W. Anderson, Eric G. Hawkinson, and Aaron Markuson "to clarify some issues" (Robinson, 80). It seems that their opposition to a visit from the Pastoral Relations Commission may have been motivated by the fear that such a visit would be in the nature of a disciplinary inquiry in relation to the pastor. In any event, the Covenant refused the church's option, further evidence, I believe, of the delicately balanced power situation.

With the exception of eight oppositional members who, according to one observer, represented "the old Covie stand," the church was now solidly behind Doughty and saw itself and its pastor as the injured parties. This, in any event, was to remain its stance throughout the succeeding weeks.

Another source of unhappiness on the part of the church was the intrusion of the Board of Ministerial Standing into this matter. The church recognized that the board had general supervision over the pastors, but rejected the notion that the Covenant system need be so hierarchical that it precluded the questioning of decisions and actions by the board. The Mt. Vernon church also felt that its pastor had the right to refuse to obey a summons to appear before the ministerial board if he felt that the reasons for so doing "appear inadequate and insufficient" (Robinson, 82-83).

The church was particularly troubled by the mandate of the Board of Ministerial Standing that Doughty was "to refrain from all oral or written public or private judgments." The church saw these prohibitions as a "serious abrogation of its pastor's rights to discuss these matters with his own family and with his church family . . . it is also made the more serious in that the mandate rests upon the flimsiest of grounds and to us it smack of police state methods which are foreign to our heritage" (Robinson, 83).

There was an appended warning that "if proceedings are continued against our pastor on the basis of the alleged reasons given by the Board, which the church considers woefully inadequate, it could endanger the relationship of the church to the denomination" (Robinson, 82-83).

The efforts of Bethany Covenant Church to minimize the seriousness of Doughty's violation of ministerial order and discipline, nonetheless, had little permanent effect. For although it is true that some of the Covenant leaders who were charged with the maintenance of ministerial decorum at this time may have used questionable judgment and may have overreacted in some of their decisions, it is also true that Doughty's actions throughout reflected a curious lack of knowledge of and sensitivity to the Covenant ethos, of solidarity with his pastoral colleagues, of graciousness in dealing with those he saw as his adversaries, of respect for facts and logical inference, and even of a garden variety of courtesy.

Doughty seemingly had little interest in accommodating himself to the Covenant as a family of faith or to its leadership and procedures even

when no violation of principle was at stake. One has a feeling that ultimately he was more interested in tailoring the denomination to his own
wishes and conceptions than in finding ways in which he and the Covenant might live and grow together under their common Lord.

In any case Doughty was summoned to appear before the North
Pacific Ministerial Association Board on April 17, 1958. Ostensibly this
was to be the first step in a hearing process for the purpose of determining if Doughty had been guilty of an infraction of ministerial discipline or
decorum or had violated his ordination vows. The intention was also to
formulate a recommendation for the Covenant Board of Ministerial
Standing on which appropriate action could be taken. But confusion
reigned from the beginning. Apparently no procedure had been worked
out, the composition of the meeting was faulty, and by a strange inadvertence Doughty managed to cast himself in the role of plaintiff and
prosecutor. He had prepared a long paper on "Causes for Concern"
which was passed out and read by the assembly, but no one seems to
have known why this was done or what to do next. It is probably true
that a good spirit prevailed, as the record indicates, but as a stage in a
process, it got nowhere. Finally someone asked Doughty if he felt that he
had broken his ordination vows, but to this question he gave an
emphatic "No."

After the chairman indicated that no action could be taken because the
meeting was improperly constituted, the process came to an end. It is difficult to determine what Doughty felt and thought. Donald T. Robinson
makes almost too much of the fact that a good spirit prevailed, though it
is probably true that Doughty felt liked by the group. But he could
hardly have felt supported, or better yet, exonerated. The summons to
Miami still hung over his head and the meeting had done little to relieve
his anxiety in that regard. But worse was to come.

THE DECISIVE STEP

Following the meeting on April 17 Doughty decided to have his paper,
renamed "A Cause for Concern in the Covenant," printed and distributed. I think that this action must be seen as a response to the rather confused and feeble performance of the conference ministerial board at the
meeting alluded to above. Doughty came to feel that he had little to
expect from his fellow ministers and that if anything was to be accomplished, it would have to be done by an "informed and aroused Covenant lay constituency" (Robinson, 102).

He may have had some hope that the meeting of the ministerial board in Portland in connection with the annual meeting of the conference in May of 1958 would make a positive recommendation on his behalf, but that was not to be. The board simply passed the matter on to the Covenant Board of Ministerial Standing.

Doughty claims that he felt "very disappointed and let down." He saw himself as rejected by the men of his own conference, in effect, "kicked upstairs." And he expected little sympathy in the higher echelons. As a consequence and because he hoped to motivate an "informed and aroused Covenant laity" to consider the errors he had uncovered and to do something about them, he decided to print and distribute his pamphlet.

It was one of those decisive steps which, for the hero in classical tragedy, carries him beyond the point of recovery. As events developed, Doughty must have had a strong premonition that his future in the Covenant was bleak. He speaks in one place of knowing that his "goose is cooked." Wisely or unwisely he had been mandated to silence, "muzzled," as he expressed it, after the Midwinter Conference in Denver, 1958. Despite this, as we have seen, he used his summons to a meeting of the North Pacific Ministerial Association Board to present the first draft of his pamphlet. He did more. He proceeded to print and distribute his paper in pamphlet form not only to a selection of Covenant pastors but to representative laypersons. He even sent it outside the "family" to people like Carl McIntire, who must have understood what Doughty was doing.

Finally, and this was perhaps the most questionable stroke of all, he gave wide circulation to his method of securing and publishing information which violated the canons of good taste as well as Christian courtesy. It became clear that in order to make his case, Doughty had secured the services of a friend reasonably skilled in shorthand who made verbatim reports on some of the lectures in the seminary that smelled of "neo-orthodoxy." These became the substance of the pamphlet.

The ethics of the case need not be labored. But the strategy of the effort deserves comment. It was consummately unwise. Doughty made one of the least vulnerable professors of the seminary his prime target. Donald C. Frisk was known for an incisive and well-trained intellect as well as for theological sophistication. But he was also known and appreciated for the devoutness of his Christian walk and for his individualized concern for his students. This inward quality transformed the theological materials he used into a focused testimony of his faith in the Holy Scriptures and in the living Lord.

In a subsequent conversation with Donald Robinson, Doughty recalled his feelings after distributing his pamphlet:

> I really had no illusions as to what the ultimate outcome of the situation
> was going to be . . . I felt that in good conscience I was not going to be
> able to obey that [the Ministerium] and I was going to have to send my
> paper out. I knew that action would hang me; I had no illusions about it
> at all (Robinson, 105).

Doughty's apprehensions were well founded. When Vigil D. Wickman, in his capacity of secretary of the Board of Ministerial Standing, directed him to appear before that board on Saturday, June 14, 1958, Doughty immediately asked his church to insist that the proceedings be recorded in some formal way. The church responded affirmatively by having Robert Elde, the chairman of the Bethany Covenant Church, direct a letter to Wickman with a request for a recording of proceedings. If the assurance of such a recording was not forthcoming, Bethany church felt that Doughty ought not to appear before the Board of Ministerial Standing in Miami.

The board's refusal to comply with this request was sent to Doughty and Elde prior to the meeting. Doughty would be allowed counsel during proceedings but such counsel would not be permitted to participate in the deliberations. Elde responded to this communication on behalf of his church by reiterating his stand on procedures and expressing concern on plans for the meeting. (It was later revealed by Doughty that the reason for the concern was an arrangement to have the ministerial boards for the North Pacific and Central Conferences present at the June 14, 1958, hearing.)

THE RESPONSE

On June 4, 1958 the president and secretary of the Covenant, in response to the distribution of "A Cause for Concern in the Covenant," sent a letter to all Covenant churches, indicating that Doughty had been asked to maintain silence in regard to the matter at issue until the meeting of the Board of Ministerial Standing in Miami.

Doughty responded to the above letter in which he had been accused of unethical procedure in "going over the head of the Board of Ministerial Standing in carrying the message directly to the people and not staying within channels" by saying that "this would be true only if history and experience showed that procedure through channels could bring basic corrections to grievances. But this they do not show" (Robinson, 107).

Doughty then goes on to point out that although the Covenant Annual Meeting is "our highest constituted authority, the great mass of Covenant people at the grass roots, who have a very remote and tenuous relation to the annual meeting, are our final and real authority and our last court of appeal" (Robinson, 107).

Stripped of their specifically religious content, Doughty's words could serve as the justification of almost any form of anarchy, for they repudiate the validity of all constituted authority, a development much feared by the Apostle Paul, as is indicated in Romans 13. What complicates Doughty's logic at this point is that in 1952 Doughty had, by his own decision, placed himself under the authority and discipline of the Board of Ministerial Standing through the solemnity of an ordination vow.[2]

This board, in turn, functioned under the duly constituted authority of the Annual Meeting. Doughty's impassioned words about the "final and real authority" and "last court of appeal" belonging to the "great mass of Covenant people at the grass roots" may be moving rhetoric but they lack social and political substance.

By intention or inadvertence Doughty had now placed himself in an untenable position if he wished to continue as a Covenant pastor. He had challenged the right of the Board of Ministerial Standing to follow its own procedures in the hearing and when the board refused to yield to his and his own congregation's strongly worded request that this be done, there was nothing for the Board of Ministerial Standing to do but to finalize its disciplinary action. This they did by 1) a Resolution of Censure charging Doughty with "an unchristian spirit and a willful method of procedure," and 2) a Resolution of Withdrawn Privileges. Doughty's ordination credentials were taken away for one year although he was allowed to retain a ministerial license (in order that there might be opportunity for repentance and reconciliation).

Beyond this a committee was appointed to investigate the issues. But the final resolution of the matter was almost predictable. On July 18, 1958, William C. Doughty resigned permanently from the Covenant Ministerium. Given his first principles and his method of relating to the Covenant Church and to his colleagues his action was probably a mercy both for Doughty himself and for the Covenant.

2. Doughty had resigned from the Ministerium on February 27, 1958 (effective June 15 of that year) and had later asked to have the action rescinded. Hence, when he chose to disregard the directive of the Ministerial Board, he was still a member of the Covenant Ministerium and accountable to it and the board, all rhetoric to the contrary notwithstanding.

CHAPTER THIRTY-SIX

Freedom and Theology

Elsewhere I have told the story of the "new thing" at Miami in 1958 (BOS, 638-640). As indicated earlier in this chronicle, the Doughty case was of central significance at that Annual Meeting, but a more permanent impact was provided by the emergence of a new political temper or disposition not unrelated to the "great shift" that succeeded World War II.

The shift had to do with impatience about traditional alignments in the Covenant which had existed for several decades. T.W. Anderson first became president in 1933. His close associates on the Executive Board and among the Trustees were second-generation Swedish Americans, many of whom had walked with him "from the beginning." Together they had worked their way out of a disastrous financial depression and some painful domestic conflicts in the Covenant; together they had developed an enviable esprit de corps. One of the major achievements under Anderson's administration had been the work of the Survey Commission in the development and adoption of the new constitution.

The Survey Commission, with a sincere desire to tighten loose bolts and to develop responsible churchmanship, had sought to give the nomination of the president to a special committee less politically identified with the general nominating committee. This change was agreeable to the Survey Commission but it left unanswered the question of floor nominations, an Annual Meeting prerogative which until now had caused only minor ripples.

But within the Survey Commission the issue caused a serious split

352

between those for and those against nominations from the floor. After an acrimonious battle, the floor proponents won out, and this was to have momentous implications for the immediate future of the denomination.

A THIRD CANDIDATE

At the Miami meeting the presidential nominating committee brought forward two names: Leslie R. Ostberg and A. Eldon Palmquist. Ostberg was a pastor whose pulpit and parish service had been superb. Beyond this he had earned a solid reputation as a churchman, having served as moderator of the Annual Meeting in 1946 and 1947, chairman of the Survey Commission, 1952-1957, and as chairman or member of numerous national boards and committees.

Palmquist was also an outstanding Covenant leader. He had been pastor of a number of prestigious congregations, among them North Park, Chicago; Edina in Minneapolis; and Hinsdale, Illinois. He came from a much appreciated family of pastors, had served with distinction in the development of Covenant worship and hymnody, and was familiar with both the weightier and lighter sides of the denominational chronicle.

Under ordinary circumstances both of these men would have been seen as strong candidates and the decision between them a toss-up. But these were not ordinary times. With the retirement of Anderson (b. 1889); with a new and untried constitution which had troubled the Jeffersonian regionalists because of its marked centralizing thrust; with a growing number of conservative pastors and laity moving into prominence; with the leadership of the school in the balance; and with the case of Doughty still a very central concern, the Annual Meeting was not in a mood for conformity. Doughty may have been silenced and disciplined and there were not many who wanted to share his fate, but his concerns for the Covenant were more alive than many realized.

Hence when Clarence A. Nelson's name emerged as a presidential nomination from the floor, it could not have been a total surprise that many of the delegates bolted and gave his nomination the votes it needed to prevail. It was not a total surprise because Clarence Nelson had been readied for this hour by a number of circumstances.

He was a native son of the Covenant with considerable support from well-established second-generation leaders throughout the denomination. His pedigree was flawless. He was a son of the historic First Covenant Church of St. Paul, a North Park graduate, and well grounded in the traditions of the older generation and in the aspirations of the young. He had served as pastor of the Evanston, Illinois, and Salem, Minneapolis churches where he had earned the reputation of being an eloquent and forceful preacher. He had distinguished himself by presidencies at Min-nehaha Academy and North Park College and Theological Seminary. In both institutions he had effected dramatic turnarounds not only in finan-cial solvency but in institutional image.

But his strength in terms of the work to which he was now called was his effectiveness as a preacher and evangelist. His giftedness in this area gave him access to congregations like Park Avenue in Minneapolis, which emerged from a milieu more conservative than his own, and seemed to make him acceptable to the more conservative pastors in the Cov-enant whose numbers were growing.

His close association with the Northwest Conference and his avoid-ance of an overidentification with "Covenantism" may also have served to distance him somewhat from the work of the Survey Commission, at least in the popular mind, although his commitment to the Covenant ideal could never have been questioned. In any event, his victory was impressive and launched him into his new responsibilities with massive denominational backing.

Nelson did not assume the Covenant presidency until a year after Miami. This procedure was later changed to eliminate a "lame duck year," but after the 1958 conference Anderson remained president for another twelve months. Theoretically the new Council of Administrators had assumed its duties in 1957, but it was not until 1959 with Nelson's assumption of the presidency that the new format was fully actualized. However, subsequent to the Miami meeting several important programs were initiated.

A NEW COMMITTEE

In order to deal more competently with the grievous issues introduced by the Doughty controversy, the denomination in 1958 authorized the as-sembling of a committee on freedom and theology.

From the time of the organizational meeting in 1885, the creedless stance of the Covenant had seemed to be an adequate means to deal with the creedal scholasticism of the Swedish Lutherans. But such dogmatic freedom carried with it a number of unexpected liabilities. It first invited the ecclesiological formlessness of the Free Church with which I have dealt sufficiently; then it invited the proselyting activities of a number of minor Swedish American sects; still later it helped to create a battle arena for the Fundamentalism of the twenties.

At this point, however, we need to emphasize something that is some-times ignored. The creedlessness of the earlier period of Covenant histo-ry did not imply the absence of uniting forms. There is a legend about the mythical smith Hephaestus that he could hammer a thread so fine that it was invisible and so strong that it was unbreakable. So fine and strong a thread hammered out of shared faith experiences bound the early Mission Friends together. If you were a Mission Friend, you knew you were not a Baptist or a Methodist or a Lutheran. And no translation of what you sang or believed or taught into a set liturgy or a formulated creed would make your character or identity any clearer.

But, as we have observed, the erosion of the Swedish language changed all that. With the coming of Americanization and the rapid integration into the fellowship of persons without much orientation in the Covenant's view of the Bible and its freedom in relation to it, new problems emerged in the denomination and particularly in its training of ministers.

When the Swedish language and religious culture dominated the scene, the physiognomy of the Covenant was too obvious to require definition. This, for example, was true for the Covenant of Sweden during the 1920s when it was forced to define its identity in relation to the higher criticism present in the theological schools of the state universities. The Covenant of Sweden in the ensuing decades reached a fairly comfortable fusion of evangelical fidelity to the Scriptures with considerable freedom to discuss, to differ, to accommodate perspectives, and to develop new guidelines (see pp. 251-254).

Hence it managed to live through its "third generation" with much less trauma than the Covenant in North America. For while the Covenant of Sweden continued to live within a framework of shared theological tradition with the Church of Sweden[1] as well as with the benefits of a somewhat controlled cultural context, the American Covenant was, in its Americanization, confronted with an evangelicalism almost consistently Fundamentalistic. Not only did many of the new people coming into the Covenant assume that devotion to the Bible meant a commitment to verbal inerrancy, they also encountered a large number of Covenanters who, because their orientation in the Covenant identity was partial, tended to equate loyalty to the Bible with verbal inspiration. And who, as a corollary to that perspective, viewed a non-Fundamentalistic approach to Scripture as heresy.

In that situation something needed to be done. Perhaps a creed would have reduced the disorder to some kind of order. But a creed was unthinkable and the work to provide one would have issued out in even greater divisiveness.

Hence the Covenant Board of Ministerial Standing, responding to the

1. Although at present SMF seems more closely allied with a Reformed rather than with a Lutheran perspective.

action of the Annual Meeting of 1958, appointed the Covenant Committee of Freedom and Theology "to plan and prepare a study of the real nature of our highly cherished freedom in the Covenant and of our theological position within evangelical Christianity" (*YB* 1958).

In appointing this committee, the Miami meeting specified the following assignment: a) to study the scope and nature of Covenant freedom, and b) to study the Covenant theological position as it is related to its biblical heritage.

The committee worked under the chairmanship of Leslie R. Ostberg for a five-year period from 1958 to 1963, submitting its final report at the Annual Meeting in the latter year. In addition to Ostberg, the membership of the committee consisted of Arvid F. Carlson, Donald C. Frisk, Paul P. Fryhling, Henry A. Gustafson, Eric G. Hawkinson, Irving C. Lambert, secretary, Karl M. Nelson, Wesley W. Nelson, Robert H. Peterson, and Walter Thorell. Of this group six were clergy and four laity. Carlson and Thorell resigned "for personal reasons" before the committee completed its work.

AIMS AND ACHIEVEMENTS

During the time that the committee worked, it performed the significant task of producing some work papers that were submitted for discussion to ministerial meetings in 1959, 1961, and 1962. A finalized report appeared in June of 1963. To achieve this task the committee held numerous work sessions, engaged in protracted conversations with pastors and laity in the congregations as well as with college and seminary students, and provided the Covenant with reports of progress.

Much of the materials in these annual reports was edited and rewritten and justice cannot be done to the entire mass. But the 1963 report, "Biblical Authority," provides a type of summary of the five years of discussion and will form a basis for a concise summation and a brief analysis.

The summary report is divided into two main sections: a) the authority of the Bible, and b) freedom within authority.

In the first section the Bible is seen in its historic development within the Covenant fellowship as an authoritative revelation whose "essential content is the gospel of our Lord Jesus Christ."

The statement goes on to say, "The Scriptures are both the witness to God's redemptive action in history and the interpretation of that action. Both the redemptive action in history in which God discloses Himself and the interpretation . . . which the Scriptures give of that action constitute revelation." The statement continues:

The church sees in such revelation the glory and mystery of God who condescends to speak his Word through the words of men, and finds in it a mystery which can be compared to the incarnation of the Eternal Son in the man Jesus. It looks upon the revelation, writing, gathering, and preserving of the Scriptures as a great work of God.

While the Scriptures address themselves both to the mind and the heart, the proof of their authority is not determined ultimately by the test of human reason but by God Himself as He bears witness to the Word through the inward work of the Holy Spirit in our minds and hearts. Because there is no other channel through which the redeeming knowledge of God is now disclosed to man, the church is bound to the Scriptures. . . .

Because the Scriptures have arisen within history and are transmitted to us through historical processes, the church in its educational task is obliged to use the best available methods of scholarly research to answer questions pertaining to the text, authorship, circumstances of origin, context, and meaning.

Because the Bible is the Word of God, the church is obliged to treasure its message, guarding it against every temptation to obscure its plain teaching or evade its truth, and humbly submitting itself to responsive obedience in the Holy Spirit.

The introductory statement, having established the relation of the Scriptures to the redemptive work of God in Christ, then goes on to ask what the constitutional faith statement (that the Covenant is a community of people which "believes in the Holy Scriptures, the Old and the New Testaments, as the Word of God and the only perfect rule for faith, doctrine, and conduct") actually means for understanding ourselves as a Christian community. It gives three meanings:

1) It means that we are people of a book . . . the Bible is a means by which God has chosen to reveal himself to us.

2) It means that we believe the Bible stands in judgment upon our sinfulness . . . [nonetheless] the message of judgment is only the context for the more positive function of the Bible. It is not only a book that judges. It is also a means of grace. . . .

3) Clearly implied in our statement of faith is the conviction that a spiritually healthy Christian community must be sustained by a right use of the Bible. . . . To receive these words of judgment and renewal we must restore the Book to the place which our fathers gave it. It must be the center of life and worship. . . .

In the second section of its study which deals with "freedom within authority" the committee sets itself the task of inquiring into the *nature of Christian freedom, the way the Covenant has experienced that freedom, and the ways in which that freedom may be maintained."*

Of especial interest in the historical context in which the document was developed is the section on "maintaining freedom in our intellectual pursuits." Although the committee's study was not perceived as contextual, that is, as growing out of the Doughty controversy, some of the issues of that protracted struggle may be glimpsed in the deliberations of the committee. A few quotations from the 1963 summary will illustrate this: "True scholarship is an essential activity." "The most significant battles of our time are those which are being fought in the world of ideas." "Scholarly pursuits, therefore, should be considered worthy of the dedication of our finest minds and most devoted hearts." "There is a difference between true scholarship, which is open to all truth, and intellectual sophistication which often looks on the Gospel as foolishness. A Christian who gives himself to scholarly pursuits may be expected to be humble and devoted to his faith. Even such a person, however, faces problems which are peculiar to the nature of his work. The attitude of objectivity, of openness to new ideas, and of freedom from restrictions on thought often leads him to conclusions which are contrary to popular opinion. Some within the Christian fellowship may become alarmed at these conclusions for fear that they may be contrary to sound Christian doctrine and they may with complete sincerity and earnestness raise questions about them."

This section concludes with some significant statements of which I shall attempts a digest:

> Neither stifling freedom of thought nor granting the scholar immunity from criticism can produce harmony. On the one hand we must recognize that we can remain active and vital in our interpretation of truth only as we permit the scholar to be honest about his conclusions. . . . On the other hand, we must recognize that the scholar is also human, subject to the temptation of pride of learning and to the common frailties of the flesh. . . .
>
> The solution to our problem is to accept the scholar, as we accept others, on the basis of his Christian testimony. . . . His actions as well as his words should bear witness to his respect for the Bible as the Word of God, his devotion to his Lord, his faithfulness to the Gospel, and his participation in the life of the church.
>
> Having earned the respect of his fellow Christians, the scholar should be rewarded with the freedom which intellectual pursuits require, but this freedom must be under the authority of the truth as revealed in the Bible. *In order that harmful tensions shall not arise between the scholar and those who may question whether this principle of freedom within authority is prevailing, there must be a continuing communication with the church in order that the truth may be further clarified. Thus the principle of freedom within authority also becomes the basis for our intellectual pursuits* (italics mine).

Since the committee's study was produced at a considerable outlay in time, in creative energy, and in denominational funds 1958-1963, it is appropriate to assess; a) its intrinsic merit as a study document, as well as b) its theoretical and practical impact on the Covenant Church.

In terms of its intrinsic merit, it can be said that the work of the committee represents a peak achievement in Covenant history in biblically based theological and ethical thought, in nobility of motive, and in apt and eloquent expression. The document reflects great credit on the members of the committee and particularly on those chiefly responsible for writing it.

It has been said that it is characteristic of theologians to write for theologians, and it may be said in commendation of the document that it achieves a high level of theological competence. It would serve admirably as a study document for a seminary class in ecclesiology or as a work paper for a week-long seminar of theologically interested pastors.

The erudition or sophistication reflected in the paper is its strength when placed in the context of scholarship; it is perhaps its disadvantage when related to the political situation which gave it birth.

The Committee on Freedom and Theology came into existence at a time when, as we have seen, the denomination and Ministerium were torn apart by a sense of incompetence, confusion, and guilt. The Doughty case had not been expertly handled, especially at the conference level, and the separation of William C. Doughty from the Covenant Ministerium was not exemplary.

This is not to say that there were not instances of masterful leadership in the handling of the case nor that Doughty did not merit censure and dismissal. He had manifested traits of character and of behavior which made his continuation as a Covenant pastor virtually impossible.

But the bill of particulars drawn up in his case, the reasons why his behavior was deemed indefensible, and the ultimate scenario developed for dealing with his discipline—all this seems to reflect a good bit of uncertainty.

Some justification for the procedure can undoubtedly be found in the circumstances. This was the first time that the disciplinary procedures of the Ministerium were applied in a case so unusual and complex. The major reason for this was the presence of many servicemen who, as pointed out earlier, were not fully acquainted with the Covenant ethos. Most of these men were gifted and adaptable, and readily found the Covenant a place to do what they were called to do—serve Christ as preachers of the Gospel. Doughty, however, belonged to a minority of applicants who had problems with fitting in. This was not a matter of doctrine but of adaptability to a particular context and to a particular kind of people. Doughty never did get oriented; instead he spent a good part of his time trying to get the denomination reoriented to his own ethos. As we said earlier, he assumed the role of prosecutor.

Hence we are led to wonder if the study committee might have done better by devoting itself to a more specific contextual investigation rather than abstract concepts of authority and freedom. The former was certainly what the Covenant expected. Perhaps if the committee had considered some of the history of doctrinal or procedural struggles in the Covenant, for example the Canada case, the A.B. Ost controversy, the questioned ordination of C. Victor Nyquist, and the polemical jousts with Gustaf F. Johnson, to name only a few, some light may have been thrown on how the denomination and the Ministerium had historically addressed its grievances and problems.

In trying to arrive at some clarification of the way in which the committee saw its task now more than a quarter of a century ago, I tried to make contact with some of the members of that body. Of the eleven original members only Donald C. Frisk was available for an opinion, but he was able to provide some very illuminating insights.[2] It is clear that the task as assigned was almost totally detached from the circumstances that prompted it. Frisk remembers it as an effort to give a broad perspective to Covenant theology, to provide a kind of summa of Covenant thought, particularly in the areas of biblical authority and Christian freedom. The study would thus furnish benchmarks for future dialogue which, one would hope, could prevent confusion and misunderstanding.

But in general the discussion was quite theoretical and abstract, Frisk recalls. For example, he cannot remember a single reference to the Doughty affair in the meetings of the committee. One wonders if the impending accreditation of the seminary by the Association of Theological Schools may have played a part in giving the committee's dialogue this general character.

In any case, the hope that the document would serve as a set of denominational guidelines was not realized. The presentation of the finalized report in 1963 caused barely a ripple. In the Council of Administrators and the Executive Board it was accorded little recognition beyond a formal expression of gratitude. It was not, so far as I have been able to determine, made a matter of serious discussion in any official forum of the denomination, and I have wondered if it was ever seriously consulted as a body of first principles.

More particularly, the work of the committee may have exacerbated

---

2. My conversation with Don Frisk took place in August, 1985.

rather than healed the wounds of the Doughty affair. An honest attempt was certainly made to have the personnel of the committee representative, but the document was seen, at least by some, as a piece of special pleading for the seminary. Two seminary deans and three professors constituted a fair percentage of the membership of the committee, and the rhetoric of the final document bore the imprint of the theological thinking then current in the seminary.[3]

In any event, the underlying tension between the biblicistic conservatives and the more moderate evangelicals of the Covenant seems not to have been relaxed appreciably by the work of the committee. There was stormy weather ahead and there may have been reasons for this.

CHANGES AT NORTH PARK

When Clarence A. Nelson was elected president of the Covenant in Miami in 1958, the action of the meeting was one of the real surprises provided by the history of the denomination. It was probably a response to a growing impatience with the structural strengthening of the Covenant reflected in the 1957 constitution. It may also have been related to the change in the constituency which had brought a more congregational point of view to the fore. We remember that Doughty and others were troubled with what they saw as increasing centralization.

Be that as it may, Nelson's election left a vacancy in the presidency of the school which needed to be filled by 1959, particularly since both college and seminary were preparing for the process of accreditation as degree-granting institutions. My candidacy for the presidency of North Park was launched with some solid support by the faculties of the academy, the college, and the seminary, with the subsequent approval of the board of North Park, and finally with acceptance of that nomination by the Executive Board of the denomination.

In commenting on the approval of the nomination by the Executive Board, I want to be as accurate as possible. I do not know the final vote in that body, but I know that my candidacy was opposed by a significant segment of administrative leadership who for personal reasons or honest doubts about my acceptability by the Covenant at large hoped for a more promising candidate.

Because of this uncertainty, some members of the North Park Board of Directors suggested to me that I should make a whistle-stop tour of the

---

3. I would not want to leave the impression that Professor Frisk in his conversation with me about the committee in any way played down the significance of its work. He saw the labors of the committee as necessary, substantial, and of lasting merit—an important contribution to the ongoing dialogue of the seminary and the church.

Covenant to let the constituency become better acquainted with me. I accepted that suggestion with as good grace as I could muster, but the motivation for the journey left something to be desired as far as I was concerned. The reason for the tour could not have been that I was not well enough known to the Covenant. Virtually my whole life had been spent on the reservation and in one way or other I had appeared in print in denominational publications, spoken in churches and conferences, taught classes in college and seminary, sat on boards and committees, and had significant contact with our sister Covenant in Sweden as much as or more than any other major candidate for office that I could recall. For me the problem was not that I was not well known but that I was probably too well known. And this can be related to a phenomenon already referred to. The constituency of the Covenant was changing rapidly and the image that I had projected among the newer members of the family—and perhaps among the older—may have rendered my candidacy suspect.

The reservation about my presidency was reflected also in the prodigious efforts put forth before and during the Annual Meeting to provide more than one candidate for the presidency. I have told that story in *By One Spirit* (pp. 640-641) with a more sanguine twist, finding the reason for this legislative stratagem less in personal opposition to my candidacy than a protest about procedure.

But more than twenty years have passed since I formulated that conclusion, and I now believe that the Rockford debate on the number of candidates for the presidency, concealed a deeper concern among many for the future of North Park. There may have been some sound democratic instincts abroad, urging a wider choice of nominees than was provided by the one candidate, but the fundamental anxiety had to do with the kind of theology that would be enthroned on the campus. Here too the conflict between biblicists and moderates was apparent.

During the life of the Committee on Freedom and Theology, the seminary, looking forward to full accreditation, had added Fredrick Holmgren, F. Burton Nelson, Wesley W. Nelson, and Werner E. Lemke to its ranks. Wesley Nelson came out of a strongly evangelical background in Turlock, California, and had had the reputation of being a pillar of biblicism. However, while serving as pastor in the Oakland Covenant Church in the 1950s, he had been influenced by the life and ministry of Roy Hessian, and had embarked on an inward pilgrimage, the dimensions of which are suggested in his autobiographical book, *Crying for My Mother*. The change was probably more one of interpretation and attitude than of theological conviction, for in 1954 he could write an article for *The Covenant Weekly* "You May Call Me a Fundamentalist."

But even if we leave Wesley Nelson's state of mind unresolved at this time and give byes to Werner Lemke and Glenn P. Anderson—who was to join the faculty in 1964—we are still left with four of the teachers who came to campus from 1954 to 1964 singularly devoted to the ecumenical cause. They were Earl C. Dahlstrom, Henry A. Gustafson, F. Burton Nelson, and Fredrick Holmgren. And their arguments, which they stated clearly enough, had a great deal of validity. The Covenant of Sweden, no less conservative than the North American Covenant, not only belonged to the World Council of Churches but was to provide some of its top leadership through the years. Furthermore, the National Council of Churches was so definitely Trinitarian that it would not accept denominations without this theological emphasis.

The problem for the Covenant of North America was nevertheless complicated by a widespread fear among the more conservative elements of "guilt by association." A not inconsiderable number of Covenant churches and pastors were closely identified with the National Association of Evangelicals. For that organization the National Council of Churches was quite unacceptable because several of its member churches held a latitudinarian view of the Scriptures. And here the words of Paul to the Corinthians were often quite literally applied: "For what partnership have righteousness and iniquity? Or what fellowship has light with darkness? What accord has Christ with Belial? Or what has a believer in common with an unbeliever? What agreement has the temple of God with idols?" (2 Corinthians 6:14-16).

The commitment of Covenant pastors and laypersons to the NAE was given particular focus when in 1955 Paul S. Rees, pastor of the First Covenant Church in Minneapolis and much admired teacher in the denomination, was elected president of the association. During the next decade (1955-1965) these alignments both on the side of the WCC and NCC on the one hand and the NAE on the other were to lead to increasing polarization and misunderstanding, as we shall see directly. As recently as this summer I was reminded by a former student and good friend of many years how outspoken my criticism of Paul Rees's association with the NAE had been at Turlock in 1952. I cannot now alter the feelings of 1952, which I am sure at the time were honest enough, but I can repent that so much of my energy went to bruise and not to heal.

When I became president of North Park in 1959, I brought with me into the position a certain interest in ecumenism, particularly in the WCC. This was due in part to the close association of the Covenant of Sweden with that body and the involvement of some personal friends.

Nevertheless, assuming responsibility for the denomination's college and seminary gave me a different perspective on my role than I had held as a member of the faculty. It became evident to me, as I was brought in closer contact with the Covenant family, its pastors and laity, that some of us had been operating with a great many unfounded assumptions about the ecumenical interest of our people and that we needed an instrument, however crude, to determine what the "big picture" in the denomination actually was. The result was that I began to favor a straw vote for the assessment of ecumenical preferences which was finally scheduled in the year 1964-1965.

In taking this position on the straw vote, I disappointed some of my friends and colleagues whose commitment to ecumenism of a formal order was probably more of a spiritual matter than I had considered it. In any event, controversy around ecumenical alignments materially increased the stress in the Covenant in the middle sixties.

THE DES MOINES CONFERENCE

In trying to describe the history of the Covenant in the period 1955-1965, it is tempting to use a well-worn phrase of Arnold Toynbee in his history of civilization—"A time of troubles." I shall not press an analogy between Toynbee's spacious chronicle and my own, but only draw a simple parallel. A "time of troubles" occurs when things cannot go further. This certainly describes the situation in Des Moines, Iowa, at the Midwinter Conference of 1965.

The theme of the conference was to be "The Bible" with papers by a number of professors from North Park Theological Seminary as well as by Douglas Cedarleaf, who was then completing ten years of ministry as pastor of the North Park Covenant Church in Chicago. In 1963 the biblical faculty of the seminary had been strengthened by the addition of Werner E. Lemke, who was completing his doctoral studies at Harvard Divinity School. He had begun his studies at North Park Seminary some years before, had made many friends in the campus community during his time as a student, and was now being given an opportunity to serve in his career as a teacher and interpreter of the Word. I had hoped that we would be able to present him to the Covenant Ministerium at the Midwinter Conference.

At a planning meeting of the Council of Administrators in the fall of 1964, I consequently recommended Lemke's name for one of the speaking slots at the Midwinter. But my suggestion was not accepted. Instead, Henry A. Gustafson, the gifted professor of New Testament who during ten years on the campus had made himself known and appreciated for his devotion to the biblical word and his insightful teaching, was given the assignment. His topic was "The Authority of the Inspired Word," and he was to be succeeded by Glenn P. Anderson whose topic was "The Adequacy of the Indwelling Word." Donald Frisk was to follow with "The Supremacy of the Incarnate Word" and Douglas Cedarleaf would conclude with "The Reliability of the Prophetic Word."

Because of faulty scheduling, I found myself committed to a week-long program on the West Coast at the very time the Ministerium met in Des Moines, and I was unable to attend this very critical assembly. I have since tried to reconstruct the progress of the meeting from the formal reports and also from informal memories and reflections.

Henry Gustafson gave the first lecture. After a brief historical introduction in which he called attention to the devotion of the Covenant to the Bible as the Word of God, he launched into his lecture:

> This, however, is not the end of the matter. The Bible, which we claim to be authoritative, is for most of the people in our twentieth century a strange book. Its outlook is dated by its Oriental-Hellenistic worlds. Its relevance is not always apparent to us who are orbiting the earth, or attempting to create life in the test tube, or seeking to understand man's personal problems in terms of guilt feelings. In fact, committed Christians often regard the perspectives of the Bible as impossible for men living in the modern world. They are not sure whether they should accept it as God's Word or treat it like any other religious work of antiquity. Thus the question of authority catches the church in confusion. Simultaneously it experiences feelings of reverence and skepticism.
>
> This situation is not to be wondered at, for the fact of the matter is that the authority of the Bible is a limited authority. The book is not God. It is man's response to God's action. It is written in man's language and by human instruments who reflect the cultures of their people and the knowledge of their times. Because human cultures change and human knowledge grows there are aspects of thought, knowledge, and behavior in the Bible which are not authoritative for us today.

Gustafson then proceeded to outline ways in which the Bible is not and cannot be authoritative for us. He instanced certain kinds of behavior and certain mores presented in the Bible which cannot be authoritative for us. He spoke of the Bible's nonscientific outlook and its lack of objectivity in presenting historical materials as "areas in which we do not and cannot regard the Bible as authoritative."

The speaker then went on to outline ways in which the Bible is truly authoritative and concluded:

> Further, the church believes that the Bible is authoritative because it has discovered that he [God] speaks through it. . . . This is to say that there is a kind of intrinsic authority to this book. It establishes itself. It is what it purports to be. . . . Or, more adequately, it is authenticated by

what the church has called *testimonium internum spiriti sancti*—the inner witness of the Holy Spirit. The Spirit of God who dwells in us witnesses to the truth of the living Word, Christ, as he is presented to us in the written word, the Bible. Thus the Bible shares in the authority of the Holy Spirit. It is he who authenticates its message to men of faith by speaking through it. Hence biblical authority is not primarily an intellectual affirmation which a Christian ought to make. It is rather a personal faith claim, the recognition of which ought to lead to a life of obedient faith in which we read our Bibles, listen to God speak, and then direct our lives to do what he demands.

Although neither radically novel in content nor especially out of character for the speaker, the lecture fell like a bolt of lightning. Much in the presentation itself as well as in what was said in the ensuing discussion created an unprecedented furor among many in the assembly.

I have asked some of those present how they account for this disproportionate effect. Granted that the authority of the Bible is an explosive topic, how explain this megatonic result?

Some have responded to my questions by saying that the "lead-in" was not particularly adroit; it did not invite to consideration but assumed the point at issue; others have said that the problem was not so much *what* was said in the lecture as *how* it was said; still others that the manner in which questions were handled exacerbated the pain of the formal presentation.

Glenn P. Anderson, a reliable source for both written and oral history, has provided a brief vignette of the scene in Des Moines at the conclusion of the Gustafson lecture. A Covenant pastor, not especially known for impassioned utterance, rose to his feet and said to Henry Gustafson, "I repudiate your right to teach in our seminary." To which Gustafson's rejoinder was, "And I repudiate your right to repudiate me."

What followed was a scene worthy of the pen of Henry Fielding or Miguel Cervantes, but it was not a scene designed to carry forward the unity of the spirit in the bond of peace. It led for a time to what seemed an unreconciled and irreconcilable splintering of the Ministerium.

At one of the informal evening gatherings of the conference some of the unrest found a focus in a protracted discussion about Gustafson's lecture and in some consideration of what might be done about it. I have not had access to the details of that conversation, but the upshot of it was a petition, addressed to the Board of Directors of North Park College and Theological Seminary, dated Thursday, February 18, 1965, and having the following content:

Dear Brethren:
    Since there comes in the course of events a time when concerned men must speak their convictions or be untrue to their consciences, the

undersigned are compelled to make clear:

1) Our unreserved commitment to the orthodox and classical doctrine of the inspiration of Scripture which affirms the integrity of the writers and the complete reliability of the record; 2) Our deep disappointment that the approach to the Bible in our seminary continues to be in opposition to the conservative view of the infallibility of the Scripture; 3) Our continuing anxiety that the conservative view of Scripture is not represented on the faculty in the biblical field of our seminary; 4) Our determination that our conservative ministerial students have the benefit of a theologically representative faculty or approval for study elsewhere.

Fifty-seven signatures follow, two of which have proved illegible. We shall hence be dealing with the signatures of fifty-five Covenant pastors. I have carefully reviewed the names and available ministerial records of the pastors signing the petition but have decided, despite their great historical interest, that the particular names will not be entered into this volume. I hope this is a wise decision.

Instead of dealing with names, I shall content myself with profiles of the signatories. Of this group four were born before 1900 and were thus reaching retirement age by this date. Fourteen of the signers were born between 1901 and 1910, twenty-three between 1911 and 1920, eight between 1921 and 1930, and five between 1931 and 1940. These five had the birth years 1931, 1932, 1933, 1934, and 1937 respectively.

I give this detailed picture to point out that there is no age group not represented. The signers, in fact, describe a fairly standard "bell curve," that is, they fall into expected age categories and do not represent a disproportion in terms of either age or youth.

Of the fifty-five signers thirty-nine had spent significant time at North Park, that is, a year or more, and of these nineteen seem to have pursued what was at the time of their study considered the full theological course. Four in the group completed the North Park summer course held at Covenant Bible College in Prince Albert 1955 and 1956 and had been qualified for ordination. Twelve had had no academic contact with North Park.

Thirty-nine of the fifty-five had studied at schools thought more conservative than North Park. Of these Moody Bible Institute, Wheaton College, Bethel Theological Seminary, Fuller Theological Seminary, and Northwestern Schools were attended by six or more students. Smaller numbers had spent some time at Seattle Pacific, Trinity Theological Seminary, Dallas Theological Seminary, Nyack Missionary Institute, Gordon Conwell Divinity School, Faith Seminary, Lutheran Brethren Seminary, Biola, Minnehaha Bible Institute, Prairie Bible Institute, and St. Paul Bible College.

An interesting category is represented by Minnehaha Bible Institute which came into existence in the early 1920s. A Bible institute was started at about the same time on the North Park campus. The original intention with these institutes was to provide training in the Bible and in the methods of Christian education. They attracted many more women than men, probably because the seminaries at that time did not encourage women candidates for the pastoral ministry. Bible institute students were invited to take appropriate courses in the seminary.[4]

Gustaf F. Johnson, whose role in the Covenant has been discussed earlier, was a strong advocate of Bible institutes, a commitment he shared with others of his apocalyptic and ecclesiological position. Johnson's preference for Bible institutes was based on the fact that they were a more direct route to service for young people who felt a calling to a career in evangelism or missions.

Johnson made a significant contribution to pastoral and lay education through his support of the Minnehaha Bible Institute and his participation in its program. But it would be difficult to state the theological position of the institute with any exactness since its teachers seem to have covered the spectrum of Covenant doctrine. In the twenty-five years of its existence Herbert E. Palmquist, Milton A. Freedholm, Joel S. Peterson, E.O. Franklin, Clarence A. Nelson, and, as indicated, Johnson among others taught courses at the institute.

In any case, seven signers of the petition had spent some time at that Bible institute.

Beyond this, it would be possible to draw further inferences about the signers by studying their dominant milieus and looking at the nature of their friendships and associations. But in view of the rather well-established contexts in which these persons moved, nothing much would be added. Those of us who were their contemporaries and colleagues in ministry saw the majority of them as mature and stable pastors who shared a devotion to the biblical Word and a concern about winning people for and nurturing them in the Gospel of Christ. Without exception they would have seen themselves as identified with the more conservative end of the theological spectrum of the Covenant.

What is troubling about them is not their indignation at Des Moines and the translation of that indignation into an instrument of protest. What is troubling is their conviction that their position was not being perceived by those of us in leadership. They honestly believed that their fears for the orthodox and classical doctrine of inspiration; their disap-

---

4. I share Marcus Ch'eng's evaluation of the women students he encountered in America. They were often not only better students than the men but they were more strongly motivated. They were nevertheless confined to the Court of Women.

pointment with the seminary's opposition to the conservative view of an infallible Scripture; their anxiety that the conservative view of Scripture was not represented on the faculty of the biblical field; and their determination that conservative ministerial students have the benefit of a theologically representative faculty—their concern was that these things were not making a dent.

I have somewhere described or heard this kind of petition described as a cry to be heard or a cry for help. Those of us who had the privilege to read the text of the petition and scan the signatures very soon understood that here we were not dealing with a polite paper but with a primal scream.

A COURSE OF ACTION

As soon as it was possible to arrange a meeting with the seminary faculty, I conveyed my feelings to that body and indicated a course of action I thought we needed to follow in order to show good faith with the petition and the petitioners, but without being drawn into passing judgment on the Gustafson lecture. (It is significant that despite the high feelings that surrounded the Gustafson presentation this was not formally seen as even the trigger cause of the petition or any subsequent action. What I believe this says is that the accumulated feelings which express themselves in the petition had an extended history and a multiple source.)

Two especially sensitive issues faced the Annual Meeting of the Covenant scheduled to be held on the campus in June. The first was the tenure of Fredrick Holmgren, assistant professor of Old Testament. The second was the Des Moines petition.

When Holmgren joined the faculty in 1960, tenure provisions required that after completion of the doctoral requirements and a satisfactory period of service the candidate must be presented for tenure to the Annual Meeting of the Covenant. Holmgren was a Ph.D. from Union Theological Seminary and had met all the professional requirements for tenure. He did not hold to the doctrine of verbal inerrancy, but he subscribed to the faith statement in the Covenant constitution relative to the Bible and his teaching and contact with students were good.

Then came Des Moines and the routine turned extraordinary. Some counselled that in this situation the question of Holmgren's tenure be postponed. But it seemed to us that such an action would put our academic integrity in jeopardy. We had, in effect, promised Holmgren tenure if and when he fulfilled the conditions. Refusing him this credential would violate policy and bring us no closer to a solution of the vexing problem then confronting us. Hence we insisted on proceeding with tenure while at the same time doing something substantial about the unrest behind the petition.

In an address to the Ministerium of the Covenant which I gave in response to their request for clarification on June 21, 1965, I spoke on "The Theological Posture of the Seminary and Covenant Faith." I developed the thesis that the Covenant faith began as a life movement within the State Church of Sweden and that throughout a century of our life as Mission Friends in this country, we have clung to the primacy of that life. I then went on to say that the life we have by faith in Christ is indistinguishable from our faith in the Holy Scriptures, the Old and the New Testament, as the only perfect rule for faith, doctrine, and conduct.

I then indicated that the strife that we were experiencing in 1965 was not around the question of our faith in the Holy Scriptures but how we interpret that faith. I said:

> There is now controversy—serious debilitating strife. Such controversy does not emerge in a vacuum. The present distress arises from the fact that the full spectrum of Covenant theology is allegedly not represented on the faculty of North Park. There is considerable feeling that the seminary is parting company with the church and that it is unfaithful to the Covenant's historic tradition on the inspiration of the Scriptures. The result is that some of our pastors and some of our churches feel alienated from the school and doubtful about the future of the denomination as a whole.
>
> It is not my task in the few minutes allotted to me tonight to present a defense of the seminary. I would like rather to delineate as clearly as I can what the Covenant has believed about the Scriptures in the eighty years of its history and where the seminary stands at present with respect to its scriptural faith.
>
> I have already argued that the central affirmation of the Covenant, viz., that life in Christ is primary cannot be divorced from the denominational position on the Scriptures as the Word of God. If we are Covenanters at all, we believe in the divine authority of the Bible.
>
> The point at issue, then, is not the authority of the Scriptures but how that authority has expressed itself. Put simply the question is this: if God wants to talk to men, how does he do it? On this point there has been a division of opinion among us at least since the emergence of Fundamentalism.[5] One group has held that God has chosen to communicate to us through inspired men and that, though the record manifests the errors and inconsistencies of human communication and transmission and reflects the thought patterns of particular cultures and particular periods of the world's history, the Bible as a whole is authoritative and perfect as regards faith, doctrine, and conduct. Another group has held that the Bible is without error *in the original writings*. Whatever incon-

5. As I have argued earlier, there was a strong presence of pre-fundamentalist dispensationalism among the mission friends in the 1870s.

sistencies or errors the Bible now manifests are the result of faulty translation or transmission. When God spoke to the authors of the Bible, and these men transcribed what was spoken, *that record* was without error.

We have spoken about the past and something of the present. But what of the future? In 1914, Gustaf F. Johnson became pastor of the Minneapolis Tabernacle, now the First Covenant Church of that city. He was a man of tremendous influence in the Covenant, a charismatic personality with something of the Old Testament prophet in him and something of a Southern senator, a self-taught popular theologian and rhetorician, and a fighter without fear. When he decided to ally himself with the Fundamentalist movement in America he introduced a new and significant factor into Covenant life and thought. During the 1920s Johnson and his colleagues gave voice to that emphasis upon verbal inspiration and inerrancy which is still with us, and although Johnson and many others are no longer alive, their position on the Scriptures, accepted by laymen and younger pastors, has attracted thousands of Covenanters to its banners. It is their voice which speaks in the Des Moines petition.

Now it is not my place to state the rightness or wrongness of any position. But it is my responsibility as a Covenanter and as the president of the seminary to determine the facts and to act in such a way that the life of the church may be preserved from harmful division and ineffectiveness.

The first fact is this: the seminary has not in its attitude toward the Scriptures proved unfaithful to the fathers.

The second fact is this: the position of biblical inerrancy and verbal inspiration is not now represented in the biblical field of the seminary. This does not make the seminary heretical, as I have tried to show, but it accounts for the desire expressed by the petitioners.

It is these two facts which lie behind my recommendation to the Board of Directors that the question of tenure be kept separate from the question of study. These two questions should be kept separate because the candidate for tenure is qualified within the present criteria. The question which needs to be studied is if the criteria should be revised. If so, such a revision will require study. To introduce new, unstudied criteria at the moment when the old *must* be applied creates an academic situation impossible to administer, at least impossible for me. I welcome a study and I welcome to that study those who are presently unhappy about the situation at the seminary as well as those who are happy. But we need to pray for patience and for charity.

This statement was made to the Ministerium on Monday, June 21, 1965. On Thursday of that week, June 24, I brought the double recommendation of the Board of Directors to the Annual Meeting, viz., the tenure of Holmgren and the appointment of a committee to study the seminary. I made clear that without granting tenure to Holmgren, my position as president of North Park would be untenable. I was accused, and justly so, of having used my position to effect a decision in the assembly, but I believed then and I believe now that the integrity of the institution and a promise given and accepted in good faith were at stake.

The meeting was stormy and at times acrimonious and one of the tragic losses was the resignation of Arvid F. Carlson from the Covenant Ministerium. Arvid Carlson and I were not intimate friends, but he had served
the Covenant and the school well, working on several boards and serving for a time on the Committee on Freedom and Theology, and I valued
his presence. I have sometimes heard pastors and laypersons deplore that
the Annual Meetings in the Covenant are now too housebroken and lack
drama, and this may well be, for power of whatever kind hopes for tranquility, but if our example of drama is 1965, we may need to adjust our
perspective. For 1965 was not just a vigorous difference of opinion but
the unleashing of destructive hostility on both sides of a question, the
ecology of death not life.

I have summarized the aftermath in an earlier history and I print it
here with some minor corrections:

> The petition led to some re-examination of the Covenant's view of Scrip-
> tures and, at the Annual Meeting of 1965, to the appointment of a
> "Committee to Study the Seminary." The committee, chaired by Rev.
> Wilbur Westerdahl, served until 1967 when it presented its basic recom-
> mendations to the Annual Meeting in Pasadena. These recommendations
> were:
> 1. We recommend that the Covenant Annual Meeting affirm the
> desirability of making North Park Theological Seminary a true model of
> the Covenant community in action through the fostering of a spirit of
> acceptance and respect for divergent views within the context of our
> historical commitment.
> 2. We recommend that a fully trained and qualified teacher who holds
> to the more conservative position on Scripture should be appointed to
> the biblical field at the seminary.
> 3. We recommend that a special committee be established composed
> of representatives of the seminary faculty, the seminary committee of
> the Board of Directors of North Park College and Theological Seminary,
> and the Seminary Study Committee to develop a procedure for the
> implementation of the above recommendation. The appointment of this
> committee is to be made by the Board of Directors of North Park with
> the concurrence of the Executive Board of the Covenant (FF, 120,121).

The Annual Meeting voted favorably on the recommendation for
greater theological balance in the teaching of Scriptures, and after some
very careful study of options, a committee under the chairmanship of the
Rev. David Larsen recommended the candidacy of Dr. Donald Madvig
of the North American Baptist Seminary, Sioux Falls, South Dakota.
Madvig was subsequently (1969) appointed to the chair of New Testament at North Park, a position made vacant by the resignation of Dr.

Henry A. Gustafson the previous year. Madvig remained in the position until 1974 when he was succeeded by Dr. Klyne Snodgrass, the present incumbent.

Before the Committee to Study the Seminary presented its recommendation to the Annual Meeting in Pasadena in 1967, it was shared with the seminary faculty, which had been invited to attend the meeting. The committee assured the faculty that the appointment of a more conservative scholar would not result in any change of personnel. No one was being asked to leave. The members of the faculty may not have been entirely happy with the recommendation, but they accepted its implications with apparent good grace. It was hence an unexpected and painful development when in April, 1968, Henry A. Gustafson presented me with his formal resignation from his chair in New Testament at North Park Seminary and shifted the scene of his scholarly labors to Pilgrim House, the United Church of Christ Seminary in New Brighton, Minnesota.

PART SIX

The Emergence of a Union 1967-1985

CHAPTER THIRTY-SEVEN

Balm in Gilead

In one of the more notable of Plato's dialogues—*The Symposium*, usually translated *The Banquet*—the Athenian comic playwright Aristophanes (455-375 B.C.), known to most schoolchildren of an older generation for such comedies as *The Frogs* and *The Clouds*, is introduced by Plato as a fictional character. Aristophanes contributes a myth on the universal human desire for unity and community. In the myth he tells of the original human being, a creature in which male and female characteristics are mingled. These double beings are shaped like apples or eggs and because of their unity, are endowed with prodigious strength. Aristophanes proceeds with his myth:

> The primeval man was round, his back and sides forming a sphere; and he had four hands and four feet, one head with two faces, looking opposite ways, set on a round neck and precisely alike; also four ears, two privy members, and the remainder to correspond. He could walk upright as men now do, backwards, or forwards as he pleased, and he could also roll over and over at a great pace, turning on his four hands and four feet, eight in all, like tumblers going over and over with their legs in the air; this was when he wanted to run fast . . . they were all round and moved around like their parents. Terrible was their might and strength and the thoughts of their hearts were great, and they made an attack upon the gods" (Edman 1928, 354).

Because they were such a present danger to the gods, Zeus arranged to have them cleft through the middle and thus permanently divided. But since that day the halves have dreamt of and striven for a reunion.

377

I am not sure that I understand Aristophanes' myth in any detail. Nonetheless, I am able to sense some of the emotional impact of his images. He gives me a glimpse of the desperate universal search for relationships and of the elusive character of any merely human dream of unity and community.

An older, more authentic account of beginnings is the Bible's chronicle of a rupture that split the universe in several ways, leaving people divided from God, from one another, and within themselves.

This is not the place for any further reflections on *The Symposium*. Plato's formula for unity has its own unique premises. But we observe in it a common longing for oneness and the stress we experience when that longing is frustrated.

As we have observed, the longing was frustrated in the Covenant for many years. That could not have been because the denomination and its leaders were unacquainted with Ephesians 2:14-16:

> For he is himself our peace. Gentiles and Jews, he has made the two one, and in his own body of flesh and blood has broken down the enmity which stood like a dividing wall between them; for he annulled the law with its rules and regulations, so as to create out of the two a single new humanity in himself, thereby making peace. This was his purpose, to reconcile the two in a single body to God through the cross, on which he killed the enmity (NEB).

Perhaps it was less a matter of ignorance of the truth than uncertainty of how to apply it practically. But my role is not to sit in judgment, for who is equal to these things? Rather, we are seeking to identify the influences that brought about the beginnings of that functional unity which enabled us to celebrate the Centennial as one church and one people.

The founding fathers did not give the Covenant an easy road even to functional unity. Within the twenty centuries of its life, Christendom has been served by ethnicities, languages, dogmas, liturgies, polities, and lifestyles as organizing centers. But if Covenant unity rested, as the fathers claimed, on nothing more cohesive than our companionship in faith and obedience, what wild divergences of belief and practice were not possible? And if these divergences were not to splinter us, what did we share that could bind us together? Of what spirit could we drink that would integrate us into a more stable family of faith?

Earlier we have presented our corporate identity—a covenant of believing and participating congregations as a source of oneness. The battle for that concept and reality was fought prior to 1885. The victory on that issue made impossible every subsequent ecumenical effort to form alliances, however plausible, that would lead to an abrogation or even significant limitation of this idea or its institutional expression.

We know well Abraham Lincoln's insistence that he had been made president not to abolish slavery or to safeguard it but only to *preserve the union*. As a Covenant Church we live and work under a similarly irrevocable mandate. Under God, we would preserve the Covenant, even while we recognize that this body shares in our human frailty and lives only by God's grace. These are the ideas I tried to incorporate into my "Choric Interlude" dealing with the Covenant seal (see chapter seventeen).

Now it is a truism that a body does not exist without spirit. And it is a Christian truism that the vitalizing, illuminating, uniting spirit of a church body is totally dependent on the presence of the Holy Spirit, the third person in the Trinity. The Holy Spirit, in Augustine's comment on this most blessed doctrine, is the ethical moment in the godhead, the "love that moves the sun and the other stars."

A church body cannot achieve and maintain life and unity unless it is moved by love, a love conveyed by the Holy Spirit. This also is a truism. In its historic existence the Church has sometimes doubted the unifying effect of love and has gone seeking for some other source of coherence, for example that of ideas. Such coherence has to do with the historic existence of the body and should not be ignored. Unity or community of concepts is a need in the life of any community. The paradox of faith needs support from the simplifications and complications of reason.

But reason and rational conclusions cannot unify the Church. In the fourth century it was the zeal of the monastic revival and not the outcomes of the theological controversies that revealed Christ afresh and saved orthodox faith. The living Christ was perceived within the fellowship of believers and was loved and thus believed in.

A MOVEMENT TOWARD UNITY

The question is, What gives us this unifying vision of Christ? I am now entering a very controversial area, and I confess that I do so with great fear and trembling. I shall be asking the question: what in 1965 helped to initiate the process that began to knit the Covenant together?

I shall have to answer the question with an intuition. I perceive that for a long time a number of things have been encouraged to sprout and grow in the obscure places of the Covenant Church. These things include a deep trust in and love for the Scriptures in their most common and simple form: the Bible read, shared, listened to, and believed in. Also in the wake of that experience is the growing assurance that what the Scriptures say to receptive hearts is "most certainly true."

The situation might be described as the Bible being for many people, both young and old, a house of holy experience and of faith. And in this house, this lowly place, the Lord Christ is revealed. Phillips Brooks says it in a well-known carol:

> How silently, how silently,
> The wondrous gift is given!
> So God imparts to human hearts
> The blessings of his heaven.
> No ear may hear his coming,
> But in this world of sin,
> Where meek souls will receive him, still
> The dear Christ enters in.

The house and the holy guest belong together. The Bible and the Savior are different expressions of the Divine charity, but they are also one. Without Christ the Bible can become harshly dogmatic, and without the Bible—the Old and the New Testaments—the figure of Christ may lose its historical rootage and its clear outline. Hence we celebrate the interdependence of the Scriptures and of Christ and their real presence in time.

We have earlier outlined the divisive process marking our history from the first emergence of Waldenström's doctrine of the atonement, through the conflict with the "Free," the wasting conflict around Fundamentalism, and the aftermath in the hassle around neo-orthodoxy.

But there is a balm in Gilead. During almost a century from 1872 when the first Waldenström rocket was fired in the atonement controversy to the Covenant Annual Meeting in 1967, when a real step toward the redress of grievance was taken by the seminary and the church, something else was underway—an effort to translate faith not into dogma and controversy but into holy living, that is, piety if by piety we mean being joyous and not merely pious.[1]

This movement toward holy living has deep roots and makes us the kin of St. Paul, St. Augustine, St. Anselm, St. Francis of Assisi and his seraphic pupil, St. Bonaventura, but also of John Wesley with a "heart strangely warmed" and of Jonathan Edwards with his thirst for the "religious affections."

The love of the Bible not as a herbarium but as a meadow fresh with

1. Zinzendorf.

flowers is celebrated[2]—and also the love of Christ, not as he emerges in the stiff brocade of the creeds and the canons, but in his work clothes among living people, smelling, as one writer has described it, of "fresh caught fish."

These loves prevailed and because of them, a third was activated—the love of the body of Christ—the family of faith in potency and act. The phrase "the friends of Jesus" has actuality among the Covenanters.

I tried to give this "life in Christ" theology substance in a talk given to Covenant ministers at the Midwinter in 1953, which I called "Covenant Beginnings: Mystical." I would not change much in that lecture except that since writing it, I have become more aware of the strong impact of Dwight L. Moody and the Sankey hymnody on the piety of the Covenant both in Sweden and here.[3]

Quite apart from the Darby influence on the Lutheran Mission Friends in the direction of negative ecclesiology, apocalypticism, and biblicism, the Moody process, enriched by Keswick holiness, served to nourish the loves to which we have already alluded.

AN EVANGELICAL WITNESS

In our history, as indicated in earlier chapters, the Covenant has had some difficulty maintaining its identity in the face of strong doctrinal

2. See, for example, David Nyvall's memorable comparison of the Scripture and the creeds: "Compare this [the New Testament] with the third article of the Apostolicum, confessing the fact of the ideal union of the church, Catholicism, quite in an Augustinian fashion. And then, at last comes a summary report on the fruits of salvation. Were it not for these, pointing to the forgiveness of sin, the resurrection of the body, and life eternal, the whole Apostolicum is sadly deficient as to life interests. It is a safe and sound confession of the triune God, strangely silent on the mystery of godliness. It is a cut and dry herbarium compared with the rich flora of the New Testament. As a first aid for memorizing a lesson it is no doubt valuable, as the following greater creeds are for more advanced learning. As a means of education these and other creeds are indispensable on the condition that they are frequently revised. Textbooks must be kept young" (Nyvall and Olsson 1954, 107). Nonetheless, however much we find ourselves resonating with Nyvall's lyrical appraisal of the New Testament in contrast to the creeds, it should probably be recalled that the latter did not originate so much as textbooks as battle cries in the support of cherished doctrines just then threatened by the assault of new and ingenious, not to say quite plausible, heresies.

3. In "Covenant Beginnings: Mystical" I allude to a collection of books from the library of A.E. Wenstrand just given to the seminary library. Among these were, in addition to the Lutheran and Pietistic classics we might expect, a number of hymnals from the nonconformist circles in Stockholm such as *Pilgrimssånger*, *Andeliga sånger för barn*, *Sånger till lammets lov*, and *Hemlandstoner*. Wenstrand was a pastor in the Mission Synod before the organization of the Covenant in 1885 and served as a Covenant pastor until his death in 1920. He was a staunch loyalist and a representative of our classical piety. Hence the mixture of hymnals is significant. The first two come from Baptist circles in Stockholm, the third is the well-known Nyström collection of translations of Sankey's *Songs and Solos*, the fourth was published by G. Edvard Alfvegren in Stockholm in 1884. Alfvegren (1846-1911) was a noted pastor among the Free Lutherans in Sweden. He was known for his devotional writings, particularly *Hvilostunder på vägen*, reflections on the pericopic texts, which appeared 1886-1906, in four massive volumes.

currents emanating from dispensational and Fundamentalist strongholds particularly in the West. But we cannot forget the incalculable debt we owe to the devotional impact of these movements, especially on our laity. American revivalism as it was presented by Dwight L. Moody and expressed itself in mass evangelism, Bible conferences, and eventually in Bible institutes gave emotional reinforcement to certain evangelical maxims that are still an integral part of our life and thought: the emphasis on the Bible as the Word of God; on Jesus Christ as the crucified, dying, and risen Lord; on our new birth in Christ and our deciding for him as the keystone of our Christian experience and the matter and form of membership in his body; on the living and reigning Lord whose coming in glory we await; and on the imperatives of evangelism and mission. All this accentuated Christology is, of course, not an original gift of any one person or agency but its centrality in the Covenant has been enabled at least in part by the close proximity of that evangelical community which emerged from the Moody circle.[4]

Out of that community directly or indirectly came literature, radio and television programming, evangelical song and music, and youth organizations like Youth for Christ, Hi-C, and Young Life. But its supreme gift was the evangelistic witness of William Franklin (Billy) Graham.

Graham first emerged as a religious leader at the end of World War II. To begin with he was closely identified with Youth for Christ and a group of evangelical radio personalities in the Chicago suburbs, but his considerable gift of communication, his imposing presence and cha-

---

4. In his recently published autobiography, *Landmarks of the Spirit*, David H. Sandstrom—a Covenant pastor until 1936, when he left the denomination for a ministry in the Congregational Christian churches (now UCC)—devotes a chapter to "Revivalism/ Conversion/Confirmation." In this chapter he summarizes some of his experiences of and reaction to the earlier revivalism of the Covenant. Many of Sandstrom's negative impressions no doubt parallel our own and those of our generation. But I wonder if the total impact on those of us who experienced this revivalistic culture, with its roots in the work of D.L. Moody, have fully appreciated the gift we were given. Sandstrom writes: "I have encountered many aspects of revivalism and many great evangelists during my life. Although the outstanding evangelist Dwight L. Moody died in 1899, I almost felt that I knew him directly because I had 'lived' him through Father and his contemporaries. I observed for myself revivalism in Father's Salem Church in Minneapolis and later in churches where I was preaching . . . " (p.79).

Sandstrom then goes on chronicle various types of revivalism and evangelism with which he had contact from his first experience at the age of seven through a succession of campaigns and meetings, some of dubious quality, until a traumatic encounter with Frank Mangs, a Finnish-Swedish evangelist, in the mid-nineteen thirties. This experience helped him crystallize his decision to leave the Covenant.

I have read this account with great interest and considerable empathy, and I agree with many of the writer's conclusions about revivalistic methods and their traumatic effect on some people. But I continue to wonder, as I have throughout my life and ministry, about the alternatives. The birth of young, whether animal or human, is an awesome but not a pretty experience. Perhaps the "new birth" of which our Lord speaks is connected with an unavoidable trauma in which the church must share if she is to remain alive.

risma, and his qualities as a leader suggested a force that would not be long contained within the more traditional structures.

By 1946, when Graham was still in his late twenties (he was born in 1918), he had become a national figure. He gained stature rapidly by his personal humility and devotion, his effectiveness as an evangelist, and the manner in which his campaigns were organized and staged. Already in 1962 Kenneth Scott Latourette, in his mammoth work, *Christianity in a Revolutionary Age*, could say about Graham:

> However, it was not too early to make a characterization of Graham. . . . He clearly belonged in the tradition of the great evangelists of the nineteenth century, especially Dwight L. Moody. Transparently sincere, not seeking personal recognition or prestige, at the first advent of fame and the flood of invitations to preach, feeling appalled and inadequate but trusting in the Holy Spirit for strength and wisdom to meet the challenge, Graham belonged in the Evangelical tradition embodied in the denominations which enrolled the large majority of the Protestants of the country, especially those of the pre-nineteenth century stock. He did not profit financially from his campaigns but drew a stated salary from his organization and one which was not as large as those of numbers of the clergy (V:27).

As I write this (Autumn 1985) Graham has been presented in one of his campaigns in California just before his departure for Communist Rumania. Seeing him on television in a personal interview with his old associate Cliff Barrows and in some of the great public gatherings in Anaheim is a powerful confirmation of the fact that although the great evangelist has undergone some understandable changes in the last thirty-five years (he is, for example, noticeably older and gentler), he is still the same fervent witness to the Gospel of his youth and still a master of his methods of mass evangelism.

In his interview with Barrows he confessed to some financial embarrassment in his organization for the first time in its history and asked for help in the distribution of his newly revised edition of *Peace with God*, first published in 1953.

I believe that an overview of Graham's statements in spoken and printed word during the past thirty years would witness to the same consistency. His messages have never raised any doubts about his belief in the reliability of the Bible. Virtually every major principle in Graham's proclamation is taken from the Scriptures. His frequently used phrase, "The Bible says," is never a rhetorical tag but always proof of how utterly Graham depends on the Scriptures for the substance of his preaching.

In his use of the Bible Graham never suggests that he has any doubt about the veridity of the historical accounts as they are presented in the

Old and the New Testaments. None of the vexing questions of sources, reactions, disputed readings, authorship, or dating that interest and sometimes trouble biblical scholars get into his public proclamation. Graham sees himself as a messenger of the Word, and as far as I can determine, that word to him is the infallible Scriptures.

During his four decades of public ministry Graham has published hundreds of articles and numerous books. A reading of these books beginning with *Peace with God* (1953), which appeared in the company of a number of "peace" books such as Fulton Sheen's *Peace of Soul*, and Lieberman's *Peace of Mind*, down to his more recent apocalyptic titles such as *Till Armageddon* (1981) and *Approaching Hoofbeats* (1983) indicates that although Graham may moderate his topics and shift his point of view in congruity with changing times, he never ceases to be utterly dependent on the Scriptures nor does he change his evangelistic intention or method.[5]

In making my evaluation I am, naturally, speaking from my vantage point as an interested but not especially knowledgeable observer. I have met Billy Graham on several occasions, but we have never exchanged more than minimal and polite greetings. There is no particular reason why he should be aware of my existence or that I should have access to any information not available to everyone else.

I mention this to make clear that I have no reason whatsoever to believe that there is more than one Billy Graham. I believe firmly that what Graham says publicly he believes privately. I was once invited to a breakfast for pastors in which he did us the favor of speaking more theologically than would have been appropriate for a more public meeting, but even on that occasion he had no trade secrets or arcane information intended only for the ministerial ear.

Latourette writes about some responses to Graham:

> In 1960 *The Christian Century* published an interview with Graham which provides an excellent summary of his understanding of himself. I quote, "Graham was quite aware that he was not a scholar, but he took account of the intellectual currents of the day including those in theology and biblical scholarship. Yet after doing so he said that his faith was confirmed in the Bible as the Word of God and in the crucifixion and resurrection of Christ. He was certain that God had acted decisively in history through Christ. He also believed in the completion of history and the final triumph of the Kingdom of God in the second coming of

5. As we might expect, Graham is a prolific and widely read author. Some indication of the topics which he has addressed in the last thirty years is provided by the titles of a selection of his books: *The Challenge* (1957), *My Answer* (1960), *The Jesus Generation* (1971), *Angels* (1975), and *The Holy Spirit* (1978).

Christ, but he refused to set a date for the event or enter into debate as
to precise details. He recognized the contrast between the revival of
religion of his day and the increase in the forces of evil—the growth of
both the wheat and the tares—but he did not doubt the ultimate victory
of Christ. He did not stress social reform, for he held that if men were
basically changed they would work for reforms. . . . He felt that he had
earlier been too narrow in defining the boundaries of the church, but
that he had come to place more emphasis on the Church, rejoiced that
he had found true Christians in every visible church, and was happy
that the cooperation of churches of many denominations in his
campaigns had made for Christian unity" (Latourette 1962, V:28).

Hence, in spite of his frank biblical conservatism, it seems to be an
almost unanimous verdict that Billy Graham has done more to motivate
and unify evangelical Christian churches across the whole spectrum of
their diversity than anyone else in our day. This is one of the conclusions
of William J. Abraham in his recent book, *The Coming Great Revival.*
Beyond this, Graham has gained the respect of other churchmen who,
although they do not share his conservative views of the Scriptures,
nonetheless see him as a powerful spokesman for Christendom.

What is this Graham mystique and what specifically has been its
impact on the process of unification in the Covenant? I raise this question
for although I would have to characterize myself as a late and somewhat
reluctant convert to the person and method of Billy Graham, I see his
presence as of great significance in the life of the denomination.

I believe that Graham's impact on the Covenant in the direction of
greater unity has been due to two major themes: a) his experiential and
noncontroversial commitment to the Bible as God's Word and to the sav-
iorhood and lordship of Christ, and b) his strong insistence that although
he will retain his conservative commitment he will "intend to go anywhere, sponsored by anybody, to preach the Gospel of Christ, if there
are no strings attached to my message." He continues, "I am sponsored
by civic clubs, universities, ministerial associations and councils of
churches all over the world. I intend to continue. . . . The one badge of
Christian discipleship is not orthodoxy, but love. . . . We evangelicals
sometimes set ourselves up as judges of another man's relationship to
God. . . . I have found born-again Christians in the strangest places,
under the oddest circumstances, who do not know our particular evangelical language. But their spirit witnesses to my spirit that they are truly
sons of God. There is a great swing all over the world, within the church,
toward a more conservative theological position. The old terms, fundamentalism and liberalism, are now passe. The situation has radically
changed, since the days of Machen, Riley and other defenders of the faith
a generation ago" (Abraham 1984, 20-21).

The fusion of evangelical commitment and inclusive churchmanship in Graham is reminiscent of his great precursor and model, D.L. Moody. Graham's openness to all those who are ready to hear his message and support his effort, regardless of denominational affiliation or theological brandname, has given him access to a wider public than just those who have embraced his type of conservatism, and this has certainly been true also within the Covenant. In this way he has served the cause of unity also within the denomination.

The same may be said of Paul S. Rees, who has been closely associated with Graham. As far as I can judge, Rees has retained his own thoughtful biblical conservatism much in the same way as Graham. But Rees's evangelicalism has been melded with a perceptive and warm-hearted churchmanship which has made him an effective witness to the Gospel in very wide circles. This "catholicity," to use the word in its most ancient and authentic meaning, has also given Rees the opportunity to "bond" the people of the Covenant (and here use I "bond" in its modern sense as binding, uniting, relating) in a most telling way.

In reviewing the life process of the Covenant during the past twenty years, I have tried to find some of the major causes for the gradual change in ambience which can certainly be perceived, and which has resulted in that functional unity we are now experiencing.

I see Graham and Rees as significant in that process. But there has also been a major internal impact to which we must now devote ourselves.

OCCASIONS FOR CHANGE

F.M. Johnson's use of Psalm 119:63 at the opening session of the organizational meeting in February 1885, "I am a companion of all them that fear thee, and of them that keep thy precepts," has often been used to indicate the wide boundaries of the Covenant, but despite this generalism, efforts go on to identify the *real* Covenanter. During the past few years typological schemes, dividing the Covenant into identifiable segments have also been developed to help define who we are. Some think we are four different parts; others settle for three.

I am sorry to say that this kind of Hegelianism doesn't take me very far. I am too much of a particularist to divide people into types and assign appropriate behavior to each and then make predictions on the basis of it. I am more prone to look at the historic process in an individual or community as representing normal and non-normal developments. Such non-normal or exceptional situations are not to be seen as evil or good in themselves, but as possible occasions for change. For example, I see the arrival of Gustaf F. Johnson on the Covenant scene in 1914 as such an occasion. His coming was no doubt associated with considerable pain for some people, but who can say that it did not spell ultimate growth for the larger Covenant, and that it did not finally conduce to a dynamic unity?[6]

The same may be said of the Des Moines crisis. The grief generated by that happening may, as in Paul's dealing with the church at Corinth, have caused a "godly sorrow not to be repented of" (2 Corinthians 7:10-11). We know that it had two consequences: the acceptance by the seminary of a more representative faculty in the biblical field (which gave the Covenant the assurance that the school was ready for creative interaction), and, not long after this, a program of visitation to the churches by the faculty of the seminary which promised a continued program of mutual help and support.

As far as the Covenant is concerned, we must certainly conclude that improved seminary-denominational relations did play a role in the change and served to facilitate the process toward unity. Glenn P. Anderson, who served as dean of the seminary from 1968 to 1982, helped enable this rapprochement, as did the members of the seminary faculty who subsequently served Covenant congregations on call in addition to their excellent academic work. In response to the denominational request

---

6. David Sandstrom, in the book already referred to, includes an episode from his early ministry. The year was 1925. Together with the faculty and students of North Park Seminary he attended a Bible conference in Chicago at which Gustaf F. Johnson was to speak. Sandstrom writes:

"That afternoon he [Johnson] was on full offensive. He deployed all the forensic skills in his arsenal to attack what he interpreted as defections of belief and dangerous worldliness in the Covenant, implying charges especially against the seminary. His standard of criticism and judgment was the five fundamentalist positions of the Christian faith regarded as essential because based on the Bible as the inspired, inerrant word of God. . . . Enlarging upon these propositions, Johnson rejected the Darwinian theory of evolution and the historical research into the Bible, often referred to as 'biblical criticism.'

"Johnson concluded his caustic, innuendo-filled speech by inviting responses from the audience, in particular from the school. It drew a long and, what I felt, agonizing silence. I could take it no longer. I was on my feet. What precisely I said I cannot recall. But I remember verbatim Johnson's reply: 'I am neither a prophet nor the son of a prophet, but I predict that twenty-five years from now, young Sandstrom will be the leading modernist in the Mission Covenant.' The session soon came to a close" (p.99).

Sandstrom then describes a short encounter immediately following the lecture in which Johnson has occasion to pass the North Park group:

"Apparently he [Johnson] was in no mood to shake hands. Standing nearby, Professor David Nyvall put his hand on Johnson's shoulder and said, 'Johnson, I'm sorry for what you did to one of my boys this afternoon.' Johnson replied, 'History repeats itself.' [Meaning presumably that this is what Nyvall had done to one of his boys.] Nyvall retorted, 'What do we know about history?' " (p.99).

Sandstrom then goes on to detail the impact of this and subsequent experiences on his decision a decade later to leave the Covenant.

for greater theological balance in the biblical field, presented in 1967, two highly qualified teachers in Bible, Donald R. Madvig (1969-1974) and Klyne Snodgrass (1974-) have served the North Park faculty. Not only have they been an academic strength to the school but they have provided the opportunity for dialogue both with colleagues and with the denomination at large, which was seen as a desideratum by the 1965 committee.[7]

Time and space would fail me were I to attempt to add specifics to this account. Faculty members in both seminary and college, pastors and lay-persons in the churches—all have worked together to achieve the sense of inclusion, comity, and affection so essential to the unity of the family of faith.

A NEW ADMINISTRATION

But I would be less than faithful to my topic as well as to my understanding of history if I failed to put these decades squarely into the political and communal contexts. Those who had felt disenfranchised by the Covenant prior to the period 1965-1967 undoubtedly had something to do with the election of Milton B. Engebretson in 1966. (He assumed office in 1967). And the election in 1968 of Earl M. VanDerVeer as the first executive secretary of the ministry, instead of the rival candidate Robert L. Erickson, who was thought by many to be a shoo-in, could not have been a fortuitous act. Some chickens were probably coming home to roost.

Milton Engebretson, was, of course, the ideal candidate. Aside from his personal charisma which earned him friends even among the ground

---

7. I cannot assess precisely the causes for the undulation in seminary enrollments in the sixties and seventies. Nonetheless, I believe that the dramatic increase must be related at least partly to increased confidence in the seminary and in the leadership of the Covenant. (I say "partly" for the dramatic influence of the Jesus Movement of the early seventies cannot be ignored. Collating the figures from North Park in this period with other seminary enrollments should help us to a more accurate estimate of causes.)

The figures, which were compiled by Glenn P. Anderson in a study he completed in 1984, are as follows:

1959	83	1968	80
1960	64	1969	61
1961	73	1970	64
1962	75	1971	54
1963	64	1972	79
1964	64	1973	93
1965	67	1974	137
1966	71	1975	147
1967	72		

In the period 1976-1985 the total has stayed above 140.

troops serving the Army Air Force in North Africa and Italy in World War II, he was politically qualified, perhaps overqualified. I summed that part of it up in 1975 for *A Family of Faith* and it's probably as well as I can do even on one of my favorite topics:

> The old Covenant mystique—rooted in Swedish-American ethnic patterns and the old life in Christ theology and nourished by the association of Covenant headquarters with established institutions like Covenant Press, Swedish Covenant Hospital, and North Park College and Theological Seminary—had not been entirely hospitable to the new people who joined the ranks after World War II. Theoretically, the Covenant was an Americanized church desiring to be "a companion of all those who fear thee." Practically it was still in many ways an ethnic denomination with its significant leadership in the hands of second and third generation Swedish-Americans.
>
> The election of Milton Engebretson to the presidency must be seen as a conscious or unconscious effort on the part of the Covenant to break that mold.
>
> In the first place the new president was not of Swedish but Norwegian descent. But of even greater significance, he was not of Covenant background. Born in Grand Forks, North Dakota, December 29, 1920, he was nurtured in the faith in a small, intensely-pietistic Norwegian group called the Church of Lutheran Brethren.
>
> After service in the United States Army Air Corps in World War II and the completion of undergraduate studies at Seattle Pacific College and the University of Washington, Seattle, Milton Engebretson enrolled at North Park Theological Seminary in 1950. His only previous contact with the Covenant had been in Seattle, Washington, where he became a member of the First Covenant Church in 1947. He met Rhoda Hollenbeck, a member of First Covenant Church, Minneapolis, during the war and married her in 1945.
>
> During his North Park stint he spent a year of internship at Stotler, Kansas. Upon graduating he served the Mankato, Minnesota, Covenant Church 1954-1957, and the Elim Covenant Church of Minneapolis, 1957-1962. In the latter year he became secretary of the Covenant, a position he held until assuming the presidency in 1967.
>
> These personal data are significant insofar as they establish the fact that Milton Engebretson was a Covenanter by choice and by adoption and not by birth. He was hence closer to the growing number of adopted Covenanters than his predecessors (*FF,* 128,129).

In any case, Engebretson set a deliberate course to make himself as useful as possible to the Covenant. He did this:

1. By remaining himself. He was from the beginning a theological conservative although not a Fundamentalist, and he has maintained this doctrinal posture throughout his many years of service. Nonetheless,

his conservatism has been the background of his thought and action, not the obtrusive foreground.

With his ideological sympathies he has combined a wide interest in reading, and although he has certainly spent days and nights reading stacks of informative materials appropriate to his many bureaucratic functions (inhabiting the Jumbo Jet of organization, as it were), he has drawn his stimulus from solo flights among fresh, stimulating, provocative, even shockingly novel ideas.

The qualities of warm friendliness and eager intellectual curiosity have made him the appreciated colleague of American church leaders and earned him the honor of a repeated chairmanship in that unorganized assembly of top people from the whole spectrum of church life in the United States.

2. By being a most effective churchman to Covenant structures and substructures, regional conferences, hospitals, retirement homes, schools, publications, conferences, youth camps, but most important of all to local Covenant churches, pastors, and laypersons.

In *A Family of Faith* I noted the point-counterpoint of his first months on the job; a) a consultation of church leaders b) a tireless visitation of the whole field. He has continued in the same rhythm. In 1979 he called his second consultation of church leaders. Some of his top lay advisers were less than happy about this deliberate exposure to question, suggestions, helpful hints, and even revisionary tactics, but the president did not share this devaluation and has even incorporated some of the more positive ideas into his subsequent planning. In any case, COLECO gave him what he wanted—living contact with the living church.

Engebretson's churchmanship has also extended to constant examination of the denominational structure given to the Covenant in the 1957 constitution. He has wanted an organization which would help the church and its leadership carry out its prioritized functions and meet its emerging concerns.

He has wanted a *unified* Covenant and a *growing* Covenant. Consequently he has worked to make room for the wide diversity of theological and practical viewpoints which abound in the denomination, and he has stressed—and in the opinions of some sometimes overstressed—the matter of numerical church growth. But Engebretson had learned from the computerized projections available to him that with the established giving patterns as they manifest themselves in the Covenant, a membership of 150,000 would be needed to support the present denominational program.

Hence it is not without significance that the nintieth anniversary of the Covenant was celebrated with the theme "Giving for Growing." In 1975, after a time of careful preparation under the general leadership of Paul W. Brandel and the executive direction of Ralph P. Hanson, Covenanters pledged in excess of $7,500,000—the largest sum by far until that year—to expand denominational frontiers both at home and abroad.

The emphasis was not limited to quantitative growth, although this was certainly dominant in the statement of aims. The president wanted to stimulate church growth in several ways, specifically by human resource development, evangelism, church planting in target metropolitan areas and central cities, and making funds available on a matching basis for the reduction of debt in regional conferences, local churches, and other specific areas of need.

Although Engebretson has made no secret of his disappointment in reaching growth goals, especially in evangelism and membership increase, in 1967 when he assumed the office of president the Covenant had 66,037 members in 550 churches; in 1984 the total was 85,385 members in 584 churches.

There can be no doubt that the president had wanted to close out the century with closer to 100,000 members. Comparisons with the past, nevertheless, provided some heartening facts for his 1984 report. He then said:

> The rate of growth in Covenant church membership almost doubled in the decade from 1973 to 1983 over the previous decade (19.9 percent versus 11.1 percent). Another factor to be considered is the rate of churches being received into Covenant membership. The 85 new churches that came in during the years from 1974 to 1983 is an increase of 57 percent over 1964 to 1973 (54 new churches). If the past is the basis for describing the future—10 of the 20 largest Covenant churches as measured by attendance were started after 1950—the planting of increasing numbers of new churches today bodes well for the growth of the church among us for the years ahead (YB 1984, 13).

There have been fundamental problems faced by Engebretson's administration in the area of the relationship of membership giving figures to annual denominational budgets. The Covenant as a people is exemplary in its total giving. Income to and through local churches reached a total of $54,400,000 in 1983 for a per capita contribution of $681. But of this amount 84 percent went to local congregations, 7 percent to the Covenant Coordinated Budget, 2 percent to nonbudgetary Covenant causes, 4 percent to regional conferences, and 3 percent to causes totally outside the Covenant. Hence, despite an increase of a total giving by a hefty 6 percent, congregations fell $200,000 short of meeting the budgetary commitments to national work voted by the previous Annual Meeting. This shortfall added to those of previous years gave the Covenant a cumulative operating deficit in 1983-1984 of close to $700,000. Since there are no established reserves for such deficits, the money to meet commitments for essential expenses, such as salaries and operating costs for missions and other high priority agencies, must come from borrowing at going commercial rates.

This curious combination of exemplary liberality, which helps fill the coffers of the local church and of the regional conferences, with a shortfall in the resources for national work may be due at least in part to the increased regionalization and localization of giving interest. Thousands of Covenanters, and these are growing in numbers every year, continue to think of Christian ministry as largely performed in and through the local church. Some who are edified and inspired by nondenominational programs on radio and television may limit their stewardship transactions to a periodic gift to one of these programs.

Hence one of the major tasks for evangelical denominations, unsupported by historic endowments, is to direct the attention of benevolent but not fully informed donors to the crucial needs represented by denominational efforts in missions, evangelism, Christian and higher education, publications, and benevolence. Engebretson and his staff as well as pastoral and lay leaders throughout the land have been struggling with ways of giving the essential national ministries of the Covenant more effective exposure.

Much has been done toward attaining this goal by imaginative programming for Midwinter Conferences and Annual Meetings. A great deal has been done through publications and Covenant Video. Awareness has also been increased through creative programs in public relations for the major agencies and institutions of the Covenant.

THE GREAT CELEBRATION

Nothing so unifies a people as a common cause eloquently presented and enthusiastically embraced. Those of us who during World War II saw Winston Churchill rally his battered country by a rare rhetoric know the truth of this observation. The "lifting up of the banner" of Covenant mission—to use a favorite nineteenth-century trope—has been done superbly by Milton Engebretson throughout his time in office, as it was by his storied predecessors. But at no time was this done with greater éclat than in the planning and execution of the Centennial celebration in June of 1985. This was done in two major stages:

1. A major fund-raising effort called Century 2 Campaign (C2C) which envisaged an unprecedented goal of $20,000,000 for major funding in the areas of world and home missions, of higher education, and programming for the needy. The five-year campaign, under the general chairmanship of Quintin A. Applequist, was directed by Marilyn J. Peterson, who worked with four area coordinators—H. Russell Anderson, Herbert R. Johnson, Glenn L. Lindell, and Clarence G. Winstedt. As executive director, Peterson gave strategic leadership to this impressive effort. (As this is being written, the serious financial difficulties in several areas of our national economy and as particularly experienced in several of the major congregations have kept the coveted goal from being fully attained. Despite this, a total of $16,225,000 has been pledged to date.)
2. A major program of celebration which involved a) the writing, publication, and distribution of significant texts (confirmation, Covenant history and commentary, Christian spirituality, an encyclopedia of Covenant hymnody, and a festival hymn book of merit), and b) a stupendous festival climax in Minneapolis (June 17-23) which drew as many as 11,000 celebrants to some of its happenings—the largest gathering of Covenanters ever on this side of the ocean. The entire event from beginning to end was grandly conceived, meticulously planned and orchestrated, and brilliantly executed by James R. Hawkinson, general chairman, Clifford Bjorklund, general coordinator, Russell Cervin, Centennial coordinator in Minneapolis, and a host of dedicated Covenanters who served faithfully on the many committees and subcommittees. Ultimately the event belonged to the thousands who provided the enthusiasm and support for a celebration of this magnitude.

It was a panorama of shared gratitude, faith, and hope; a fusion of memories, experiences, and expectations; a scenario of testimonies, conventicles, prayers, sermons, lectures, debates; a potpourri of mini-performances by choirs, bands, ensembles, quartets, soloists, acres of exhibits, and of crafts and art displays, youth adventures, kid construction efforts, green-grass fair events, barrels of coffee and soft drinks, hot dogs and sweet rolls and pizza wedges eaten in haste in a perpetual passover from friend to friend.

It was an exhibition of lovingly and beautifully wrought banners from churches around the globe, jubilantly carried.

It was a succession of dazzling presentations of choral and instrumental music in the grand style; of solemn rituals of ordination and communion with enough folksy informality to make them like a conventicle; of Covenant historical pageantry and of Covenant imagery on the big screen.

It was a constant flutter of personal and affectionate responses; of gleeful shrieks of reunion and hearty back slaps; of liberated laughter; of spontaneous hugging in aisles, lobbies, ticket lines, parking lots; of shared snacks and meals with an outfumbling for checks; of notes pinned on the bulletin boards like bread cast on the water; of wallets crammed with snapshots appearing from nowhere.

It was glad tears at meeting. It was sad tears at parting. It was the bitter-sweetness of time running out. And it was the faint far glimpse of "the joyous gathering" at his appearing and his kingdom.

It was also a fitting summation to almost a quarter century of distinquished service to the Covenant and all its activities and people by Milton Engebretson in the tasks of unifying, healing, organizing, motivating, and moving hundreds of churches and agencies and thousands of believers here and abroad toward the objectives spelled out and blessed by the forebears and cherished by this family of faith.

We began this chapter with reference to Plato's great dialogue on the search for unity and the One. For Plato the searching for and the finding of unity is the consequence of the solemn processes of the philosophic mind. But the unity for which this church has prayed and labored since its inception is ultimately a gift of God's love and of the grace of our Lord Jesus Christ who, though he was rich, yet for our sake became poor.

Unity comes through the power of God and the wisdom of God— through energy properly distributed and problems solved through the gifts of faith and vision. But ultimately unity—at least the functional unity we look for in this world—comes through kenosis, the emptying which is the mind of Christ, through praying for the truth spoken in love, and through receiving that balm in Gilead which is to forgive and to be forgiven. Through the work of the Spirit in us, it means ultimately the absorbing of the enmity for the sake of the unity.

CHAPTER THIRTY-EIGHT

FUNCTIONAL ONENESS: A PRECARIOUS ACHIEVEMENT

In his "State of the Union" message to the Ninety-first Annual Meeting of the Covenant Church, held in Tacoma, Washington, June 23, 1976, Milton Engebretson concluded by saying: "The message is true, accomplishment is within reach, let us follow our convictions and act with dispatch. I am convinced that the Covenant's finest days are immediately before us. Praise be to God!"

Fortunately the ground for this hope was not in circumstances in which America found herself on the eve of her 200th birthday. The national waters were indeed rough. There were, of course, some real causes for a national rejoicing the church bells proclaimed ten days later. But in 1976 the mood in the United States and the world at large was hardly cheerful.

During the decade immediately preceding, that is 1966-1975, some of the most humbling events in the history of the nation had transpired. We had, to be sure, succeeded in a manned moon landing and taken a giant step for humankind; we had witnessed the conclusion of Vatican II with its encouraging modification of Roman intransigence; our president had visited The People's Republic of China and the Soviet Union, and Brezhnev had returned the courtesy; we had started the SALT talks with the Soviet Union, had worked out an Ocean Floor agreement, and had contracted for a Nuclear Non-Proliferation Treaty with the Soviet Union and ninety-six other sovereign states; Indira Gandhi had become the strong prime minister of India, and Pakistan and Bangladesh had, with some encouragement, gone appropriately separate ways.

But France had walked out on NATO when it could not get a larger role in command functions. In Germany the Baader-Meinhof gang and in Italy the equally vicious Red Brigade proved such a real threat to European security that sleepy frontiers were suddenly guarded and entering travelers meticulously searched. Such incidents were a gloomy portent of a decade of escalating terrorism engineered by addled amateurs like the Muslim Fundamentalists or cynical sovereign states like Iran and Libya.

But the shame of the United Sates went deeper. Having been drawn into playing a confused savior role in Vietnam, it landed in the Southeast Asia morass, which had already a decade earlier been explored and abandoned by the more realistic French. The unquestioned American military strength in World War II, which had been less decisively tested in the Korean war, was, for whatever reason, found inadequate for the mission entrusted to it in Vietnam. Complicating the conduct of the wars both in Korea and Vietnam was a divided public opinion and a lack of unifying sentiment. This was especially true of the latter conflict in which the intentions and deportment of the South Vietnamese were chronically cloudy and often suspect and where a ground for a comfortable and permanent comity seems not to have existed. If we read accurately the "gut" reactions of American combatants, many of them felt abandoned by their top leadership and, worst of all, unsure about their mission.

As a result, many caved in emotionally and others became victims of drugs already in ample supply in that disorganized land. A further complicating factor was the growing capacity of the media not only to report happenings but to impact public opinion almost at will by a vastly more powerful technology than previously existed.

Another source of American embarrassment was the development of the long-harbored and intense hostility of the Arab world. The involvement of the United States formally or informally in the establishment and growth of Israel was not a comforting experience for some of the Arabs, and their pain was acutely exacerbated by the almost miraculous military success of the Israelis in the wars of 1948, 1956, 1967, and 1973. So impressively effective was the Israeli war machine in contrast to that of their adversaries that in the confrontation of 1967 (June 5-10) only six days were required to bring the Arab forces to heel.[1]

But the Arabs controlled another kind of power. Aware of the diminishing oil reserves of the western world and the crucial dependence of industrialized nations on their oil, the Arabs imposed an embargo on oil

1. I recall the civilized concern expressed by a Jewish businessman at a Chicago luncheon during those dramatic days. He was, of course, impressed by the victorious outcome, but he said, "I am fearful that every victory of this type will make it more difficult for Israel to find its place in the Middle East. And what we hope for Israel is a chance to live in peace with her neighbors."

shipments in 1973 and simultaneously raised the price of crude oil. These actions were, as one might expect, wrapped in the rhetoric of environmental restraint and ecological salvation. The West needed to help the Arabs conserve this precious commodity etc., etc.

The consequent panic at American gas pumps that resulted in unmanageably long lines and general frustration was probably, at least in part, contrived by those who had something to gain from this real or simulated shortage. But this embarrassment did have a salutary effect on western consumers who had grown indifferent to the conscienceless waste of fossil fuels since the dawn of the automobile and airplane eras. Now suddenly the role of individuals and corporations in safeguarding our future supplies of energy became a priority. We learned to wear sweaters, turn down thermostats, use wood stoves, and build and drive pigmy cars.

But the embarrassment was not limited to the fuel economy, trying as that may have been. The resulting oil prices fueled an inflation abnormal except in wartime; its effects on the poor and those living on fixed incomes were disastrous, and it impacted institutions dependent on endowment income and unable to raise fees enough to keep pace.

And so it was that the national birthday had not so few sputtering candles when July 4, 1976, rolled around.

But the deepest shame was not our military reverses in Vietnam, the behavior of our French friends in the NATO hassle, the cunning of the oil rich Arabs, or even our own economic woes. The darkest ignominy for Americans was the moral treason within—the breakdown of public responsibility and accountability, the erosion of integrity in the events of Watergate.

Those who survived the sixties on American campuses remember the excesses of the more radical student protesters—the dreary vandalism, the violent obstruction of academic process, the thoughtless indignation that ususally found the wrong target. We remember student records defiled with excrement, precious paintings razor-bladed into ribbons. But under this nauseating "acting out" there was not seldom a distorted idealism, an absence of craft and guile.

But what could the American people say of their esteemed public leaders who governed under an oath of fealty to the nation but sold their "sacred honor" for a mess of pottage and then tried to conceal their chicanery behind bravado, stonewalling, and the Big Lie?

This was America in the middle seventies and the context in which President Engebretson spoke at the Tacoma meeting. His report did not, as in some previous and more obviously turbulent years, directly address the national crisis. Despite this or perhaps because of it, he conveyed insights on the significant task of the Church in any age—in the world but not of it—to transmit the heritage of the Spirit to its own and succeeding generations. In closing his address he said:

> As our nation celebrates its Bicentennial the people of the United States measure their stature and performance against the hardy heroes whose character and determination formed a government of democracy and freedom which has lasted for two hundred years. We also present a new birth of freedom for humanity which has lasted for almost two thousand years. In fact, Christianity alone can be accredited for providing the basis for the freedom within this nation. We must also measure ourselves and our integrity of perfomance, not against the stalwarts of yesteryear but against the power within us and the degree to which our dimness of vision has been enlightened by the continuing presence of the Holy Spirit. "The Spirit of the Lord is upon (us)." He anoints, equips, inspires, and encourages us. . . . He also shows us what the Christian ought to be doing, to proclaim the Gospel, minister to the needy, and raise the understanding of all in Christ.

Earlier in his address Engebretson had stressed that, "we must keep the operation alive with 'business as usual'! But," he said, "Covenant 'business as usual' is no mean existence." He continued:

> It is mission, it is education, it is publications, it is healing, it is caring, it is righting wrongs, it is freeing people, and it is preaching the Word. It is mobilization, evangelization, and rehabilitation, it is also managerial, financial, and custodial, and much, much more. It is some operation. Our calling is to keep it functioning, serving, living, and progressing. "Business as usual" is the day-to-day performance of God's work which is by far the most important of all we do. But all too often it is the least glamorous and the most difficult to dramatize enough to evoke an adequate volume of support.

Engebretson's words in Tacoma a decade ago, "Business as usual," might well be placed as a memorial frieze over ten years of Covenant work. The phrase includes everything except the element of celebration. But, as a Baptist friend of mine says or quotes, "You've got to have a victory before you shout, 'Hosanna.' " And in 1976 Milton Engebretson was not yet ready for the celebrative shout. That would come later.

CENTRAL ADMINISTRATION

Although the work of the denomination in the decade 1976-1985 was carried out largely through the structure that had been obtained since the adoption of the new constitution in 1957, there were some changes. These will be noted directly. The composition of headquarters has remained amazingly stable during the past ten years. Five of the nine members of the Council of Administrators served the entire decade: Milton B. Engebretson, president; Clifford W. Bjorklund, secretary; David S. Noreen, executive secretary of Christian education; James R. Hawkinson, executive secretary of publications; Nils G. Axelson, president of Benevolent Institutions.

Robert C. Larson, lately executive secretary of church growth and evangelism; Earl VanDerVeer, executive secretary of the ministry; William R. Hausman, president of North Park College and Theological Seminary; Doris R. Johnson, executive secretary of Covenant Women; and Raymond L. Dahlberg, executive secretary of world mission, served five years or longer.

To this roster of servants of the council during the decade must be added Paul W. Anderson (home mission until 1978); Russell A. Cervin (world mission until 1977); Lloyd H. Ahlem (North Park College and Theological Seminary until 1979); Arthur A.R. Nelson (acting president, North Park College and Seminary 1979-1980); Erma G. Chinander (Covenant Women until 1980); Randolph J. Klassen (evangelism until 1980); and James E. Persson (evangelism, 1982-1983).

Another role which deserves to be mentioned as a vital adjunct to the presidency of North Park is the deanship of the seminary. Glenn P. Anderson served in this office with distinction from 1968 to 1982. In the latter year he resigned the deanship to continue his teaching and writing in the field of church history. He was succeeded in the deanship by Robert K. Johnston in 1982.

REGIONAL ADMINISTRATION

We have noted the stability of the Council of Administrators during the decade 1975-1985. This has also characterized much of "middle management"—the regional conference superintendency.

Warren D. Swanson served the Midwest Conference as superintendent from the time that division was formed by the merging of the old Midwest with the Iowa Conference on September 26, 1969.[2] Clarence G. Winstedt was superintendent of the Central Conference from 1976 (when he succeeded A. Eldon Palmquist, 1968-1976) to 1983 when he resigned to become director of church growth and evangelism in the Pacific Southwest Conference. Luverne W. Sands served the Pacific Southwest Conference from 1977 to 1985. Superintendents of other regional confer-

2. On October 20, 1985, as this was being written, Warren Swanson died unexpectedly from a heart attack at age sixty-two. He will be mourned as a gifted and devoted churchman and a great friend of many.

ences who have served for some time in the decade 1975-1985 are as follows. (A date beside a name in the following list indicates the year in
which the superintendency began.)

Canada: Albert R. Josephson (1970); Keith C. Fullerton
                     (1978); Gerald V. Stenberg (1982).
Central: Clarence Winstedt (1976); Donald A. Njaa, acting
                     (1983); Herbert M. Freedholm (1984).
East Coast: C. Leslie Strand (1952); Paul A. Johnson (1977);
                     Robert L. Erickson (1980).
Michigan—Middle
East, now Great
Lakes: Harry V. Swanson (1965); David S. Dahlberg
                     (1982).
Midwest: Warren D. Swanson (1969).
North Pacific: Raymond L. Dahlberg (1973); Delmar L. Anderson
                     (1978); Edward Larson (1981).
Northwest: Carl H. Janson (1967); Stanley R. Henderson
                     (1981).
Pacific Southwest: Edward Larson (1964); Luverne W. Sands (1977);
                     Clarence Winstedt, acting (1985).
Southeast: Robert C. Larson, acting (1976); Chester E. Larson
                     (1983).

Earlier we have indicated the revised role of the superintendents in the
administrative structure of the Covenant. Whereas superintendents were
once the victims of a somewhat undefined process which made them
accountable only to regional conferences or, worse yet, to the ad hoc
needs of conference churches, the 1957 constitution attempted to introduce a measure of order and predictable procedure. The 1957 constitution left the major responsibility of the election, remuneration, and tenure of service with the regional conference, but gave the Executive Board
of the Covenant the responsibility of consulting with the conference in
the choosing of a superintendent. The regional conference, now an
administrative unit of the Covenant, must also submit proposed constitutional changes to the Executive Board for approval to assure that such
revisions are in conformity with the Covenant constitution. The integration of the work of the Covenant and conference has been significantly
improved since these changes were made. In effect the superintendents
now function within a frame of double reference. They serve both the
conference and its churches as well as the larger interests and programs
of the denomination. Through the Superintendents' Council, the Com-

mission on Pastoral Relations, and their place on a number of commissions and committees, the superintendents provide effective representation for a wide range of denominational activities.

THE MINISTERIUM

Another important link between the Covenant in its capacity as a family or body of churches and the local church is the Covenant Ministerium. From the beginning of the Covenant Church there has been a Ministerium, that is, a gathering of the denominations' ordained or licensed servants for the purpose of ongoing training, and edification, as well as the establishment and clarification of procedures.

The early opposition to church organization carried over also to ministerial affairs, but the need of a ministerial committee to handle rules of ordination and licensure and eventually related matters of discipline was recognized early. This grew gradually into a Ministerial Board which was later renamed the Board of Ministerial Standing and finally got its present name, the Board of the Ministry. This name seems more accurately to state the board's total function. The Board of the Ministry is governed by its rules. These rules must be adopted by the Annual Meeting of the Covenant after the approval of the Ministerium and are printed with the other instruments of order and procedure in the *Covenant Yearbook*. The rules were completely revised in 1973.

Perhaps a point of clarification may be in order. Pastors and laypersons joining the Covenant often come with a misapprehension about the role of the denomination in the life of the local church. They assume, as is the case in many independent churches, that the local congregation has the final say about the credentialing and discipline of its pastor. But while it is certainly true that the Covenant does not normally interfere in the internal decisions of the local churches (in this respect following a congregational principle), it is also true that the ministers licensed or ordained by the Covenant work under the ultimate supervision and discipline of the denomination. Because of this, the denomination and the conference have considerable interest in the type of pastor called by local congregations. Hence good churchmanship dictates that the local church work closely with the regional conference and the Covenant in the selection of a pastor.

The Ministerium as an organized body is a much later phenomenon than the committee or board of the ministry. However, the consitution of 1957, Article VII makes formal provision for such a body. The rules of the Ministerium are also printed in the *Yearbook*. The interaction of the Board of the Ministry and the Ministerium is constant and close. Provision for such interaction is made in both the rules of the Ministerium and the rules of the board. An important principle governing the work of both bodies is that the Ministerium has formal access to the Annual Meeting of the Covenant Church only through the Board of the Ministry. On the other hand, adequate checks and balances exist. The rules of the board stipulate that "the recommendations of the Board relating to the ordination, licensure, and discipline of ministers, or policy statements relating to its work, shall be submitted to the Covenant Ministerium at its annual meeting for approval." Non-approval of a matter results in a referral back to the board for further consideration (*YB* 1984:442).

Another significant point is that the Board of the Ministry is the only body that submits its recommendations directly to the Annual Meeting without the intermediate approval of the Executive Board.

COMPOSITION OF THE MINISTERIUM

Because the Covenant Church provides a considerable measure of theological freedom, it has been troubled throughout its history with a number of fruitless controversies. No community which allows itself this much freedom can avoid differences of opinion and vigorous debate (both of which give depth and power to the common life), but a shared level of theological awareness can probably prevent much of the kind of clash that leads nowhere.

If this is so, the gradual normalization of educational requirements for pastors in the Covenant will probably serve, not to eliminate debate, which would be a serious loss, but to assure the kind of interaction which informs, illuminates, and blesses the church.

In the period 1972-1985 a total of 346 candidates were ordained by the Covenant. Of these, 239 had earned the Master of Divinity Degree (the so-called M.Div.) at North Park Seminary. Of the remaining 107, eighty-six had earned an equivalent degree at an academically acceptable school. Of these, thirty-six had been educated at Fuller Seminary, twelve at Bethel, and six at Trinity. Thirty-two had completed their M.Div. at one of a wide range of seminaries, although there is no clear indication of preference in this group: seventeen came from less conservative and fifteen from more conservative schools. The remaining twenty-one candidates fall in special categories and are of limited statistical significance.

On the basis of the loosest sort of computation, it is possible to say that of the 346 ordinands earning the M.Div. degree from 1972 to 1985, 80 percent had been significantly subjected to the moderate conservatism of North Park Seminary or its equivalent, whereas 20 percent had had their most meaningful contact with seminaries theologically farther to the right.

By 1985 the Covenant had 922 ordinands. On the basis of the 80:20 proportion, this would mean that 700-plus of the ordinands had had an opportunity to be significantly impacted by the seminary and its more moderate position, whereas roughly 200 had spent more quality time in seminaries of a more conservative stamp. The presence of such an influence cannot give us any certainty about its prevalence in any particular student. It can only suggest the degree to which the seminary was given the opportunity to communicate its spirit and its theological ideas to the denomination's future pastors. And the general probability is that the greater the chance for impact, the larger the degree of lasting influence.

A source of ordained clergy other that the educational pool provided by the seminary has been the clergy of other denominations who, for valid reasons, desired to affiliate with the Covenant Ministerium. In the period 1972-1984, of the sixty making application for transfer, 75 percent have come from denominations which in one respect or another are deemed more "conservative" than the Covenant.[3]

They include eighteen of the following denominations: Korean Methodist, Korean Presbyterian, National Baptist Convention, The Wesleyan Church, Free Methodist, Evangelical Free, Nazarene, Christian and Missionary Alliance, Independent Fundamental Churches of America, Pilgrim Holiness, Baptist General Conference, Conservative Baptist, Evangelical Mennonite, Assemblies of God, Lutheran Church—Missouri Synod, The Missionary Church, Conservative Congregational Christian Conference, and Church of God (Anderson, Indiana).

Of these denominations the Korean Presbyterian, Evangelical Free, Nazarene, IFC, and Baptist General Conference provided the largest number of transfers: twenty-five.

Fifteen of the transfers (25 percent) came from churches generally considered more liberal than the Covenant: American Baptist, United Methodist, Lutheran Church in America, and Presbyterian. Of these the United Methodists provided by far the largest number: nine.

The transferring in of these pastors leads to some question the Covenant may want to consider. The issue of paedobaptism (the baptism of

---

3. "Conservative" is not a very precise term. Thus theological conservatism may mean fidelity to the doctrine of the verbal inspiration of the Bible, but it can also mean devotion to the creeds and confessions. Behavioral conservatism may mean the refusal to drink alcoholic beverages, coffee, or Coca Cola, or to use tobacco, play cards, or wear scanty swimsuits. Thus the Lutherans of the Missouri Synod have a conservative view of the Scriptures, but are liberal about alcohol, and, at least until recently, about the use of tobacco. The members of the Covenant of Sweden do not generally accept the doctrine of verbal inerrancy, but affirm total abstinence from alcoholic beverages.

infants) versus adult baptism has been a delicate one for many years and the accession of disproportionate numbers of pastors from either persuasion is bound to have an effect. The same may be said of pastors who wittingly or unwittingly disturb the delicate balance of inerrantists and more moderate Bible believers. A *sine qua non* of Covenant comity is the willingness of both parties to live and let live so long as basic fidelity to the Scriptures is maintained. This is not an easy achievement and precious ground can be lost to bigots of either persuasion if we forget that ceaseless vigilance is the price the Covenant pays for its freedom. But here the vigilance probably concerns one as much as the other.

Although the transfer in of the pastors from other denominations is of great significance, the transferring out of pastors also seriously affects the church, particularly if those who leave are, as is so often the case, a true embodiment of the denomination's image and spirit. Elsewhere I have made reference to a recent book by David Sandstrom, a pastor who left the Covenant Ministerium in 1936 and became affiliated with what is now the United Church of Christ. Every Covenanter interested in what has given the Covenant Church in its communication of the Gospel a touch of true greatness, but also what has served to skew it from its historic identity, will do well to read the Sandstrom memoirs.

In any case, during the period under consideration (1972-1984) twenty-five ordained Covenant pastors left the denomination. Two of these affiliated with groups more conservative than the Covenant; twenty-three transferred to what, for want of a better term, I shall call less conservative groups such as: Lutheran Church of America (three), United Church of Christ (five), Presbyterian Church, U.S.A. (eight), United Methodist (five). One joined the American Baptists and one became an Episcopalian.

I shall now allow myself one observation. It would probably be well if, in a self-study of the denomination, we pay more attention to motivation than we have done heretofore. It is probably true that among the forty-five pastors of conservative background who joined the Covenant Ministerium in the period 1972-1984 many were drawn by the promise of greater theological freedom. It must also be true that of the fifteen transferring in from a more liberal sector, some were attracted to what they saw as a more evangelical denomination. And, finally, of the twenty-five who left, there must have been a goodly number who felt that the Covenant was too restrictive. But whatever the reason for coming or going, the Covenant has a stake not so much in arguing with the feelings as in determining what the real reasons are for the turnover in pastors whether such a turnover benefits the denomination or not.

As Krister Stendahl pointed out at the Centennial celebration in Minneapolis, anniversaries can tempt us to exaggerated self-adulation, especially if we forget that the measuring stick is not a heroic history or present outward success, but devotion to the Gospel that calls us to the community of death and resurrection.

As a historian of a denomination with which I am strongly identified, I sometimes feel that our emphasis on numerical growth may actually impede that growth which is implied in John 12: "Unless a grain of wheat falls into the earth and dies, it remains alone; but if it dies, it bears forth much fruit" (v. 24).

If this is a valid judgment, the kind of pastors and laypersons we should probably continue to pray for in the work of the Covenant are those whose witness and example encourage us to "go forth to him outside the camp, and bear the abuse he endured" (Hebrews 13:13).

During this decade the stabilization of the Ministerium through a fairly uniform program of theological education contributed to the unity of the Covenant. But in some areas the understanding of doctrinal freedom may have set the stage for controversy. Most directly affected by this situation were:

1. The interpretation of irreducible faith as defined by the Covenant constitution.

     The publication of Fredrick Holmgren's book, *The God Who Cares: A Christian Looks at Judaism* was a cause for concern for David Larsen, then pastor of the First Covenant Church of Minneapolis. Larsen charged Holmgren with heresy before the Board of the Ministry.

2. The manner in which Scripture is used or misused to arrive at decisions at Covenant meetings.

     In 1984, a Covenant church brought objections to Klyne Snodgrass, professor of biblical studies at the seminary, about the way in which the issue of women in ministry was dealt with by the Covenant Ministerium.

     In 1985 the Calvary Covenant Church of Poway, California, urged the Covenant to assure better biblical preparation for the discussion of major issues at Annual Meetings and used as an example the handling of the issue of the sanctity of life and abortion.

The background of these issues is as follows:

In 1979 Holmgren put some concepts he had been developing and presenting in his classes in Judaism in *The God Who Cares.* His main thesis was that Christians have historically misunderstood Judaism and the Old Testament, seeing the Jewish faith as largely an emphasis on Law and reducing Judaism to a joyless, often tedious, and even dead observance of many minute regulations. Christians, on the other hand, have tended to glorify their own faith as a religion of grace, life, and freedom.

In presenting his thesis Holmgren tried to show that Judaism and Christianity have much more in common than Christians have allowed and that the differences emphasized by Christians have tended to separate the two peoples and to exacerbate the negative feelings toward Jews which have been held by Christians throughout the centuries.

In his statement of charges Larsen claimed that Holmgren's book had fallen short of the irreducible minimum of Covenant faith. "The Covenant Church," said Larsen, "has always aligned itself with the reformation doctrine of salvation by faith in Jesus Christ. This is the irreducible minimum in our heritage that cannot be compromised." Larsen continued, "the author [fails] to take a position that adequately proclaims that salvation is in Jesus Christ alone. Such failure is tantamount to heresy."

In dealing with the charges the Board of the Ministry did not concern itself with a detailed scrutiny of the Holmgren book but with the question of Holmgren's faithfulness to what the Covenant believes about the Bible as spelled out in the constitution. The result of these deliberations was that the Board of the Ministry found Holmgren not guilty of the charge of heresy.

Another example of stress with some possibility for disunity (this one in connection with statements and actions at Covenant meetings which failed to conform to biblical principles) related to the explosive issue of women in ministry. A Covenant pastor, whose identity I shall not reveal, took issue with Klyne Snodgrass, professor of bibilical literature at North Park Seminary, for his share in a position paper on women in ministry. Pertinent to this matter is the fact that the appointment of Snodgrass came as a result of the Pasadena decision of 1967 relative to a greater balance in the biblical department of the seminary between more and less conservative views of the Scriptures. Snodgrass, as did his predecessor Donald E. Madvig, belonged to the more conservative position. It is of particular interest that a person with such fidelity to the Bible should have been singled out for censure by our anonymous correspondent.

Snodgrass defended his position on women in ministry by careful biblical exegesis. The unnamed pastor, speaking from a most conservative position on this topic, had argued that women may not properly occupy a position of pastoral authority because the Scriptures nowhere give women the right to "oversee an elder."

Snodgrass answers his correspondent not by the use of "modern" arguments but by reliance on the texts. He suggests four approaches to the problem: exegesis, authority, ministry, and humanity. In none of these areas, as presented in the Scriptures, does Snodgrass find any support for refusing women the call to ministry.

Still another area brought under scrutiny is the Covenant's handling of "sanctity of life and abortion." At the annual meeting of the Ministerium held in Minneapolis on June 24-25, 1985, the Calvary Covenant Church of Poway, California, through its pastor, John E. Thill, presented a resolution regarding biblical position papers. It was the desire of the congregation that such papers be prepared and distributed to delegates prior to Annual Meetings so that these representatives might be biblically informed before considering and voting on significant issues.

Together with this general resolution the Poway church presented a paper called "A Biblical Affirmation on Abortion and the Sanctity of Life." The paper took a very absolutistic position on abortion, allowing abortion only when by means of it one life might be rescued rather than two lost. A list of justifications for abortion often invoked, such as potential birth defects, the rape or incestuous experience of the mother, or severe hardship in the family, were all disallowed.

This paper was presented for discussion at the Annual Meeting, having first been distributed to the Ministerium, but was not generally supported. A milder resolution was presented, discussed, and favorably acted on by the assembly (YB 1985).

CHAPTER THIRTY-NINE

Functional Oneness: Through Ministry and Mission

One sign of the dynamism of the Covenant in the decade has been the growing number of men and women committed to formal ministry and the preparation for it. During this ten-year period the Covenant ordained 296 pastors—a 44 percent increase in the credentialed leadership category. Earlier we indicated the trends in the preparation of Covenant pastors during a slightly longer period (1972-1985) and showed that there was a ratio of approximately 4:1 between those who received their primary theological training within the Covenant Church and those who got it elsewhere.

The Covenant has not been able to arrive at an optimal mix of these groups. It is obvious that having 100 percent of the pastors trained by North Park might not be desirable. On the other hand, having more than 50 percent trained by seminaries other than North Park would certainly not be optimal either. In the Covenant, being what it is in terms of significant individuation, the particular preparation is not indifferent. If the Covenant represented a more generalized type of evangelical conservatism with a fixed set of terms and tenets, adequate ministerial training might be gotten in any one of a dozen seminaries. Conversely if the denomination were comfortably liberal, a theological education could be secured in an even larger number of schools. But pastors serving Covenant churches in our time face a peculiar set of problems to which a generalized theological approach, whether conservative or liberal, is not adequate.

This is not because the denomination or seminary cherishes an illusion of academic superiority or has fervent commitment to an ethnic identity, but rather because there is a fear of too ready homogenization in any direction. Given the present historical circumstances, there is stronger likelihood that such homogenization would have an evangelical character, but whatever the outcome, the question of "mix" is not without meaning.

There will be occasion directly to return to the question of the ultimate character of Covenantism. But at this point we confess a lack of clarity about the optimum mix of "insiders" and "outsiders." It may indeed be an unanswerable question.

It is certainly true that, as the typologies developed by Lloyd Ahlem and Milton Engebretson suggest, the "Covenant mystique has expended far beyond the Swedish Pietistic individuation it once possessed." Nevertheless, some of the evangelicals and neo-evangelicals now being welcomed into the fellowship may be making too easy an equation between Covenantism and the conservatism of biblical inerrancy. This is an error made by Harold Lindsell in his *Battle for the Bible* and repeated in a second book, *Balance in the Bible.* The Covenant, despite its love for and commitment to biblical faith, never has been and probably never will be a Fundamentalist church. In all likelihood it will continue, as up to the present, to welcome into fellowship those of conservative, even inerrant views, but it will also continue to safeguard the right of less conservative Christians to belong to this family of faith as long as they confess their belief in the Scriptures as reflected in the Covenant constitution.

Historically the Covenant has also manifested a stubborn resistance to being forced into any other ideological mode. It is cool toward the reduction of biblical faith to sterile orthodoxy; it is equally cool toward any form of rationalism that seeks to reduce the Scriptural paradoxes. In another direction it is cautious about absolutizing charismatic experiences, expectations, and controls within the community.

Like the great faith tradition within Judaism, the core of the Covenant has been content to be defined by its story, its particular history. This story has ultimate meaning insofar as it is also the story of God's ongoing action in history. "This is the Lord's doing and it is marvelous in our eyes."

There are some risks and perils. One of these is to overidentify our own actions with God's and to refuse to see that much of our history needs to be repented of rather than glorified. Another corollary danger is that we become so preoccupied with the ritualization of our past history that we refuse critically to examine our present and our future. But if our form is a free, creative obedience to God's design, however it emerges, we can rely upon the Holy Spirit to illumine and energize.

It is in this spirit that much of the ongoing and pulsating work of study, writing, discussion, worship, witness, and celebration is presently carried on in the Covenant Church. The insistence that all pastors intending to serve in the Covenant spend some time, however modest, in studying on the North Park campus does not, then, arise from the narrow assumption of intellectual or spiritual superiority. Rather it comes from the desire to share what is uniquely the Covenant's gift with all those who choose to walk in the company of the denomination and its pastoral leadership.

THE ROLE OF THE MINISTERIUM EXPANDS

One of the agencies enabling the integration of the diverse pastoral elements of the Covenant into a unified group has been the Ministerium. Although present as a self-aware body within the denomination from the very beginning, until recently it lacked a substantial role. Initially it was only a *matrikel*, a list of names of pastors credentialed by the Covenant. Then gradually it found purpose in arranging pastoral meetings and conferences associated with annual meetings of regional conferences or of the national body. But with the growth of a sense of identity in the regional conference and its enlarged role in administering the work of the Covenant within the region, the role of the Ministerium expanded as well.

In 1968 the Covenant Ministerium was significantly strengthened by the creation of the Office of the Executive Secretary of the Ministry. This office found an important support system in the regional and national ministeriums. By 1973 the chairmen of the regional ministeriums were meeting with the executive group of the national Ministerium for informal discussions, and in 1977, through a constitutional change, the regional chairmen were made permanent members of the national executive committee with funding provided for their meetings at the national level (YB 1978, 162-164).

Through this new structuring the regional and national bodies have been able to consider issues on which the Covenant at large is seeking guidance, for example, marriage and divorce, ministerial compensation, abortion, and perhaps, most significant of all, the role of women in pastoral ministry.

After careful deliberation by the Board of Ministry and the Ministerium, the issue of women pastors was brought to the Annual Meeting of 1976. Considering its large consequences, the recommendation was very simply stated: "The Board of the Ministry, with the approval of the Covenant Ministerium recommends to the Ninety-first Covenant Annual

Meeting that the church go on record as favoring the ordination of women" (YB 1976, 178).

Even though the recommendation was opposed by some prestigious church leaders and even though it resulted in a "lengthy debate, pro and con, revolving around such issues as the scriptural basis of ministry, the meaning of ordination, the respective roles of men and women in the ministries of the church, and the practicality of women serving as pastors, it was passed by the assembly" (YB 1976, 178).

That it did so with relative smoothness must be attributed to a large extent to the growing influence of the Ministerium on the forming of Covenant opinion and on Covenant decision making.

The result of this action has been the subsequent ordination of at least seventeen women: Carol Shimmin Nordstrom and Sherron Hughes-Tremper (1978), Adele O. Cole (1979), Carla Lang (1980), Janet R. Lundblad, Mary V. Miller, and Marilyn S. Sandin[1] (1981), Isolde K. Anderson and Jean C. Lambert (1982), Catherine J. Bouts, Patricia N. Dickson, Karen L. Palmatier, Jan Potts, and Marie C. Wiebe (1983), and Frances M. Anderson, Helen M. Casey, and Lynne B. Floto (1985). Of these the great majority have pastoral placements as of this writing.

THE ROLE OF THE CAMPUS

No agency exerts a stronger formative influence on Covenant leadership than the academic community, particularly the campus of North Park College and Theological Seminary. Most of the ideas and attitudes as well as visions which eventually impact the churches of the Covenant have their origin and reinforcement in that community—its chapels, classrooms, libraries, and lecture halls, but also its numerous places for the informal exchange of ideas and experiences.

The campus continued during the decade 1975-1985 under the leadership of Lloyd H. Ahlem (1970-1979), Arthur A.R. Nelson (acting, 1979-1980), and William R. Hausman (1980-). Clarence A. Nelson (1950-1959) and Karl A. Olsson (1959-1970) had devoted themselves to building a virtually new campus at a cost of almost $8,000,000 with the result that long-term debt grew and operating deficits accumulated. Both were the price paid for dramatically upgrading both the college and the seminary. Under the leadership of the Department of Development significant initiatives were taken to strengthen annual giving and to broaden the base of capital funding. LeRoy M. Johnson (1965-1978)

---

1. Marilyn Sandin transferred her ordination to the Presbyterian Church (U.S.A.) in 1984.

expanded the scope of Friends of North Park and actualized the President's Club, and together these efforts significantly increased unrestricted gifts. These groups also became significant support groups for other projects as well as prospective clients for the estate planning program initiated toward the end of the 1960s. In 1978 LeRoy Johnson shifted his center to denominational headquarters where he has developed a Covenant-wide estate planning program benefitting the denomination, its agencies, and institutions.

During the decade operational funding was significantly helped by a reduction in capital indebtedness. Under the leadership of the then chairman of the Board of Directors, Dr. G. Timothy Johnson, a program of reducing a capital debt of $1,700,000 by the payment of $900,000 was successfully completed.

Dr. Johnson also chaired a Committee on Campus Location that struggled with the perennial problem of whether the school should continue in its present location or move elsewhere. After an intensive and detailed analysis of alternate situtions, the committee recommended that the school remain in its present location.

During these ten years the college has maintained its academic quality largely through the competence and devotion of a faculty that remains loyal to the institution in spite of what most often seem trying circumstances, particularly financial limitations. At the conclusion of the 1985 academic year a number of members of the faculty, administration, and staff have completed at least a quarter century of outstanding service. They are: Dwain Dedrick, C. Hobart Edgren, Alice Iverson, E. James Kennedy, J. William Fredrickson, J. Melburn Soneson, Zenos Hawkinson, Betty J. Nelson, Vivadelle Odell, Elder Lindahl, Gladys Sandquist, and A.T. Johnson.

During the decade 1975-1985 a large number of long-term faculty members, administrators, and staff retired from service on the campus. A list of their names is a true roll of honor: Betty Jane Highfield, Margaret V. Peterson, Philip Liljengren, Theodore Hedstrand, Harold Reever, Ralph Lowell, Paul Larson, Gladys Larson, Carroll Peterson, Reynold Vann, Dorothy Vann, Elmer Ost, Ruth Ost, Margaret L. Peterson, Evelyn Lindgren, Theodore D. Johnson, Robert Byrd, Ivar Wistrom, Harriet Wistrom, Inez Olander, Dorothy Johnson, Elvie Kangas, Herbert Pankratz, Melvin Bergquist, and Harriet Stengl.

This time also brought significant changes to the theological seminary.

Earl C. Dahlstrom, professor emeritus of pastoral studies; J. Irving Erickson, professor emeritus, librarian and chaplain; Donald C. Frisk, professor emeritus of theology; Wesley W. Nelson, professor emeritus of pastoral studies; and Sigurd F. Westberg, professor emeritus of missions, reached retirement age. Dean Emeritus Eric G. Hawkinson and Peter P. Person, professor emeritus of Christian education, both full of years, died leaving "an empty place against the sky."

Since 1973 several members have joined the faculty of the seminary: C. John Weborg, theology (1973); Klyne R. Snodgrass, biblical literature (1974); Frances M. Anderson, Christian education, and Wayne C. Weld, missions (1975); Richard W. Carlson, ministries (1978); Philip J. Anderson, church history, and Norma S. Goertzen, director of library (1979); J. Robert Hjelm, pastoral studies (1980); John E. Phelan, dean of students and biblical literature (1981); Edwin A. Hallsten Jr., pastoral care and counseling, and Robert K. Johnston, dean and theology and culture (1982).

Special mention should also be made of Fredrick Holmgren and F. Burton Nelson who completed twenty-five years of teaching, research, and writing. Glenn P. Anderson, who had served as professor of church history since 1964, and had assumed the deanship in 1968, retired from his administrative duties in 1982 after giving himself with exemplary faithfulness and competence to an institution becoming every year larger and more complex. Enrollment rose from eighty students in 1968 to 155 in 1980-1981. With the increased student interest came an enlarging clientele and growing pressure for the modification of the requirement that candidates for ordination from other seminaries spend a portion of time in orientation at the Covenant seminary. Anderson, troubled by what he felt was the risk of erosion of historic Covenant piety by the presence of so many pastoral candidates who "knew nothing of Joseph," tried to temper the trend by rigorously but compassionately applying existing standards for ordination. More positively, he sought to counteract the trend by presenting Covenant history, theology, and pastoral studies relating to them in a most persuasive manner.

No one has loved the broad sweep as well as the significant particulars of the Covenant chronicle more than Glenn Anderson—for him every tick of the grandfather's clock has its special meaning. Even during his long and wearing battle with cancer, an illness that stole energy from him unit by unit, he continued his meticulous research, his enthusiastic teaching, his attentive recording of what he had learned.

But all this took its toll, for when he stepped down from the deanship in 1982, his illness had already begun to shadow his path. As this is written Glenn Anderson is involved in his own Armageddon, fighting for a chance to finish his work. His unyieldingness toward his illness is combined with a deep faith in God's victory and an openness toward the way he himself must walk. He has become an exemplar of the Christian believer and the serious scholar to all those who live in his presence.[2]

Anderson's retirement precipitated the need not only to choose a new administrator but to determine more precisely the direction that the seminary and the leadership of the Covenant would go. No "favorite son" candidate emerged from the ranks of the institution or the Ministerium with enough strength to prevail, and, after considerable contest and scores of suggested candidates, the mantle finally fell on the shoulders of Robert K. Johnston. Although a Covenanter all his life and an ordained pastor in the denomination since 1975, Johnston had followed an untraditional path for a Covenant leader. Growing up in the Pasadena Covenant Church (which, for many years, had seemed to have as much interest in Fuller Seminary as in North Park), Johnston had completed his baccalaureate degree at Stanford and his B.D. at Fuller Seminary. Eventually he earnd his Ph.D. at Duke University and taught at Western Kentucky University from 1974 to 1982. His primary contact with the North Park Seminary was his year of orientation 1970-1971.

Johnston's candidacy was hence controversial. No one questioned his academic or overall professional qualifications, but the point at issue was where he might be placed on the loyalty spectrum. He was by inclination, sympathies, and association more of a neo-evangelical than a Covenant Pietist. In 1978 he had written *Evangelicals at an Impasse* (published in 1979), a work, which, while scholarly and objective enough and certainly irenic, seemed to place him in the evangelical camp. Such a designation is not intended to identify him as a Fundamentalist, a classification he would properly repudiate, but it did identify him with the Fuller group, against which bitter, albeit courteous battles had been fought by some in the seminary community for more than a quarter of a century. The situation was not improved but the assumption of the presidency of the school by William R. Hausman two years earlier.[3] There was some feeling that the reins of leadership and influence had been torn from the hands of the Covenant loyalists.

Now three years later, the new dean's administrative skills, his ability to enlist the energy and loyalty of the seminary for the shared task, his respectability as scholar and writer, and his willingness to be collegial

---

2. During the production of this book, on November 22, 1985, Glenn Anderson died. He was sixty-three years old.

3. William Hausman, elected to the presidency of North Park College and Theological Seminary in 1980, was not "a son of the congregation." He was an active member of a Covenant church, he did his seminary orientation at North Park, and he was ordained into the Covenant pastorate in 1971, but at the time of his election he was registrar and director of admissions at Trinity Evangelical Divinity School in Deerfield, Illinois.

without self-consciousness or slick accommodation have won for him the confidence of the seminary community.

WORLD MISSION

During the decade the goal in the Department of World Mission for full-time career missionaries was the almost legendary 159 inherited from the late 1950s. In 1976 there were 119 missionaries located on seven fields, although twenty-six of these were short termers.[4] Consequently there were in actuality ninety-three career missionaries (YB 1976, 94). By 1978 there were ninety-eight career missionaries and thirteen short-termers. By 1981 the missionary corps numbered 102 career missionaries with thirty-seven short-termers; two years later the total of career missionaries and short-termers was 130. Interest in short-term opportunities continued at a high level, attracting forty-six applicants in 1983 and thirty-nine in 1984. By 1985 there were seven fields: Zaire, Mexico, Ecuador, Japan, Taiwan, Colombia, Thailand (with two missionaries serving in Sweden) with a total church membership of 93,049. There are now 104 career missionaries, thirteen having been consecrated at the Centennial conference in Minneapolis. There are forty short-termers and 2,508 national workers.

The seemingly disproportionate size of the church in Zaire (57,000 in the late seventies, 75,000 by 1982, 79,000 by 1983, and by 1985 85,000) is related to the amazing grassroots revival throughout the sub-Sahara region of Africa where, apparently, Christianity has developed its own distinctive ethos and its own dynamic.

The statistical data is, of course, a poor instrument for measuring the presence and the power of the descending dove. The 1984 World Mission report contained some glimmerings of glory not measured by quantity:

1. The Zulu Falls hydroelectric project at Karawa of which Milton Engebretson, Arden Almquist, and I saw the humble beginnings in 1970, has now been completed through the skill and devotion of Bob Thornbloom and his people.
2. Money has come from a German foundation to assist in the establishment of an eye clinic in Central Africa from which Covenant medical missions will benefit.

4. The record is not always clear about those included in the category "missionaries." In this report the 119 missionaries included twenty-six who are short-termers, that is, serving without any long-term commitment. But in checking with the Department of World Mission, I learned that now when the term "missionary" is used by itself, it always means career missionary, whereas the noncareer worker is given the designation "short-termer" or "short-term missionary." The goal of 159 has reference to career missionaries.

3. The Young Foundation, which has had a strong African interest for years, has given money for a hospital chapel, a new maternity building, and some major equipment at Karawa.

4. Kathryn Sundstrand, whose heroic educational exploits, despite mountainous discouragements, have continued for decades, is completing twelve volumes of curriculum materials in the indigenous dialect for twelve years of Bible study. Like many of her colleagues she has to struggle with limited financial resources and a scarcity of trained helpers.

5. Gordon and Geneva Christenson, long-time workers in Zaire, have returned to Bumba on the Zaire River where they see fields white for harvest.

6. Dr. Leo Lanoie spent a year at the University of North Carolina studying public health, an ongoing priority for Zaire.

7. The Wasolo Hospital—remembered for the presence there two decades ago of Dr. Paul Carlson—has now been restaffed.

8. After months of toil on a joint project with the Wycliffe translators and the pastors of the Ngbaka tribe, the New Testament has now been completed and is ready for use by those who possess the reading skills. A short-term missionary, Kenneth Satterberg, helped with a literacy program for the tribe, and special financial help was provided by Covenant Women.

9. Of special interest has been the holistic program initiated by James and Joan Gustafson in Thailand, where work began in 1971. It is a very practical effort to meld the two petitions of the Lord's Prayer: "Give us this day our daily bread" and "Forgive us our sins that we may forgive those who sin against us." Because Ray Dahlberg's report on Thailand is so crisp, realistic in detail—filled with flavor and fragrance and the fluttering of wings and the flapping of fins—and luminous with feeling, I have taken the freedom to quote a part of it. It deserves to be chronicled:

> Our holistic ministry, which brings together our agribusiness and evangelism and church planting, continues to grow. We now have seventy-two house churches, several of which have started daughter churches with a combined membership of 850 believers—an increase of 21 percent. Local leaders in each village are trained by our staff to be worship leaders and pastors. We now have forty-eight paid staff most of whom are connected with our farm and all of whom are supported by proceeds from the farm business. The faithful support of Covenant World Relief has made this entire agribusiness project possible.
>
> The farm also has been growing. We now have 150 sows and six boars, and they have bred at the rate of twenty-five per month. We will soon be farrowing 250 baby pigs each month and marketing about the

same number at a finished weight of 220 pounds. This should make the entire farm operation self-supporting.

The fish part of our operation is making a profit, and so is our duck production. We now have 1,500 ducks—all male—and are growing these only for meat. We pay about a nickel for each baby duck, feed it pig manure for four months, and sell it for $1.50. Our real need is for more manure; we hope the added number of sows and growing pigs will supply that.

We have started about six new pig-fish-duck cooperatives for supporting local churches. James Gustafson has received some financial support from Australia to fund these new co-ops. I visited one that had its own sow, about twenty-four little pigs, and also a couple of dozen ready for market. We had a worship service with the village people next to their pig farm and between two of their fish ponds. They also had about twenty-five ducks ready for market just in time for the Chinese New Year.

We are also growing some of the finest vegetables and fruit trees on the banks of these manure laden fish ponds. In addition to marketing 300 pounds of fish each day, we also sell fruit and vegetables. . . .

People working on community development and self help relief projects have come from all over the world to observe our work with the hope of implementing it in their own countries. There is no better example of Christian ministries being linked to economic development anywhere than what is being done by the Covenant in Udon Thani, Thailand. To minister to the whole person and his needs is our goal.

We continue to be involved in writing verse by verse commentaries, writing hymns, compiling a hymnal, and teaching people to play indigenous instruments for worship and praise to God. Evangelism, church planting, and church development teams constantly minister to an ever-widening circle of villages as the church spontaneously grows and multiplies as empowered by God's Holy Spirit (YB 1984, 183-186).

CHURCH GROWTH AND EVANGELISM (HOME MISSION)

Church growth cannot be measured merely by membership figures. This is a truism, but in an age of simple quantification it needs to be remembered. Nevertheless, as long as we are in the body, membership facts do have a negative or positive implication even for the spiritual growth of the church.

Considering the facts that the Covenant stewardship policy has tended to penalize inflated membership figures in the local congregation, the painfully slow but real growth in the statistics is reassuring. During the decade the denominational total rose from 72,926 in 1975 to 85,942 in 1985. The growth index follows: (It is figured on December 31 of the year indicated.)

Year	Number of churches	Total membership	Average membership
1975	537	72,926	135.8
1976	536	74,623	139.22
1977	539	75,213	139.54
1978	544	75,000	139.35
1979	552	77,205	139.86
1980	562	78,541	140.46
1981	565	80,759	142.94
1982	573	82,542	144.05
1983	577	84,139	145.82
1984	584	85,942	147.16

An informative analysis of church attendance is conducted each fall. The area of study is twenty of the best attended churches in the denomination, and the facts are gathered from the first two Sundays in November. The following chart is from the 1984 survey:

Rank		Church and Location (averaged for morning services, Nov. 6 and 13)	Attendance
1	(1)*	Rolling Hills Estates, California	1754
2	(2)	Burnsville, Minnesota	1218
3	(22)	Chicago (Oakdale), Illinois	857
4	(3)	Minneapolis (Redeemer), Minnesota	855
5	(4)	Oakland, California	821
6	(6)	Prairie Village, Kansas	762
7	(5)	Mercer Island, Washington	761
8	(15)	Arvada, Colorado	746
9	(8)	Sacramento (First), California	735
10	(18)	Redwood City, California	706
11	(17)	Bellevue (Newport), Washington	694
12	(11)	Minneapolis (First), Minnesota	685
13	(14)	Grand Rapids (Evangelical), Michigan	670
14	(7)	Loveland, Colorado	655
15	(16)	New Brighton, Minnesota	648
16	(13)	Pasadena, California	630
17	(10)	Rockford (First), Illinois	629
18	(9)	Chicago (North Park), Illinois	597
19	(25)	Modesto, California	556
20	(12)	Los Angeles (First), California	535

* Rank from previous year

Of these twenty churches, eight are located in Minnesota or east of that state. Ten of the largest, as measured by attendance, were founded after 1950. Several of these had received substantial help from Frontier Friends. Seven of the twenty were founded before 1900 (*YB* 1985, 160).

A somewhat different phenomenon from the numerical growth of essentially white, middle class, perhaps north European churches has been the parallel, although still modest, increase in congregations serving particular ethnic groups. The Covenant, remembering its own immigrant beginnings, embraces these congregations with especial interest. As the century closed, there were forty such churches divided as follows:

Korean	11	Assyrian	1
Black	6	Estonian	1
Native American/		Spanish speaking	9
Eskimo	12		

Robert C. Larson, now executive secretary of church growth and evangelism, has presented some ways in which new chuches get planted. In clarifying this he continues to use the metaphor of birth and growth. He identifies four kinds of planting.

1. *Natural growth.* This originates in an intentional commitment of a group to start new work and is clearly the preferable method of church extension.
2. *Caesarean section.* This kind of planting is often the result of the trauma of a church split. Although deplorable in itself, it may provide an opportunity which must be utilized.
3. *Adoption.* In this situation an established congregation provides members and finances for the launching of a new work.
4. *Step-parenting.* In this situation only financial assistance is given toward the planting of a new congregation.

Another type of planting much utilized by the Covenant in the past has been so-called "nucleus-building." An experienced pastor is sent into a promising community and begins building a group or fellowship "from scratch." A nucleus builder can obviously find him- or herself at work in one of a number of the situations outlined above (*YB* 1984, 164-165).[5]

---

5. The present strategy of church planting seems to be emphasizing the use of the group in starting a new work rather than depending on the gifts and energies of a builder. The latter method may have the effect of making the new church overidentified with the builder and vice versa.

Every strategy requires the resources of personnel and finances. At present the Covenant is fortunate in having a good supply of well-trained pastors, many of whom welcome the stimulus of a frontier opportunity. But a persistent problem is adequate ongoing financial support for the program. The Covenant as a national body provides funds for the regional conferences on a matching basis, but this requires a consistent and sufficient flow of mission funds into Covenant and regional coffers.

So far the funding experience for home missions as part of United Covenant Action has not been encouraging. Covenant stewardship is, in general, impressive evidence of the sacrificial spirit of Covenant people. During the decade per capita giving for all causes soared from $323 in 1976 to $641 in 1984, an increase of 98 percent. Giving for certain special causes not included in per capita averages also increased, sometimes dramatically. Thus World Relief in the years 1982, 1983, and 1984 got $624,000, $575,000, and $584,000 respectively. Church Growth and Evangelism got $175,000 through Frontier Friends in 1983-1984, and World Mission received $174,000 for four special projects. Covenanters invested $38,000,000 in National Covenant Properties, $8,000,000 in IRA's. Of this total $27,000,000 is invested in mortgage notes to Covenant churches.

Further evidence of fiscal confidence in the Covenant and of faith in its program of mission and benevolence is the $16,250,000 just pledged through Century 2 Campaign. Gross assets of Covenant institutions now total $257,000,000 with liabilities of $164,000,000. Covenant Estate Planning Services has distributed $10,000,000 since 1978 and has $48,000,000 in expectations from its program of bequests, annuities, and trusts.

But despite this glittering display of both affluence and stewardship, the Covenant continues to be plagued by budgetary woes. This has been a chronic ailment of some institutions, for example North Park College and Theological Seminary which just now finds itself in the throes of shrinking enrollments in the college and rising costs. But the headquarters budget was in rough balance until 1979 when it began to experience a down draft.

The deficit figures tell the story:

        1980 $ 93,000
        1981   88,000
        1982   244,000
        1983   158,000
        1984   194,000
        Total $777,000

The figures do not give all the facts, for they do not reflect the heroic process of reducing costs and cooking soup on a nail. But this kind of inconsistency between what the Covenant has and what it gives in support of mission programs ultimately gets reflected in the kind of work done in the field. Gifted and dedicated men and women are called to serve our aided churches. When they are placed, they expect to be renumerated for the work they do. They are willing to serve sacrificially, but they need consistent support. When that support fails or at least is seriously reduced, they have reason to ask how serious Covenanters are in their commitments and in the promises made by their congregations at Annual Meetings of the Covenant.

MIDDLE MANAGEMENT

The Covenant is "middle managed" through nine regional conferences, each under the administrative leadership of a superintendent. In 1985, for the first time, the Council of Regional Superintendents met with the Executive Board of the Covenant in a meeting of mutual orientation. Two position papers were read on Covenant and conference relationships, summary papers on the state of the conferences were read by the superintendents, and there was time for informative and animated discussion.[6]

The two position papers presented at this joint meeting were designed to state a) whàt the Executive Board expects of the regional conferences and their superintendents, and b) what the conference superintendent as chief executive officer of an administrative unit of the Covenant may expect of the latter. The president, Milton B. Engebretson, presented the first paper and senior superintendent Edward Larson, the second.

Engebretson voiced the following expectations of conferences and their superintendents (they are presented here in summary form):

1. Promoting the theological consensus and spiritual mystique of the Covenant among the churches.
2. Recognizing the Covenant as the parental organization, with a prioretal position.
3. Giving their fullest cooperation to programs, mandates, and special emphases initiated and promoted by the denomination, for example Giving for Growing, Century Two Campaign, seminary visitations, etc.

6. All the materials used and quoted in this section are taken from the proceedings of the joint session which are on file in the Office of the President, The Evangelical Covenant Church.

4. Exercising fairness in relation to other regional conferences.
5. Accepting all qualified pastors, whose credentials are in order, for ministry in their churches so that the whole denomination serves as a field of service to all pastors.
6. Working actively to develop stewardship and denominational support.
7. Giving constructive criticism of the denomination when needed. "This, in part," writes Engebretson, "fulfills the superintendent's function [as] the Covenant's ambassador to the regional conference [and the function] of the regional conference's emissary to the denomination."

In concluding his report Engebretson said, "The track record established by the Covenant has yielded strength and dignity to the office of the superintendent, status to the conference, and the position of special priority to the parent body. Together we have an almost unparalleled record of rising stewardship. Eighty-five thousand people gave $62,000,000 to their churches in 1984, plus pledging to give an additional $16,000,000 (above and beyond annual giving) over the next five years. . . .

"More important than the giving is the unity, cooperation, and sense of oneness experienced throughout the parent body and all of its divisions. There is a unity in theological interpretation of biblical truth never before experienced. . . . God in his grace has been good to the Covenant."

In his statement of expectations that the conference and its superintendents may have of the Covenant, Edward Larson spoke of *affirmation, understanding,* and *appropriate* logistics.

By affirmation Larson meant support for the role of superintendent "in the eyes of the rank and file." He suggested that "consultation with the conference and the superintendent should be a high priority in any issue involving both the conference and the Covenant." In addition to attitudinal reinforcement, Larson also spoke of ceremonial and organizational affirmation. "Although now being addressed more specifically, the office of superintendent has not, until now, appeared prominently in the flow chart of the Covenant organization."

Another area of concern for the superintendents, averred the senior superintendent, is understanding. The duality of the role of the superintendent must be seen. "He lives in two worlds with the regional world assuming an ever increasing sense of identity. The superintendent, because his role is not clearly defined, often in crises has to assume powers he does not have. Situations may force him to act hierarchically in a very congregational system."

His final concern dealt with the area of communications and planning. He writes, "The superintendent should be able to expect communication and consultation in sufficient time to coordinate conference activities with those of the denomination." He asks further, "Is there room for consultation in the planning process when prior commitments of the conference can be considered? Can one expect that every effort is being made to keep activities from coming to the conference level with the aura of a *fait accompli?*"

Larson also deplores the "diffused identity of the Council of Superintendents in the structure. The superintendent is essentially responsible to the president. But the great amount of time spent with the Department of Church Growth and Evangelism and its executive secretary contributes to the diffusion of identity and breakdown of communications. Expression of this can be read in the many times when, tongue in cheek, we [superintendents] are called bishops, but all the while we know that we have few clear lines of authority."

In fairness to Larson's total report, it should be pointed out that he concludes his statement on a very positive note, both with reference to the Covenant system—which he lauds for providing a flexibility that encourages trust, freedom, and creativity—and to the leadership of the incumbent president, Milton B. Engebretson, which he praises as being strong and supportive.

Looked at from a historical perspective, some of the frustrations voiced by the superintendents have an understandable origin. When the denomination was on its way to becoming Americanized and reaching out for recruits, efforts were made to make the Covenant as appealing as possible, particularly to American evangelicals. In the need to "sell" the denomination, terms such as "freedom," "congregational," "autonomous," and "evangelical" (meaning "Fundamentalist") were loosely and sometimes irresponsibly used.

During the last fifty years denominational historians have labored to set this record straight. They have emphasized the following principles among others:

1. The Covenant is not "free" in the sense that theologically anything goes. It has a noncreedal but not a nontheological position. Theology in the Covenant rests upon the biblical faith described in the Constitution.
2. The Covenant is not typically congregational in polity even though it gives considerable freedom to the local church in administering its own affairs. In terms of polity the Covenant is a mixed form, half congregational and half presbyterian. It gives freedoms to the local con-

gregations, as indicated, but it assumes denominational and regional responsibility for a number of activities in which it expects the solidarity of its member churches. Fidelity to the national program and budget, to which local congregations have given solemn assent in the Annual Meeting, is not a matter of caprice but of sacred obligation. The same is true of all programs to which the Covenant Church as a denominational body commits itself, including such major fund-raising efforts as Giving for Growing and Century 2 Campaign; it is also true of the programs of the regional conferences.

One activity that divorces the Covenant completely from the congregationalist norm relates to the pastoral ministry. In the Covenant the denomination and not the local church assumes responsibility for the pastor. The Covenant selects, trains, credentials, ordains, helps to place, disciplines, and ultimately pensions its pastors.[7] All these responsibilities are held by the national body functioning through the Board of the Ministry and the Ministerium.

3. But an area in which the greatest confusion prevails is that of biblical faith. The Covenant is a Bible-believing fellowship, as indicated above, but it has never officially subscribed, even under the pressures of the 1920s, to the tenets of Fundamentalism or evangelicalism if by this we mean an adherence to Scriptural inerrancy or verbal inspiration. There are many Covenanters who are Fundamentalists and there are probably many local Covenant churches that would formulate their faith in these biblicistic terms. They belong to the family of faith together with everyone else who believes that the Scriptures, the Old and New Testaments, are the Word of God and the only perfect rule for faith, doctrine, and conduct. As indicated, they share the rights and privileges pertaining to membership. But there is one right they do not have and that is to demand that all other Covenanters must believe as they do.

In his report to the Executive Board, one of the superintendents stated in his own way a problem faced by the church:

> I have lost much confidence in some identifying words that no longer carry much of their former meaning. It is not enough to call ourselves "evangelical" and expect people to know who we are as a denomination. Thus a major concern that I carry is for us to more clearly identify

---

7. Pastoral pensions have a long and complex history in the Covenant. It is reassuring to know that funds are in competent adminstrative hands and are being given the most careful stewardship by the Board of Pensions. Assets have gone from $2,400,000 in 1970 to $16,900,000 in 1985. Minimum pension payments for pastors with twenty-five years of service are now $240 per month.

ourselves in terms of freedom, the authority of the Word, and other statements that must be retained as benchmarks of the Covenant. If not we will continue to drift more and more to the right, into the morass of no identity at all.

The joint meeting itself, the reports of the superintendents, and the statements by both Engebretson and Larson suggest the opening of a new and significant dimension in Covenant polity. The meeting signals a practical acceptance of the implications of the system of governance developed in the constitution of 1957. It asks for a more clearly defined leadership role for the superintendents and better liaison between Covenant and conference and vice versa. And it ventilates some of the frustrations felt not only by Edward Larson but by other superintendents as well. Statements emanating from the superintendents and included in their reports are not untypical:

> Finances are the big frustration and the smaller the conference in terms of the number of churches, the greater the frustration. . . . There is need to get rid of some sacred cows. . . . Another frustration is the lack of authority or power to effect change. . . . I could wish for closer dialogue between national and regional administration. The distance and response between the local church and national administration continues to widen. This is reflected in the decline in the percent of income from churches to the national budget. A close look should be given to bridging that gap. I believe that conference administration is a key link in creating a ministry bond for denomination. . . . There is a necessity of merging congregations. . . . A few of our conference churches are impacted by the so-called "third wave"—a term given to the specialized ministry of the Holy Spirit through "signs and wonders." In true Covenant freedom we want to be open to all aspects of the Spirit's work and at the same time recognize the danger of excesses. . . . [Some of my frustrations stem from] a resistance to change [which might] attract younger families, e.g., music, format of worship, etc.

PUBLICATIONS

Of no small significance in the training of the rapidly expanding Ministerium and the changing laity is the development and publishing of materials providing some guidance, especially for those not oriented in the character and mystique of the denomination.

The past decade has seen the publication, distribution, and initial use of a number of significant helps for the understanding of the Covenant and its spirit. Space will allow only the most summary listing of some of these resources. They are presented in six major categories.

1. Works on the history and present life of the church and of the Covenant Church in particular.
   a. 1975   *A Family of Faith*. The Covenant after ninety years. Karl A. Olsson, president emeritus, North Park College and Theological Seminary.
   b. 1976   *Twice Born Hymns*. The story of hymnal translation in the Covenant. J. Irving Erickson, professor emeritus, North Park Theological Seminary.
   c. 1976   *Deep Tracks in Africa*. The life story of missionary Titus M. Johnson. Sigurd F. Westberg, professor emeritus of missions, and Francis J. Mason, former managing editor of *The Covenant Companion.*
   d. 1976   *Mission in Ferment*. The new challenges in World Mission. Russell A. Cervin, executive secretary emeritus of World Mission.
   e. 1980   *Covenant Roots, Sources, and Affirmations*. Translations and commentary on primary sources of Covenant history. Glenn P. Anderson, professor of church history, North Park Theological Seminary.
   f. 1984   *A Precious Heritage*. A century of mission in the Northwest, 1884-1984. Philip J. Anderson, assistant professor of church history, North Park Theological Seminary.
   g. 1985   *The Mission of a Covenant*. Placing the Covenant Church in the more general "covenant" tradition. Paul E. Larsen, pastor of the Peninsula Covenant Church, Redwood City, California.
   h. 1985   *Sing It Again!* A compendious handbook of *The Covenant Hymnal*, 1973. The stories of lyrics and melodies, authors and composers appearing in that hymnal. J. Irving Erickson.
   i. 1985,   *Into One Body . . . by the Cross*. The development of
      1986   Covenant ecclesiology during a hundred years. Karl A. Olsson.

2. Works on Worship and Hymnody.
   a. 1973   *The Covenant Hymnal*. Strikes a balance, typical of much in the denomination, between the classical hymnody of the Protestant heritage and the evangelical modes of the nineteenth-century awakenings. A special resource is its translations from the hymns of the Swedish Pietists. Prepared by The Covenant Hymnal Commission.

b. 1981 *The Covenant Book of Worship*. Produced by a special committee on the Book of Worship, chaired by Glen V. Wiberg.

c. 1985 *Come Let Us Praise Him*. The Centennial Hymnal compiled by the Covenant Commission on Church Music and Worship, chaired by J. Irving Erickson. An appealing bouquet of heritage hymns and classic and traditional works as well as Gospel and contemporary songs.

3. Works on Theology and Christian Doctrine.

a. 1974 *The Word Is Near You*. A series of sermons, lectures, and Bible discussions by early Covenanters selected and translated from the Swedish by Herbert E. Palmquist.

b. 1975 *Bound to Be Free*. A collection of essays by contemporary Covenanters reflecting on what the Covenant is and what it may become, edited by James R. Hawkinson, executive secretary of publications.

c. 1976 *Jesus and the End Time*. One view of the Covenant apocalyptic. Everett L. Wilson, pastor of College Park Covenant Church, Saskatoon, Saskatchewan.

d. 1979 *Evangelicals at an Impasse*. Biblical authority in practice. Robert K. Johnston, dean of North Park Theological Seminary since 1982.

e. 1979 *The God Who Cares*. A Christian Looks at Judaism. Fredrick Holmgren, professor of biblical literature, North Park Theological Seminary.

f. 1981 *Covenant Affirmations: This We Believe*. A theological summation of central Covenant tenets. Donald C. Frisk, professor emeritus of theology, North Park Theological Seminary.

g. 1983 *The Christian at Play*. A theological and biblical view of the relationship of play and work. Robert K. Johnston.

h. 1985 *God's Friends. Called to Believe and Belong*. Wesley W. Nelson, professor emeritus of pastoral studies, North Park Theological Seminary. The new confirmation text produced by the Board of Christian Education and a special committee.

4. Books on the Christian life. A partial list by a number of Covenanters.

a. 1975 *Crying for My Mother*. A moving autobiographical account of the intimate life of a pastor, Wesley W. Nelson.

b. 1977   *Meet Me on the Patio*. Relational Bible studies. Karl A.
            Olsson.

c. 1978   *When the Road Bends*. A Christian view of "passages."
            Karl A. Olsson.

d. 1978   *"While It Was Still Dark."* One Person's Pilgrimage
            through Grief. Adaline Bjorkman, a member of the Hins-
            dale, Illinois Covenant Church.

e. 1979   *Wild Beasts and Angels. Seeing Faith in the Arena of Daily
            Life*. Essays by Arthur Anderson, pastor of the First Cov-
            enant Church of Youngstown, Ohio.

f. 1982   *Don't Park Behind a Truck*. Wesley W. Nelson's profound
            whimsy at its best.

g. 1983   *None But a Child May Enter*. Posthumous poems by Fred
            Moeckel, (1929-1966).

h. 1983   *Marah, the Woman at the Well*. A story by Nina Mason
            Bergman, a member of the Bellevue (Newport), Washington
            Covenant Church.

i. 1984   *Poems and Prayers from the Ark*. The lyrics of children.
            Collected and edited by Priscilla Johnson, a member of Cov-
            enant Congregational Church, Waltham, Massachusetts.

j. 1985   *Listening to God, Lessons from Everyday Places*. Janice
            Kempe, a member of the Trinity Covenant Church, Living-
            ston, New Jersey.

k. 1985   *Landmarks of the Spirit. One Man's Journey*. David H.
            Sandstrom. Sandstrom was a pastor of the Evangelical
            Covenant who transferred to the Congregational Church
            (UCC) in 1936. He served in that church body as pastor and
            as a denominational leader in the area of stewardship until
            his retirement in 1967. Sandstrom's book gives glimpses of
            the Covenant Church from a very significant period and is
            thus of great historical value. The foreword is by Paul
            LeRoy Holmer, he too is one of the "sons of the congrega-
            tion" who made the difficult choice to serve elsewhere and
            thus also has much to tell the Covenant.

l. 1985   *Lift My Spirits, Lord*. Bryan Leech, Covenant pastor, free-
            lance writer, author of hymns.

m. 1985   *Alive to Christ, Alert to Life*. A study on spirituality. John
            Weborg, professor of theology, North Park Theological
            Seminary.

5. Other publications.
The impact of the printed word is not limited to books. The Covenant

informs impacts, and blesses its constituency by *The Covenant Companion, The Covenant Home Altar, The Covenant Quarterly, The World Mission Prayer Calendar*, and a spate of well-edited and tastefully printed publications. Regional conferences and in some instances local churches also publish materials to give information about their work, including a wide variety of newspapers and newsletters.

6. Covenant Video.

During the decade a promising start was made in producing videocassette materials for use in VCR's through which it was hoped that the total ministry of the Covenant Church might be dramatically and informatively presented. Originally funded by a grant from "Giving for Growing" and utilizing the skills and devotion of Ted Ericson, the program seemed to have an assured future. Unfortunately, like many other useful technical developments of the time, this program's progress was delayed by the recession of the early 1980s.

CHRISTIAN EDUCATION

During the decade the Department of Christian Education celebrated its sixtieth anniversary and, with some significant refinements and enrichments, might be said to be carrying out the mission envisaged for it by its founder Nathanial Franklin. It majored in programs of Christian training for all ages and provided both guidance and inspiration.

The department sponsored two major events for adults: "Big Sky" in 1978 and "Scene '82" in 1982 which drew a total of some 1,500 participants. Teenagers were given their training plus opportunities at the perennially popular Covenant High Congresses (CHIC) held 1976, 1980, and 1984 with an average attendance of 2,600.

In 1978 the Commission on Social Service Institutions launched a program for a different age category: Senior Adult Ministries Implemented (SAMI). This was a three-year project to develop a ministry for senior adults. The program was initially sponsored by the commission, which continued as its catalyst until 1982, but it also utilized expertise from the Board of Christian Education, the Board of Benevolence, and North Park College and Theological Seminary.

The SAMI committee was originally under the leadership of Paul W. Peterson. At Big Sky in August, 1978, SAMI arranged a special program which dealt with this ministry at the national level. The program continued under its planned scenario until its completion in 1981. Unfortunately Peterson's death that year removed the program's *primus motor*, a dedicated and imaginative leader. Nonetheless, the essential

SAMI program has continued after 1982 under the aegis of Christian Education. Much credit goes to Sylvia Larson for her selfless service through the pages of a SAMI newsletter.

A continuation of the SAMI emphasis was assured by a well-attended conference on the campus of Northwestern College, Roseville, Minnesota, immediately following the Centennial celebration in 1985. The conference theme was "Adults Over Fifty: Pioneers of a New Frontier." Evelyn M.R. Johnson had primary coordinating responsibilities.

A major publishing project of the department during this period (1975-1985) was the writing and editing of the confirmation text, *God's Friends, Called to Believe and Belong*. Written by Wesley W. Nelson with the help of a committee appointed by the board, the book has a helpful workbook for pastors and other teachers.

Sunday school enrollment went from 64,000 in 1978 to 72,000 in 1984—a promising sign of revived interest. As indicated, a promising beginning in videocassette resources was frustrated by a lack of funds.

COVENANT WOMEN

A long and significant service by Covenant Women going back to 1916 was finally recognized by the creation of a Department of Women's Work in 1978. The action was authorized by the Ninety-third Annual Meeting of the Covenant in that year. In 1981 the Board of Women's Work asked to have its name changed to "Board of Covenant Women." This revision was finalized in 1982.

Nevertheless, under whatever name and with whatever organization, Covenant Women continued its outstanding work of generous enablement and insightful training during the ten years. It remained faithful to the purpose spelled out in its constitution:

> As Covenant Women sharing a faith in Jesus Christ, we unite to: advance the kingdom of God through worshiping, working, and witnessing in all areas of our life, the home, the community, the nation, and the world; grow in personal devotion to Jesus Christ as Lord and Savior; provide for Christian edification and fellowship. We seek to achieve these goals by study, prayer, service and giving, supporting the work of The Evangelical Covenant Church . . . (*YB* 1979, 155).

In 1975-1976 the organization reported a membership of 30,000 women with a total income of $137,000, and gifts to the Covenant amounting to $100,000. Although total receipts rose to nearly $400,000 in 1982-1983, the giving ratios remained proportionate. Covenant Women gave $100,000 to Giving for Growing, $100,000 to ARM (Assisting Retired Missionaries), and over $100,000 (in money and supplies) to "Women of Zaire," a program designed to assist the women of that nation with basic skills such as reading and writing, health care, Christian nurture, Christian behavior, and housekeeping arts. Covenant Women also gave substantial assistance for North Park College scholarships, scholarships for women preparing for ministry, building improvements on the campus, and it continued to provide enabling assistance to all other Covenant causes. In 1985 and 1986 it pledged substantial assistance to a fund called Women Outreaching to Women which helps "women suffering from the pressures of societal problems, including alcoholism, abuse, and abandonment; teenage pregnancies of their daughters; disabilities; and caring for elderly relatives and friends."

Another interesting side of the activities of Covenant Women is the sponsorship of four Triennial conferences, 1974, 1977, 1980, and 1983, which each attracted over 900 participants. Triennials have been training and inspirational meetings with assemblies, workshops, discussions, devotions, musical events, and rich opportunities for personal interaction.

A celebrative and high point of the decade was provided by the Centennial Brunch which attracted 2,300 women on Tuesday morning of the Annual Meeting.

Leadership of Covenant Women changed its form during the decade. For many years it had been vested in a chairman, who was assisted in administration by an executive director. Until 1979, the chairmen for the decade had been Jean B. Nelson and Betty M. Carlson, and Erma G. Chinander had served as executive director. But in 1979 Erma Chinander became executive secretary of the Board of Women's Work. She retired in 1980 and was succeeded by Doris R. Johnson. Betty M. Carlson continued to serve in a primary post by becoming chairman of the new Board of Women's Work.

BENEVOLENCE

Since the immigrant days (1886) when Henry Palmblad, a devout and compassionate layperson in the Chicago area, first began to bring needy Scandinavians to the newly established Home of Mercy in Bowmanville (*Barmhärtighetshemmet*), there has not been a more momentous decade for the Board of Benevolence and its institutions than the present one.

That is because the hospital situation generally has become most critical with costs soaring out of reach and the government and other third-party payers being seemingly more concerned about cost than care. The amount of inpatient care the payer will pay for is constantly being reduced. As a consequence, hospital stays have been drastically reduced in length and hospital censuses dramatically decreased. While this allows general cost reduction—an admirable step for the overall economy, it works havoc with hospital budgets which are based on an anticipated number of inpatients. These budgets have in all instances been set up to assure enough profitability in the operation to reduce capital indebtedness, cover new capital outlays for essential construction, sophisticated and expensive equipment, and the maintenance cost for high-tech operations.

At present the Covenant owns and operates two hospitals: Swedish Covenant Hospital in Chicago and Emanual Medical Center in Turlock, California. A glance at the financial statements of these two institutions for one year will indicate the size of their respective operations.

In fiscal year 1983-1984 operating revenues and expenses for the two hospitals were as follows:

	Swedish Covenant	Emanual
Operating revenues	$44,268,394	$22,230,590
Other income	211,492	765,692
Total	44,479,886	22,996,282
Operating expenses	43,216,155	21,846,161
Net result	1,263,731	1,150,121

Although both hospitals managed to end the fiscal year with slight operational profits, the phenomenon of the shrinking hospital census coupled with rising costs is disquieting.

On the other side of the ledger is the rising census in Covenant retirement communities. There are now twelve campuses representing thirty-two retirement, nursing, and personal care facilities housing a total of 3,300 persons:

    Covenant Home, Chicago, Illinois
    Covenant Village of Northbrook, Northbrook, Illinois
    The Holmstad, Batavia, Illinois
    Bethany Covenant Home, Minneapolis, Minnesota
    Covenant Village of Cromwell, Cromwell, Connecticut
    Covenant Manor, Minneapolis, Minnesota
    Ebenezer Home, Buffalo, Minnesota
    Covenant Village of Florida, Plantation, Florida
    Covenant Village of Turlock, Turlock, California
    Mount Miguel Covenant Village, Spring Valley, California
    The Samarkand of Santa Barbara, Santa Barbara, California
    Covenant Shores, Mercer Island, Washington

We began this little essay about benevolence with a reference to Henry Palmblad and the Home of Mercy. Those were humble beginnings but they also reflect the enormous difference between the then and the now. Those who came to the Home of Mercy and continued to come for many decades were those who truly needed human compassion in order to survive. Because statistics are not available, we cannot say with any certainty how many people sixty-five and older today move to a retirement community as a matter of course. That number is bound to increase as the population continues to rise. There are now fewer teenagers in the United States than people sixty-five and older, and by 1990 it is anticipated that whereas there will be 31,000,000 people sixty-five and older in the United States, there will be only 23,000,000 teenagers.

This rising tide of senior adults will be looking for the kind of institution which, like those now in the Covenant constellation, provide the best surroundings for the most reasonable cost and also assure that the dimension of care, motivated by biblical faith, continues to nurture and gladden those who come.

A new organization of the Board of Benevolence is now on the drawing board. The Board of Benevolence will be given a corporate base redesignated "Covenant Benevolent Institutions, Inc." This corporation will consist of three divisions: Swedish Covenant Hospital, Inc., Chicago; Emanuel Medical Center, Inc., Turlock; and Covenant Retirement Communities, Inc. The president of Covenant Benevolent Institutions (now Nils G. Axelson, who first became administrator of Swedish Covenant Hospital in 1952) will serve as chief executive officer of the parent corporation. Dr. James B. McCormick, who became president of Swedish Covenant Hospital in 1984, will continue as the C.E.O. of the Swedish Covenant Hospital corporation, John S. Trussler, president of the Emanuel Medical Center, will continue as C.E.O. of the Emanuel Medical Center corporation, and Paul V. Peterson, who has been executive vice-president of Covenant Retirement Communities, will be the C.E.O. of the new corporation with the designation Covenant Retirement Communities, Inc.

As of January 31, 1985, the parent corporation, Covenant Benevolent Institutions, had combined gross assets of $201 million and liabilities of $135 million with a fund balance of $66 million. Henry Palmblad understood a lot of things but he probably would not have grasped that. What he would have understood was the record of faithful and skilled service given for a century by the home and hospital families and those now working at the many retirement centers.

We offer a roll of honor from Swedish Covenant Hospital and Covenant Home in Chicago—persons who in one capacity or other have completed over twenty-five years in the past decade: Esther Tornholm, Eva Wenzel, Lucille Sandquist Johnsen, Emma Sarring, Vilma Sander, Eileen Delana, Betty Greider, Alexandra Liszka, Ruth Hendriksen, Eunice Hulth, Marguerite Johnson, Minnette Levin, Caroline Bruger, Robert Chamberlaine, Lois Heavyside, Phillip Simon, David Andersson, Nicholas Portokalis, May Palmgren, Constance Nelson, Edward L. Olson, Nils G. Axelson, James B. McCormick, William Ackley, Erik Larsen, William Hutson, O. Theodore Roberg, Jr., Russell Elmer, John Kulis, Theodore Wright, Sr., Kornel Fojcik, Elias Stambolis, Robert Hulburt, Valentine Hogstrom, Thomas Baffes, William Andrews, Bradley Carr, Evangelia Zervopoulos, Nils Tunestam, Robert G. Anderson, Russell Boothe, Earl Sanborn, John Baylor, Edward Millar, Wallace Thornbloom, Kenji Kushino, Linden Wallner, Ludvig Bugsch, John Orndorff, Frank Pirruccello, James FitzGibbons, Willard Meyer, Eugene Lorant, Hilda Maisma, John T.C. Gernon, Fernly Johnson, Lester Kittilsen, John Lavieri, Norman Larson, Maynard Murray, Robert Penn, Frank Nagel, Lorin Olson, Andrew Peterson, Margaret Pijan, Karl Scheribel, and John Ursin.

From a small mustard seed planted with such love and hopefulness a century ago, a great tree has come. Now, as then, what matters is the vital essence of the tree itself, the life expressing itself in branch and leaf. What matters in the tree of charity spreading its growing shade over people, a tree in which even the birds of the air may rest (Matthew 13:31-32), is the ongoing quality of mercy, an unceasing outpouring of love in compassion and caring. Henry Palmblad would have understood that very well indeed.

CHAPTER FORTY

RETROSPECT AND PROSPECT

Zenos Hawkinson, professor of history at North Park College, has said that the Covenant in North America originated among "de få och fattiga"—the few and the poor. This is a valid insight into the origins of the denomination. It may serve as an instructive memory for a time somewhat enamored of quantity and the solidity of wealth.

But what may be true of a situation is not necessarily true for an intention. Undoubtedly the Mission Friends of the 1870s and 1880s were poor by most modern standards, but they seem not to have intended to remain poor. Unlike the mendicant orders of the medieval Church which by choice lived in conflict with affluence, the Mission Friends seemed to have yearned to enter more fully into an earthly inheritance. As a group they had no consistent theology of poverty and saw no contradiction between longing for 160 acres of tillable prairie land and hoping for a heaven where rust does not corrupt nor thieves break in to steal.

Hence it would not be accurate to suggest too sharp a contrast between Henry Palmblad and the modern relatively affluent Covenanter. Both have served charity, although in different ways. But neither of them has married St. Francis's Lady Poverty.

I had once hoped to speak prophetically of the Covenant's future. Assuming that "the past is prologue," I had thought that some sensible inferences might be drawn from our century-old profile that would help to sketch our present and our future. Drawing an insight from Hawthorne's "Old Stone Face," I had imagined that the resemblance might be traced between what we once were and what we are about to become,

435

but I am no longer confident of that.

The events of the present, and perhaps the "apocalypse" we are facing, may strip us of any illusion that we can effect a simple continuation. What we find in our future, even within the cozily constructed walls of the Covenant, may be not continuity at all but mutations, new creations, and novel, though biblical, models for change. In the face of this perhaps there are reasons for "stripping down" and confronting the future more youthfully and more athletically. The language may seem frivolous, but there are good biblical examples in 1 Corinthians 9:19-27 and Hebrews 12:1-13, as well as in Luke 12:35,36.

In the face of this I hear projections, given with the best of motives I am sure, of essential numbers for the Covenant. I hear an estimate that the denomination must achieve a total membership of 150,000 to 200,000 if we are to survive fiscally. I ask on what assumptions such projections are based. May they not be built on the premise that as things have been they (must) remain, or on the assumption that we are to draw our criteria of adequacy from the surrounding cultures. But in the Spirit of the Lord can we not free the serfs, sell off the cherry orchard, and believe that even in us God may do a new thing (Isaiah 43:18-20)?

If the writing of this book has brought me a singled focused insight, it is that the unity of the body, that is, its life, is dependent not only on the application of some common sense worldly standards—these have their good, gray legitimacy, of course—but on the application of a heavenly strategy—the luminous, paradoxical method of the cross. The body is to grow into living oneness through the saving death of its Creator/ Redeemer. He who is Lord by virtue of his emptying (Philippians 2:5-11)—that is, his kenosis—is to be the life and fullness of the body through the crucifixion and resurrection of believers. The Church is to live in that discipline and by that discipline—in constant dedication to readiness. "Let your loins be girded and your lamps burning, and be like men who are waiting for their master" (Luke 12:35). The stance is that of the fully involved athlete: strenuous and stretching, taut and eager, panting and sweating with exertion, but essentially joyous. What is asked is flexibility, mobility, commitment, delight.[1]

---

1. My students will remember my reference to Meister Eckhart's daring simile of God's delight in his identity: "In this likeness or identity God takes such delight that he pours his whole nature and being into it. His pleasure is as great, to take a simile, as that of a horse, let loose to run over a green heath where the ground is level and smooth, to gallop as a horse will, as far as he can over the greensward—for this is a horse's pleasure and expresses his nature. It is so with God. It is his pleasure and rapture to discover identity, because he can always put his whole nature into it, for he is this identity itself" (Raymond B. Blakney, *Meister Eckhart, A Modern Translation*, New York: Harper and Bros., p.205).
Perhaps it is not too audacious to say that it is only in such mobility and activity that the believer and the church discover their delight in their true identity.

A fairly simple illustration from the history of tactics may be clarifying. In the seventeenth century a trend toward simplification of field tactics developed. Under the leadership of some brilliant students of tactics the prevailing mode of military combat was gradually pushed aside by new systems stressing lightness of armament and armor and increased maneuverability of troops, whether infantry or cavalry. The safety of the heavier equipment, which had made foot soldiers into virtual mobile fortresses in the field, was sacrificed to the opportunity of the flexible and the mobile. Speed and the ability to maneuver freely became the armor of the new age. Shakespeare has Hotspur speak for this time in his reflection on the military situation, "Out of this nettle, danger, we pluck this flower safety."[2]

How can military analogies of lightness, mobility, risk, and decisiveness be applied to denominational life in the Covenant Church? Are we not inviting back some of the administrative chaos from which we were so mercifully delivered a few decades ago? I think not. I believe the tactical analogy holds. The more flexible tactics that emerged in the Thirty Years' War might have brought with them an erosion of control. But this did not happen. The art itself improved.

The same reasoning can probably be applied to tactics in the church. It should be possible to combine effective administration in the higher echelons with freedom and creativity at subordinate levels as well as in personal activities without loss of essential control.

As indicated earlier, the adoption of a new constitution in 1957 led to greater administrative effectiveness and a greater measure of justice through the specifying and integrating of functions. Before this the Covenant had been unsure of how much structure it wanted or should have. This uncertainty led to a thin and porous administration not always fully prepared for its multiplying tasks. With the new constitution came better balance. Energy could be applied more rationally.

But a problem inherent in improved administration and churchmanship (control, accountability, fewer loose ends) may be top-heaviness. With progressive refinement—taking care to eliminate random detail— the risk of ponderousness increases. Task breeds task; the increase of tasks calls for more standard procedures and more qualified personnel, and the presence of these invites the expansion and complication of management. It is probably inevitable that when management becomes grooved, its status grows more absolute, and before long a permanent bureaucracy may be at the door. The organization is developed and complicated for its own sake. Weight has been geometrically multiplied, and

2. *Henry IV*, Part I, II, iii, 11.

in the long run weight impedes function. With it comes a built-in resistance to reform and simplification.

I hear some of the younger people, both lay and clergy, affirm that although they admire the denominational leaders both as persons and as officials, they wonder about the ponderousness of the system.[3]

There is no reason to believe that any organization can totally avoid the bureaucratic traps, but the Church is particularly susceptible to such problems because it tends to rely on a built-in system of blessing its mistakes and canonizing its mediocrities. Most business organizations must show profit to survive, but some churches need only plead good intentions. Nonetheless, the Church does have an effective instrument of audit not available to the business world. The Church, as long as it remains classical in its beliefs, does have eschatology—its cherished doctrine of the last things. The Church believes with James that the Lord is at the door. "Establish your hearts, for the coming of the Lord is at hand." This conviction continues to infuse reality into the body of Christ.

A SCRIPTURAL SCHEMA

In preparation for the writing of these summary pages, I turned again to Nils W. Lund's perceptive book *Chiasmus in the New Testament* (1942) and read its concluding section on "The Book of Revelation." It provides a Scriptural schema for what I would now like to say.

Lund's thesis about Revelation is that it combines the series of letters to seven late first-century churches in Asia Minor with an apocalyptic canvas arranged with startling artistic brilliance but carried by a strong prophetic and apocalyptic intention. In other words, we are not talking about art for its own sake but about art in the service of proclamation.

The book proclaims a message of hope to the faithful in the young Church and a message of judgment on much in the environing Roman Empire. The content of the hope is obvious; heaven is on the side of the believers. Christians are to be encouraged by a vision of God's future to face and overcome both the coercive and the seductive pressures of the Empire.

Lund argues persuasively that John's message is arranged "chiastically" and derives some of its power from this. The chiastic order, unlike western literary texts that reach their consummation of emphasis at the end, places the focus of meaning at the center. A well-known passage like 1 Corinthians 12-14 will clarify the point. We recall that this block of

---

3. [See *Narthex*, Vol. 2, No.1 (February, 1982) and Vol. 3, No. 1 (February, 1983)] for some perceptive comments on Covenant organization.

material deals with spiritual gifts but that all of these gifts are exceeded in excellence by unconditioned love, that is, agape. The materials are arranged in conformity with this important distinction:

A Spiritual gifts—their distribution throughout the church, chapter 12.
B A more excellent way—love, that is agape, chapter 13
A' Spiritual gifts—their use in the worship of the church, chapter 14.

Such a chiasm is found in the letters of the seven churches in Revelation, chapters 1-3. Again the middle element is the focus of emphasis:

A Ephesus
 B Smyrna
  C Pergamum
   D Thyatira—focus of intensity
  C' Sardis
 B' Philadelphia
A' Laodicea

Thyatira's central position is indicated not only by its placement in the chiasm but by the disproportionate space it is given in the passage and by the seriousness of its situation. Lund writes:

> The Epistle to Thyatira is the center of the series. The chief danger is some peculiar form of idolatry which has already crept into the church. . . . The church is described as defiled by the practices of an idolatrous community. It is significant that the strongest representation of idolatry, namely by the woman Jezebel, and the ultimate doom of that perversion of worship, namely, when the bed of pleasure will become a bed of pain (3:22), should be found in the central epistle of the seven (Lund 1942, 337).

This idolatry, Lund goes on to say, is represented by Jezebel, the consort of King Ahab, ruler of the northern kingdom 876-854 B.C. Jezebel not only continued to worship her own gods but worked energetically to destroy the worship of Yahweh, to discredit the work of Elijah and most probably of Micaiah, and to place Baal Melkart as the national deity in Samaria.[4] Such a placement would entail not only the presence of the

---

4. Jezebel was not a Hebrew but the daughter of Ethbaal, king of Tyre. She was given in marriage to Ahab in a deal involving Ethbaal and Omri, the father of Ahab, who preceded the latter as king of Israel. Jezebel brought the religion of Baal Melkart to Israel. Unlike the rural Baalism which the Israelites encountered upon their first entering Canaan, the Baal faith to which Jezebel was devoted fostered doctrines and behavior directly opposed

repulsive pagan deity in the capital city but the more grievous substitu-
tion of the dead god and the dying culture of the Canaanites for the living
God of the patriarchs, the prophets, and the kings of Israel, as well as for
the living faith of the people. It would be a choosing of death rather than
life.

The parallel with the situation in Thyatira has already been suggested.
Here also Christians are being seduced by the total environing culture.
Suggestions have been made that Jezebel is a code name for Sambatha, a
contemporary sibyl whose cell was located outside the city, or for the
goddess Artemis, or for a persuasive woman leader of a heretical sect.
But no such identification is necessary. It may indeed be misleading, for
what seems clear from the context and the chiastic pattern to which we
have alluded, is that the problem in Thyatira cannot be assigned a single
cause, such as a person, a goddess, or an inviting heresy. The problem
for the Thyatiran Christians was a pervasive climate—an atmosphere
breathed, assimilated, and incorporated. Thyatira was what we now call
a "lifestyle." It was Jezebel all over again.

Lund calls attention to the fact that Thyatira was a city in which favor-
able conditions existed for what might be called "bread and butter" idolatry. He writes:

> [Thyatira] was, nevertheless, a great center of trade, famous for the
> number of its guilds. There were guilds of bakers, potters, workers of
> brass, tanners, leather cutters, workers in wool and flax, clothiers, and
> dyers, among whom probably the two last mentioned were very impor-
> tant (Acts 16:14). Memberships in these guilds were essential for all
> workers who would succeed in their trade. Since pagan religious cere-
> monies were a part of such fellowship, we may well imagine the prob-
> lems that would arise for Christian members. There would be sacrificial
> feasts that would often take the form of revelry and licentiousness
> (Lund 1935, 37,38).

The central panel of the chiasm thus describes an overwhelming
danger to the Christian faith which, with the increased emphasis on the
worship of the Roman state and emperor which was now developing

---

to those of Hebrew prophetism. Baal Melkart was the national god of Tyre. A rival to the
Hebrew nation and its severe monotheism, Baal Melkart was worshiped with obscene rites
including the sacrifice of infants, an activity in which he seems to have had the collusion of
his goddess-wife Ashtoreth.

We do not know enough about either Baal Melkart of Jezebel nor indeed about the Thyatiran church to know why precisely Jezebel figures in the cryptogram of the Apocalypse.
But we may conclude with some likelihood that just as Jezebel wanted to see Israel immersed
in her own lifestyle, so the paganized Christians of Thyatira beckoned their fellow believers
to experiments with "the deep things of Satan," symbolized by Jezebel (A.E. Bailey and
C.F. Kent, *History of the Hebrew Commonwealth*, New York, 1935, chapters XIII, XIV).

might well have seemed a most sinister threat to this minority faith.

This may have been the reason for a fact emphasized by Lund, viz., the naming of the speaker in the Thyatiran panel in Revelation 2:26-28:

> He who conquers and keeps my works until the end, I will give him power over the nations, and he shall rule them with a rod of iron, as when earthen pots are broken in pieces, even as I myself have received power from my Father, and I will give him the morning star.

In Revelation 22:16 the identity of the morning star is clarified. "I am the root and offspring of David, the bright morning star." The overcomer in Thyatira is to be given the supreme reward for his endurance. And that reward is the Lord himself.

The juxtaposition of the living Lord and Jezebel in the Thyatiran panel provides a contrast which may speak prophetically to the next century of Covenant life. The modern Church has two fundamental elements in common with the Thyatiran panel: on the one hand the presence of a subtle and seductive environment represented by the "bread and butter idolatry" of Jezebel, and on the other the exemplar of redemptive life and faithfulness projected by the victorious Lord, the root and offspring of David, the bright and morning star.

A persistent disciple image emerges in the New Testament. It is that of the ready servant or athlete stripped down to essentials and prepared to engage an adversary.

The imagery that clusters around these concepts of ready servant or prepared competitor is that of youthful vigor, imagination, and hopefulness. Jesus is the bright morning star and the offspring of David. And David, like the figures of Keat's Grecian urn, shines with a storied youthfulness. Despite the power politics of middle age and the impotence of senescence, David remains the young shepherd king, the sweet singer of Israel, and the guardian of his people. There is a glimpse of this cosmic youthfulness in Psalm 19 where the sun is seen as a youth whose tent is pitched in the heavens, "who comes out like a bridegroom from his wedding canopy, rejoicing like a strong man to run a race." The same juvenescence breathes in the Song of Solomon.

It is a young Christ who meets us in the Apocalypse and it is a young Christ who emerges in the primitive art of the Church; he is often pictured as a youthful shepherd carrying a lamb on his shoulders. It is an image of abundant life and of eager and unhindered commitment to the task of healing and redemption; a stark contrast to the languor, complacency, and indifference of the imperial culture—the gray mass, weight, and weariness of the world.

The last scene in John's chiasm of the seven churches is that of the church in Laodicea. There the Lord addresses that congregation in some well-known phrases:

> I know all your ways; you are neither hot nor cold. How I wish you were either hot or cold! But because you are lukewarm, neither hot nor cold, I will spit you out of my mouth. You say, "How rich I am! And how well I have done! I have everything I want." In fact, though you do not know it, you are the most pitiful wretch, *poor, blind,* and *naked.* So I advise you to buy from me gold refined in the fire, to make you truly rich, and white clothes to put on to hide the shame of your nakedness, and ointment for your eyes so that you may see. All whom I love I reprove and discipline. Be on your mettle therefore and repent. Here I stand knocking at the door; if anyone hears my voice and opens the door, I will come in and sit down to supper with him and he with me (Revelation 3:15-21, NEB).

In this passage the Lord censors the decadent tendencies he perceived in the churches of Asia Minor toward the end of the first century. This decadence is reflected in a number of symptoms, primarily complacency and self-satisfaction, the lack of zeal and engagement that characterize the spiritual middle class—a lukewarmness that in Thyatira had led to a toleration of the worst kind of evil.

Laodicea is encouraged to secure the refined gold apparently produced in the crucible of suffering, the white garments of the martyr witnesses, and the eye unguent that restores spiritual sight. In other words, it is urged to distance itself from an accommodative church in which life has oozed by without the need for commitment, discipline, and suffering and to identify itself with the heavenly hero.

The first generation of witnesses has already been gathered to its rest; the second generation, those who knew the apostles and heard their testimony, are thinning out. The refining fires of general persecution may not yet be burning but the wood is being gathered. It is time now not only to expect the chastening of the Lord but to welcome it. For behold the Judge is at the door!

A LOOK TO THE FUTURE

If this ancient message has relevance for the Covenant at the beginning of its second century, perhaps some questions are in order.

1. Is the model of faithfulness, purity, simplicity, integrity, intimacy, courage, vigor, and enthusiasm suggested in Revelation, chapters 1-3, a possible guide for the future of the Covenant Church?

2. Without suggesting forms of church life that radically set the denomination "against the world" in a manner inappropriate to its understanding of the Gospel as well as its history and tradition, what might be a workable strategy for the Covenant Church in its association with the environing cultures and their dominant values?

3. More specifically, what, if any, of these values does the Covenant see as indispensable for its continued existence and growth?

4. Again, more specifically, what that is now thought indispensable or at least desirable to our culture would the Covenant be willing to strip away in order to approach the New Testament model more closely?

In this connection we as a church are indebted to the prophetic first-century mood generated by Dr. G. Timothy Johnson in his Sunday afternoon message to the Covenant Centennial, June 23, 1985. Taking his text from Matthew 25:31-46 (sometimes called "The Great Assizes") Johnson surprised, puzzled, and certainly aroused and awakened the thousands gathered for that celebration in the Minneapolis Auditorium by his question if the Covenant Church might appropriately be identified with the sheep or the goats.

At COLECO II I read a paper on the social organization of the denomination which borrowed some of its ideas from William C. Shutz's concept of group dynamics as consisting of inclusion, control, and affection.[5] The paper was later published in *Narthex* (Vol. 3, No. 1, February, 1983) and was given some helpful interpretation by Isolde Anderson, Zenos Hawkinson, Michael Halleen, and Arthur Nelson.

If Covenant history and present process are placed over the Shutz grid, we perceive that with an emphasis on the increase in structure, particularly in central administration (and perhaps with the growth of computerized projections in the task of planning) and without a concurrent adjustment in the involvement of the periphery, not only may the control in the hands of the periphery diminish, but the sense of inclusion and affection for the Covenant as a whole may also be attenuated.[6]

5. The study was published in 1958 with the title *A Three-Dimensional Theory of Interpersonal Behavior.*
    Closely related to my paper at COLECO was Herbert J. Hedstrom's perceptive paper *The Structure of the Covenant.* In addition to the excellent contents of the paper, which was published in *Narthex*, Vol. 2, No. 1 (February, 1982), Hedstrom includes several pages of highly illuminating comment on Covenant structure which came to him in response to a letter sent to several Covenanters before he finalized his paper. Beyond that the paper has another dimension in its presentation in *Narthex.* It is followed by critical responses by Paul E. Larsen, Evelyn Johnson, Aaron Markuson, and Richard W. Carlson.

6. A parallel phenomenon is the growing isolation and independence of some of the larger Covenant congregations, particularly those, who by origin or choice, see themselves as denominations in little. When under the leadership of strong, charismatic pastors, such churches may even become autocephalous (self-headed) and practically separate themselves from both the regional conference and the denomination.

Some evidence for this is found in 1981, 1982, and 1983. In his reports for those years President Engebretson reports that although giving to all causes has dramatically increased each year (1981: $46,000,000 for a per capita gift of $568; 1982: $51,000,000 for a gift of $618 per member; 1983: $54,400,000 for a $660 average), decreased giving to denominational causes forced a budgetary cutback of 8 percent in 1981, 10 percent in 1982, and 14.3 percent in 1983 (*YB* 1982, 1983, and 1984).

Although there was a marked improvement in 1984, it is now seemingly more difficult to get day-to-day budget money for the center than for regional and local causes.[7] If Shutz is right, this points to a lessening of feelings of inclusion and affection at the periphery for the Covenant as a national body and some strengthening of positive feelings for the regional and local work.

A reversal of this trend may have been apparent in the Century 2 Campaign and in the Centennial celebration in Minneapolis in June, 1985. But in these events thousands of people had a chance to "own" the Covenant and hence to feel inclusion and affection. When the celebration is looked at more carefully, it is evident that the sense of ownership was promoted not only by "being there" but by sharing in arrangements and responsibilities. The truly significant Saturday "fair" reflected the participation of hundreds if not thousands of Twin City and Minnesotan Covenanters, who had a chance to share in the "control" of the event not so much by making the big decisions as by making sure that their part was carried out, according to plan.

Hence the Centennial celebration turned out to be not just an obligation to fulfill, however solemn and circumstantial, but a unified shout of joy! Faith had become, in Harry Emerson Fosdick's storied words, "not weight but wings."

The Covenant of the future, if I understand the generation now coming into leadership, may commit itself to a lighter and more athletic version of Covenantism than we have helped to form. In such a version impulses will travel more quickly from periphery to center and from center to periphery than is possible in a more traditional structure.

Such a Covenantism should affect every branch of our work. It will mean that personhood and personal relationships are not only cherished but made even more intrinsic to our way of working. Role identities and functions will not be eliminated, but they will more than now be leavened by the freedom and courtesy of faith. Our theology will be more relational and our lifestyle less than now determined by traditional man-

---

7. In some ways the Covenant is a fortunate exception to a trend because of the presence of an energetic and charismatic president. Milton Engebretson has often done successful personal fund-raising to avoid a deficit.

ners and methods. In many situations such as board and committee meetings there will be an expressed need to participate both cerebrally and emotionally, and Covenant will mean even more than now a true equity in Christ. The emphasis in the local church will be both on effective organizational functioning and on the development of a "family of faith" in which nurturing and caring are shared responsibilities.

With the personalizing and relationalizing of the Covenant throughout its structure, a process not only desirable but realizable because of the posture of increasing numbers of today's young people, some modifications will no doubt take place in organizational models and procedures. I shall make a brief summary of what some of these changes may be:

1. Applying some critical discernment to the older organizational model borrowed from corporate life. This model sees church administration emanating from a pyramid standing on its base. Such a highly centralized model owes much of its power to its entrenchment in business and industry, but also to its application in the military, in political structures, in higher education, and in church establishments. It has much to recommend it and it will always play an important role even in not-for-profit organizations. It is inexpensive in terms of time loss, for it emphasizes effectiveness and expeditiousness and is not entirely uncomfortable with the application of raw power. It is well-tooled for results in nonpersonal and quantifiable areas, and its methodology is often borrowed by agencies and institutions committed to achieving in just such areas.

   But whatever its merits—and these are not few—the model is probably deficient when applied univocally to the faith process, for it lacks a calculus to measure the inward maturing of the individual in grace and knowledge or the development of a faith community or the discerning, calling forth, and application of gifts, or the emergence and energizing of spiritual leadership. Put simply, the corporation model is largely applicable to the production of impersonal, measurable objects or the initiation of cold processes. It knows little about the facilitation of a process energized and warmed by the Holy Spirit. That is why Paul, perhaps concerned that the "gifts" in 1 Corinthians 12, 13, and 14 might be reduced to merely human functions, places agape love as the energizing center of his chiasm.

2. Some changes, nonetheless, may be on the way. With the development of an understanding that each aspect of life has its appropriate art or science and its proper goal setting and method, space may be provided for a life in the Spirit in the Christian community. Ray Stedman calls it "body life." Now for nearly two decades I have called it a relational

lifestyle. The crucial activity involves both product and process in this context and the outcomes are both temporal and eternal. Here the community may benefit from having the pyramid of leadership periodically placed not on its base but its apex. Beginning with some random relational maxims such as "The treasures are in all the people" and "People support what they help create," the focus may be shifted to the life and work of the body of Christ seen as a living organism with vital, diversely equipped members. In this setting a leader is not handed a mass of individuals on which to exercise his or her skills in evangelism, preaching, teaching, fund-raising, or fund management. The leader is seen as an energizer and facilitator of a process designed to equip all the members with grace and knowledge that they in turn and in conformity with their charismata may carry out the commission of Christ to go everywhere and to everyone with the glad news of grace.

The particular organizational forms that this emphasis will assume lie outside the scope of this vision. There is, nevertheless, reason to believe that the present structure of the Covenant will serve its objectives well. Modified and applied by the people to whom it is entrusted, it will permit both the flexibility and control that the new time seems to be asking for. And on the basis of my acquaintance with the new cadre of leadership waiting in the wings, I would judge that the denomination will continue in good hands.

A few people whose opinion I have asked regarding this my "apocalypse" consider me idealistic and theoretical (not to say avuncular, in short, a "blithe gaffer") in my projections. But I am not envisaging a Utopia. The options are not either/or. The organizational and communal are both prime ingredients in the denomination of the future, and they stand in a dialectical and supplemental, not an adversarial, relationship. This means that the church cannot only tolerate but benefit from the natural leader who knows how to motivate individuals and to activate the glutinous mass of the community. But it can also benefit from a leadership that devotes its energy to bonding the community through affectional relationships. It can gratefully accept a Paul in angry confrontation with Peter in Antioch or insisting on his apostolate at Corinth, as well as a Paul longing affectionately for his friends at Thessalonica or encouraging his Philippian associates to rejoice in the midst of adversity.

The book which started out to be a modest sequel to *By One Spirit* and *A Family of Faith* has grown into a book on Covenant ecclesiology. I hope it has been true to its title, *Into One Body . . . by the Cross.* In doing this work my belief in the crucified and risen life as the only basis for the unity of the Church has been immeasurably strengthened. And, as I have tried to emphasize in these concluding paragraphs, for me the crucified and risen life is a life in relationships, in which the values of truth and grace exist side by side in unvarying interaction. I believe that the future of the Covenant as "one body" in whatever we are called to do depends on our openness to that gift of the Holy Spirit which makes us one in the Spirit with God, with our own selves, with the people around us, and with the environing world. It is probably not our calling to control the people we have been given or to improve them, for those are the works of the Holy Spirit; we are called to identify with them, to stand with them "under the mercy," and to be bound with them forever in the bond of love.

Appendices

APPENDIX A

The Theology of John Nelson Darby

Because the theological ideas of John Nelson Darby were so essential to the shaping of the "Free" tradition and to informing Fundamentalism as it developed in the early decades of this century, I have felt it useful to provide an elaboration of these ideas (see pp.42-45.). This elaboration is based to a large extent on Clarence E. Bass's thorough study of Darby's theology in Backgrounds to Dispensationalism *(Chapter 1, "Distinguishing Features of Dispensationalism," and Chapter 4, "Darby's Doctrine of the Church."). What I construe to be only direct quotations by Darby or close paraphrases are set off by quotation marks.*

During the fifty-plus years that Darby lived after his disenchantment, he clung with tenacity to the following beliefs about the Church and the end time. There is no evidence that he was ever led significantly to alter them; they were hewn in stone:

THE CHURCH

A. "The true Church composed of the whole number of regenerate persons from Pentecost to the first resurrection who gather in the name of Christ, united together to Christ by the baptism of the Holy Ghost, is the Body of Christ of which he is the head and the holy temple for the habitation of God through the Spirit" (Bass, 100).
B. "The Church [as it now exists both established and dissenting] is in

451

ruins. The pristine purity of the Church as instituted by Christ has become corrupted by the orders and government of man. The universal priesthood of all believers has been usurped by the establishment of professional pastors; unconverted men are allowed to hold offices which have been instituted by man, not Christ; the presidency of the Holy Spirit has been perverted by man, and in its place believers look to the guidance of a man-made ministry; the bond of communion has been broken in general, the fellowship which was to reflect the glory of Christ—simple, direct, Spirit-filled—has been replaced by a system bearing the evil marks of corrosion" (Bass, 100-101).

"The Church has lost its unity, its power, its holiness, and has ceased to bear witness to God in the world. What is called the Church has become the center of evil and pretense. The members of Christ's body are dispersed: many are hidden in the world, others in the midst of religious corruption—some in one sect, some in another—in rivalry with one another" (Bass, 101).

"This ruin in which the Church finds itself is not merely one of denominational division; it is one in which the entire nature and purpose of the Church has become so perverted that it is diametrically opposed to the fundamental reason for which it was instituted" (Bass, 102).

"It is not merely that the Church has become corrupted, and has lost its effectiveness. The Church is in ruins! It has become a corrupt mass, an apostasy hastening to its final consummation rather than the symbol of a dispensation which God is sustaining through his faithful grace" (Bass, 103).

C. "The ruin is without remedy." Darby regards the Church as "a dispensation which, like other dispensations, has failed and must suffer the judgment of God. . . . As Israel has been cut off, so will the Church; and as a remnant will be saved out of Israel, so there is hope that a remnant of the Church may be used to glorify Christ" (Bass, 103).

D. "That the Church is responsible for its present state of corruption and ruin is beyond question. Its entire history has been a deviation from its true principles. It has become consumed with making a system, with seeking human leadership; with desire for numbers instead of genuine converts; with human righteousness, ordinances, succession, ceremonial observances, professional ministry, carnal procedures—confusing spiritual administration with human imagination" (Bass, 104).

E. "The believer has a responsibility to this Church in ruins, but not to restore it. Any attempt to restore the Church will result in utter failure, since it is neither in God's will that the Church be restored, nor does man have authority to do so; he is utterly incapable. All efforts to repair the ruins are not only sinful but quite beyond the strength of the churches. God has never restored a fallen dispensation to its original state, but has always proceeded to a new medium of dealing with man. Man cannot begin the Church again, for God is not beginning it" (Bass, 105).

F. "Believers are to forsake the government and order of man which has corrupted the Church, and assemble in simple unity. . . . The only true course for believers is to withdraw from all religious societies called churches and to meet in the name of the Lord Jesus—to call together the true assembly of God. Separation is not enough: it has in it no uniting power. Some positive principle is needed to secure the cohesion of those who have withdrawn from the corruption. This can be found only in Christ, who is the true center of unity, and whose mediatorial powers can unite the assembly of God as its redeemer, its head, and its life" (Bass, 106-107).

"This assembly must have the power of the Holy Spirit in order to gather the believers who forsake the corruption of an apostate church. . . . The assembly is to be a single gathering of all believers, without pomp or ritual, with strict adherence to the Scriptures for all procedure, and with reliance upon the Holy Spirit as the source of its power" (Bass, 107).

"The responsibility for this assembly lies with the Brethren. The presence of the Holy Ghost in the Church as one body was the grand doctrine on which the whole testimony of the Brethren was founded. The testimony was especially committed to the Brethren" (Bass, 107).

Darby rejects with utter disregard all claims of others to be the true representative of Christ's body on earth, and makes for the Brethren a sole claim to this distinction. Only the Brethren gather in his name. Others gather as Baptist, Congregationalist, etc., not as "his body." Only the Assembly (Brethren) is the Church of God on earth. (These Brethren are obviously the Plymouth Brethren.)

The constituting principle of this assembly is that it is gathered in the name of Christ. "It is not the fact of being a Christian that constitutes God's assembly, but their being gathered in the name of the Lord" (Bass, 109).

"To be gathered in his name means to conform to the provisions which he has established; namely to allow the free rule of the Spirit in building up the body of Christ without external authority or organized societies—all of which hinder the Spirit" (Bass, 109).

G. The historical genesis of the Church

1. "The true Church came into being at Pentecost. It was composed of a remnant of Israel to which believing gentiles were added" (Bass, 110).

2. The covenant with Abraham is unrelated to the Church. "It con-

tained no promise of the Church" (Bass, 110). However, there was an assembly already in the Old Testament. This was constituted by God from among the Israelites; they were known as his people. When Israel rejected Christ (their Messiah and King) the nation was judged by God and only a remnant was spared.

However, this remnant was not a continuation of the covenant with Israel; through the atoning death of Christ and his resurrection and the power of the Spirit it was integrated into and became his body on earth: the assembly of God among people. This assembly is more than just the group of called-out believers; it is the actual embodiment of Christ in the world. Though presently in the world, the Church (the assembly) has an essentially heavenly existence and waits to share in the rapture which takes it out of the world. "Only Israel has an earthly existence" (Bass, 110-111).

H. The Church (the assembly) is also to be seen as God's habitation, created through the redemptive work of Christ.

I. Christ is the head of the Church. In creation he is the head of all principality and power, of creation and all things that exist, but in redemption he is the head of the Church. The Church, consequently, is to share in his glory. While all things will be out under his feet, the Church will reign with him as joint heirs. . . . Thus the Church is the ultimate of God's plan for humankind. Darby writes, "The body if any place be spoken of, is always spoken of as on the earth. . . . The body is formed by the baptism of the Holy Ghost sent down from heaven. . . . " The purpose of the earthly existence of the Church is the manifestation of the activity of God's love and holiness through the power of the Holy Spirit. For this reason it was gathered as a remnant from Israel, and when this testimony has been completed, it will be given its heavenly character in the glory of Christ. Until that time the Church labors through its gifts "for the perfecting of the saints . . . unto the building up of the Body of Christ." The expression "Church of God" applies to a company of believers gathered in his name in the locality in which they reside. Hence there can be no universal Church in the literal earthly sense. Each assembly is an autonomous local congregation with its own administrative privileges. It answers only to the rule of the Holy Spirit . . . (Bass, 117-119).

There is, therefore, no such thing in Scripture as a central authority having jurisdictional control over a group of churches. Each assembly is independently responsible to the Holy Spirit for the exercise of gifts under its own administration. It is not bound to other churches in a union of bylaws and creedal formulas, but in a fellowship of unity which is based on a mutual obedience to the Word, coming through the guidance of the Holy Spirit (Bass, 117).

Each assembly, however, is independent in government only not in existence as the holy body of Christ, for each assembly comprises the body of Christ.

DARBY'S DOCTRINE OF THE CHURCH IN RELATION TO THE LAST THINGS

One of the distinctive features of Darby's ecclesiology is the doctrine of double issue—the belief that Israel and the Church have not only discrete identities but separate destinies.

The classical view of the relation between Israel and the Church is that advanced by N.W. Lund in his pamphlet *Israel and the Church*, originally written in Swedish but now translated and available in the Covenant Archives.

This view holds that God's design for his people is unitary. Originally God purposed that the wounds of sin were to be healed in and through his chosen people, first through the instrumentality of patriarchal faith, then through the creation of the law and the nation of Israel with its gifts of discipline and prophecy, and finally through the coming of God himself in the form of his Son, the lifting up of the horn of salvation, and the effecting of the mission to the Gentiles.

This "plan," or a version of it, was aborted by the rejection of the presence and message of Jesus, but despite this "murder," the deeper intentions of God were fulfilled in the salvational acts around the death, resurrection, and exaltation of Jesus and in the birth of the Church. Ultimately God's design will be completed in the appearance and kingdom of Christ. In this kingdom, because of God's mercy, all those who "believe" will be included. For, as the Apostle says (Romans 9), "He has included all under unbelief that he might have mercy upon all."

In this classical view of consummation the Jewish people play a most crucial role, but this view makes no allowance for a double issue. Unlike Darby's view, which literalizes prophetic portions of Scripture, the classic view treats Israel as a symbolic progenitor of the Church and treats the Church as a mystical fulfillment of what God intended with his original covenant people.

Darby, on the other hand, makes a sharp distinction between Israel and the Church. Originally God's intentions with Israel were to be achieved through a number of discrete dispensations culminating in the establishment of the Messianic kingdom.

But these intentions were at least temporarily frustrated in the rejection of the Messiah by his own people and in the ensuing suffering and death of Jesus. What followed was the stopping of the "heavenly clock" and the beginning of a new phenomenon in the coming of the Spirit and the birth of the Church. This "interruption" of the unfolding Messianic design is not directly related to the story of Israel. It is a new dispensation, a "*nova*," which will reach its own culmination in the rapture of the Church through the secret coming and in the initiation of the end events.

Bass summarizes the dispensational views of Darby and some of his followers in a number of principles which, although they may differ in detail, provide a consensus about the manner in which Israel and the Church reach their discrete resolutions.

A. Human history is, in God's economy, divided into definite periods of time "during which man is tested in respect to obedience to some specific revelation of the will of God (*Scofield Reference Bible* [New York, 1917], p.5). We may thus expect that the Bible also is divided in this manner and that each division has a specific purpose.

B. Each of these different periods or dispensations is "marked off in Scripture by some change in God's dealing with mankind, in respect to two questions: of sin and of man's responsibility. Each of the dispensations may be regarded as a new test of the natural man and each ends in judgment—marking his utter failure in each dispensation" (*Rightly Dividing the Word of Truth* [Oakland, N.d.], p.18).

C. Dispensations declare some leading principles or interference of God, some condition in which he has placed humans. The principles are God's, but the responsibility is given humans for the display and discovery of what he was and their bringing in of their infallible failure as with regard to humankind. . . . There is no instance of the restoration of a dispensation afforded us. There is only partial revival through faith.

D. Dispensations are so widely different in character that what is simple obedience and for the glory of God in one dispensation may be entirely foreign to the character of another.

E. In summary, Darby's dispensationalism insists:
1. The Church in no wise assumes any of Israel's relation to God; there can be no "spiritual Israel," the promises of the Abrahamic covenant are still inviolate.
2. The nation to whom the Lord promises the kingdom is not the Church.
3. The Church is: the body of Christ, the bride of Christ, the habitation of God by the Spirit, the Lamb's wife; but never a nation. The nation is Israel—the believing remnant living when the Lord returns (Bass, 30).

4. The Gospels: Jesus preached Gospel of kingdom; Paul preached the Gospel of grace.

5. Darby insists: the whole of God's redemptive relation to humankind is centered in his covenantal relation to Israel. Israel, as a nation, is related to God by one principle (the unconditional covenant), while the Church, as the body of Christ, is related to him by an entirely different principle.

6. The Church is an interruption of God's plan with Israel necessitated by the rejection of the kingdom by the Jews when it was offered to them by Jesus. "This idea was most certainly fathered by Darby" (Bass, 27).

7. Although the Church is "in the heavenlies," it is not a part of God's initial redemptive plan. Some statement about this "interruption" and the sharp distinction between Israel and the Church may be found in the writings of Darby's followers:

"The Church is a parenthesis" (H.A. Ironside in Bass, 28).

"The Church is an intercalation" (Lewis Sperry Chafer in Bass, 28).

"The Church did not exist before or during the earth life of Christ. Scripturally we find the birth of the Church in Acts 2 and the termination of its career on earth in 1 Thessalonians 4. Comparing then what is said in Scripture concerning Israel and the Church, we find that in origin, calling, promise, worship, principles of conduct, and future destiny all is contrast" (Chafer in Bass, 28).

8. The kingdom. Dispensationalists restrict future kingdom to a restoration of the Jewish kingdom (supposedly) offered to the Jews by Christ but which they rejected. . . . This kingdom was not a spiritual kingdom but a literal fulfillment of the Abrahamic promises. "The Gospel of the Kingdom is the good news that the promised kingdom of the Old Testament was about to be established with the manifestation of the King" (A.C. Gaebelein in Bass, 29).

F. There is also a fair amount of agreement on the scenario of last things.

   1. Pre-tribulation rapture

     a. Textual base 1 Thessalonians 4:16-17

     b. Secret, any-moment-coming

     c. Based on ecclesiology, not exegesis

"In determining the question of whether the Church will go through the tribulation, a most important factor is the definition of the Church. It is therefore not too much to say that the rapture question is determined more by ecclesiology than eschatology. . . . Any answer to the rapture question must therefore be based on a careful study of the doctrine of the Church as it is revealed in the New Testament" (Walvoord in Bass, 39).

"Those who believe in the rapture of the Church before the appearing of Christ hold that the Church has a special and peculiar character and connection with Christ. The Church's joining Christ has nothing to do with Christ's appearing or coming to earth. Her place is elsewhere. She sits in with him already in heavenly places. She has to be brought there as to bodily presence. The thing she has to expect for herself is not . . . Christ's appearing but her being taken up where he is. . . . It is this conviction that the Church is properly heavenly, in its calling and relationship with Christ, forming no part of the course of events on the earth, which makes the rapture so simple and clear, and on the other hand it shows how the denial of its rapture brings down the Church to an earthly position, and destroys its whole spiritual character and position" (Darby in Bass, 39).

2. The great tribulation

   a. Rapture—The Church is removed.

   b. Seven-year period follows. The prophetic (heavenly) clock stopped at the time of Christ's rejection by Israel and his death is now set to fulfill God's intention with Israel. Three and a half years Israel has covenant with antichrist, who breaks it. Three and a half years Satan overpowers the antichrist. The time of Jacob's trouble is now poured out over the world. During the "seven years" the gospel of the kingdom (not of grace) is preached. An elect remnant of Israel (144,000) survives the tribulation to become the kingdom to which Christ returns when the "seven years" are ended.

3. Millennial reign of Christ

   a. Restored "kingdom" is established by Christ in the millennium that *follows* the tribulation. "The millennium is that period of 1,000 years, prophesied in Scriptures of personal, worldwide, glorious reign of the son of David, our Lord Jesus Christ, who after his literal return from heaven will fulfill the promises made to the patriarchs to restore Israel to her own land and to give her the realization of God's covenantal promises" (J. Dwight Pentecost in Bass, 43).

   b. Millennium is to be the literal fulfillment of Old Testament prophecy (Bass, 139-40).

   • Government is theocratic.

   • National distinctions will continue.

   • Seat of government is Jerusalem.

   • Christ will have physical throne with David as regent.

   • All nations will be subservient to Israel since regathered tribes will be central.

• Christ will reign through Israel.
c. Relation of Church to millennium.
  • Some think Christians will reign with Christ in kingdom.
  • Others assert that Church will not return to earth but will be a part of Holy City hovering above. Joined by Old Testament saints, they will constitute eternal state (Bass, 44).
4. The eternal state
In the dispensationalist view, New Jerusalem is an actual city where the Church will dwell eternally. The city is not in heaven but will have a physical location. Saints to be transferred from heaven to this new location—for eternity. It is also the abode of God (Bass, 45-46). The city will be the dwelling place of the Trinity; the Bride—the Lamb's Wife; the Church; the redeemed of Israel; the redeemed of all ages; unfallen angels.

SOME CONCLUSIONS

In the context of Darby's (and his followers') eschatology, it is important to restate his distinction between the true Church and Christendom. The true Church contains only those who have been saved, a limited number out of the mass of professing Christians. The use of the word "saved" as designating the converted becomes more understandable when related to Darby's theology. In the historic Church "saved" is used to indicate the termination of the salvation process, not its beginning. Ecclesiastical organization has corrupted the organized Church—the external, visible Church as seen here on earth. The Church, therefore, cannot be described in terms of the organized structure which is seen today, but only in terms of the believer's (relation) to Christ. The Church is heavenly, not earthly: the individual believer is not baptized into a church here on earth, but into a heavenly relation with Christ (Bass, 46).

As indicated earlier, Darby distrusted all organized ecclesiastical systems. This dominant idea combined with that of the individual's heavenly relation to Christ (as constituting the Church) resulted in a spirit of separatism among dispensationalists. All who did not agree with Darby's interpretation were characterized as "not having the truth" or as "not understanding the divine plan of the ages" (or—later—as not "rightly dividing the word of truth") and therefore as somewhat "apostate."

The corollary of this attitude was the tendency among dispensationalists to associate themselves prominently with the theology of interdenominational and independent churches (Bass, 47). Sandeen also sees a close connection between dispensationalism and the founding of Bible institutes (Sandeen 1970, 181-83).

APPENDIX B

'Some Words to Enlighten'

As the "Free" enterprise gathered momentum in the early 1880s, the cry for the dissolution of the Ansgar Synod also increased. But, as we remember, the formal termination of the synod would have resulted in the loss of Ansgar College to the city of Knoxville. And the college had now become important to the designs of Princell and the "Free."

Hence they were anxious to promote disestablishment without risking the loss of the school. It is in this context that Martenson writes this editorial in Chicagobladet *(July 25, 1882), which, as a mirroring of the situation, I have felt merits to be translated and included as an appendix.*

Since the meeting in Moline [June 7, 1882, reported in *Chicagobladet*, June 16, June 23, June 30, July 4, July 11, and July 18] we have received several comments which require an answer. These comments in essence have been as follows:

We thought the Ansgar Synod was dissolved, since their pastors speak against factionalism, call denominationalism harlotry, and judge it to be unrighteous. But now we see that they have a long list of names of pastors in the papers, that the Synod has had its annual meeting, that it is giving licenses, and requires reporting of activity [by the pastors]—if this is so, it is a faction like any other denomination; or are just other denominations parties? Is it only harlotry to belong to other denominations but good to belong to the Ansgar Synod? Can one punish what one practices? May one not preach and does one lack the right to travel at half fare because one is not licensed by a denomination as someone has claimed?

Because of these questions we would like to say that the Ansgar Synod is not formally dissolved—*yet*. We hope, nevertheless, that this will happen.

Two years ago it seemed that the overwhelming majority within the Synod considered it wrong to belong to a party which received congregations and placed pastors, and a reform got under way immediately. [This is the situation reflected by S.W. Sundberg and K. Erixon in their letters from 1880.] Brother Erixon, who was then president of the Synod, traveled widely to the congregations belonging to the Synod and let the brethren within the Synod understand that they should withdraw from that in congregational life which was evil and to be free and independent from the Synod in carrying out their work. But a formal dissolution did not come about for several reasons. In the first place, it was feared that the fellowship would be fractured and a new synod formed if the old one were dissolved too rapidly. For there were a few prejudiced brethren who could not survive without a synod wherefore at the suggestion of a possible dissolution of the Ansgar Synod began thinking of joining the Mission Synod. In the second place, the Ansgar Synod has the right to decide about the use of the school building in Knoxville, and before the Synod was formally dissolved, they wanted to transfer this right in a legal manner to the brethren in the school society. For these reasons the Ansgar Synod has been allowed to live on until the present. This, however, is more on paper than in reality, for lately the Synod has deliberately refrained from adding any congregations or pastors. This is the greatest evil of denominationalism because in this way souls are drawn to the Synod and become the Synod's possession, and this leads to the encouragement of zeal and factionalism towards one another.

Yes, but the pastoral list of the Synod has more names than ever. Yes, but this is not a registry of the Synod's pastors but only of those to whom the Synod has granted license. When the Synod ceased "making preachers" some brethren were appointed who on behalf of the Synod would grant licenses to those who did not wish to be affiliated with a synod, but as a consequence of the generally held and distorted idea that he who preaches and solemnizes [needed a license. These brethren] felt that they should have these rights.

The synodal spirit within this Synod [Ansgar] seems to be dying, which was proved at the last annual meeting when it was almost impossible to get anyone to accept the presidency. Small wonder that with such thoughts they could join in the condemnation of the "harlot" [synodalism]. But neither is it strange that people find such talk contradictory when the Synod still exists. As far as we are concerned, we are convinced that this as well as all synods and parties, whatever name they carry, should be eliminated in both word and act, and just as well now as later, for they cause harm if they exist only in name.

Now that the Synod's rights to the school building in Knoxville have been transferred to the school society, the building should not constitute support for the existence of the Synod. And even if these rights had not been transferred, there is no support in God's Word for the existence of a faction because of material benefits. . . .

We hope, therefore, that the Ansgar Synod at its next [annual] meeting completely disappears as a synod.* We wish the same for the other synods, but so far there doesn't seem much reason for hope in that direction because they work with zeal to strengthen their encampments. And if the Synod is not pulled up by the roots, there is a danger that it will resume its growth. In that event the last confusion will be worse than the first; a topped tree is always larger and stronger when it recovers than if it had never been topped. If there is antipathy toward denominationalism and factionalism, let all the actions follow and God will be responsible for the consequences. We cannot do evil that good may come, no matter how good our intentions are. It had probably been better to let things be as they were, school and all, and to let the Synod fall rather than to preach against one's own practices . . . it is impossible to belong to a party or a synod without becoming egotistic and joining a party is evidence of factionalism—that I have an inclination for partisanship above everything else. And this factional spirit grows day by day until at last one can only desire success for one's own party, pastors, and congregations. One can speak a different language but one's heart and mind do not follow. These are realities, say what you will. . . .

*Since the annual meeting to which Martenson refers is that of May, 1882, the "next meeting" would have been that of 1883. But the end of the Ansgar Synod did not come until 1885, and by that time many of the synods, pastors, and laypersons, as well as organized congregations, had found refuge in the ark of the Covenant.

APPENDIX C

MARTENSON'S REPORT

John Martenson's report of the Altona meeting (September 17-25, 1878) appeared in the Chicagobladet *October 11, 1878 (see pp.55-57). In order to better understand the content as well as the strategy of Martenson's writings at this time, I have translated his report of this meeting.*

The mission meeting in Altona, Illinois, was pretty well attended. Several brethren from both the Ansgar and Mission Synods preached the Word and the presence of the Holy Spirit was perceived. As had been expected, the uniting of the above-mentioned synods was also discussed. We cannot report what was said, but the substance of it was that it is desirable to remove the obstacles that separate the Christians not only within the above-mentioned synods, but among all denominations. No one was able to find any support in the Word of God for the motley collection of synods and denominations. It was therefore considered advisable in this matter to be guided by God's Word and not the traditions of the fathers. Despite all their knowledge, the Christians in our day behave more imprudently than the unlearned laity in the time of the apostles. The sheep desired to be as one and together and had never set up the barriers; that work had been done primarily by the shepherds. It would be best, without delay, to remove what does not conform to the Word of God. The time is short; the matter weighty.

This was the substance of what the speakers said. At first glance these opinions seem somewhat shocking; nevertheless, on closer scrutiny one

463

shall find that they contain great truths that are worth considering. For we must admit that these party barriers have caused great evil, however innocent they may seem. It is certainly not without reason that the ungodly claim to be confused about what is right, for in our day the Christians seem not to have one faith, one baptism, one God. In no way. Rather it is now so that only they seem unified who have the same conception in these matters; wherefore there will soon be as many denominations as there are different opinions. It is certainly high time that Christians awake.

Dear brothers and sisters, within whatever enclosure we may find ourselves, whatever name or confession surrounds us, may this no longer keep us from them who share a precious faith. Those who do not want to serve the Lord but only their belly are sure to urge partisanship; but may God's people in the Lord's name bid farewell to all factions, for these things are the same as idolatry, murder, and witchcraft (Galatians 5). May it be more important for us to associate with God's people in love than to impose our convictions on them! . . .

Paul strongly emphasized the unity of Christians and sternly rebukes the Corinthians when they name themselves after Paul and Apollos; perhaps it is just as culpable and carnal to call ourselves Baptists, Lutherans, Methodists, Adventists, Ansgarians, and Mission Friends. . . .

Now every Christian knows that these different parties are a hindrance to the furthering of God's kingdom; one may even pray to God to break down the fences and bring believers together; but when it comes to practice in these matters, we are immovable. Then no one will yield, then everyone is right and no one wants to relinquish anything. Then the Methodist wants everyone else to be a Methodist and the Lutheran that everyone should be Lutheran, but to let one or the other name go and to know nothing except Jesus Christ and him crucified—that very few desire.

What can be the reason for this? Are these names so dear that for them one will sacrifice the fellowship? What holds us back?

From our point of view it is not the *name* but rather the clergy and the church that constitute the main reason. Let no one be offended by what we say but rather test the words and keep what is good. The main problem, as we see it, is that we have turned our back upon God's Word, and let the enemy introduce a priesthood which subsequently, because they all seek their own and not what belongs to Christ (Philippians 2:21), through the building of churches have caught both believers and unbelievers in a spiritual enslavement. . . . Formerly all the people of God were considered priests, but now only they are called priests who are anointed or ordained; hence the priest has gradually become a sort of

God. The name the preacher has gotten from the preacher "factory" [seminary, presumably] and the worshipers he has gotten from the name, and the idolatry has increased more and more, so that, so to speak, one has offered all to this god: the Word, the sacraments, and the ability to judge [discern]. In this way the idol has become so indispensable that Christians may speak in the fashion: "Our preacher is ungodly and we should wish to have another, but the harvest is plentiful and the laborers are few; we shall probably have to make this one do for the time being, and better something than nothing." Thus through this homage and these rights, the idol has become larger and larger until finally, "infallible" and "orthodox," he has made himself the judge of thoughts and motives.

If now this miserable situation prevailed only among the ungodly, less needed to be said. But alas, the leaven has reached also the Christians and become so deeply rooted as to seem ineradicable. It is nevertheless essential that the evil be removed lest there be irreparable damage.

But what can be done to improve the situation?

The answer is not easy. Perhaps the best would be if brethren gather and deliberate before the Lord. For our part we believe that if God's children really were aware of who they are—a royal priesthood which doesn't have to beg the pastor for the Word, communion, or baptism, but who have all this as their possession—a great deal would be done for the cause of unity. But so long as we have not made our calling sure but blindly follow human beings, the union of the people of God will not succeed. God doesn't want us to be the slaves of people because we are destined for freedom; may we not then as a hindrance to the kingdom and to our own destruction continue to take part in what is harmful. What we mean is this: may no child of God any longer seek to establish or form Lutheran or any other factional congregations; rather, if there are Christians in a place, follow the example of the apostles, for they are good leaders in the forming of congregations as well as in confession and faith. We do not need to say, as we have heard more than once, "We are only a couple of families in this place; we can't afford to support a pastor; we long to partake in communion which because of the lack of a clergyman, we have not been able to do for a long time." We are born to the priesthood and God has promised us to be in the midst of his people where two or three are gathered. Formerly Christians designated from their own midst servants and providers from which they expected nothing more than that they were faithful (1 Corinthians 4:2). What hinders us from doing that now, helping ourselves to the spiritual gifts God has given us to each one?

The unity of the children of God is of great importance; on this point all Christians are in agreement. But if we continue to keep and to embrace our denominations, we deny with our actions what our mouths confess. We certainly need to think about this before we act and we want to hear the opinions of others; but there can be no doubt, and it has been proved by experience, that synods and different denominations are an evil which can be likened to little kings who are constantly feuding and try at one another's expense to arrive at power and prestige.

Now we have in all haste and without much coherence given our opinions. May no one, if these opinions are incorrect, become embittered by them. Rather, correct us, for we neither are nor wish to be considered infallible. But when the matter was brought up, it was best to be candid and to speak honestly so that people can grasp one's meaning. It feels both difficult and risky to speak freely on these matters, for the synod, the denomination, and the preacher are the corns of the masses; beyond this, the enemy whispers that one should placate so that no one is offended and subscribers are lost because of this; but now we have a conviction—and may God grant that it is not changed—that if the newspaper is not maintained without the denial and concealment of what is evil, then may it perish. Truth is truth, whether it is hailed or hated.

APPENDIX D

Some Words Regarding the Organizational Meeting

In an effort to clarify the procedure that governed the inviting of representatives to the organizational meeting of the Covenant, February 18-25, 1885, Nils Peterson, one of the pastors opposing the "Free" tactics at Jamestown in 1883, sent the following article to Chicagobladet *on March 27, 1885. On April 13, 1885, Peterson received the article back from the* Chicagobladet *with a notification that it could not be published. Peterson then sent the article to* Missions-Wännen, *which printed it on April 29, 1885 (see p.164).*

Some of the introductory information will be found elsewhere in this work, but since the article provides additional light on how the meeting got constituted, I have translated it and include it herewith.

Although my communication is late, I nevertheless feel urged to say something of what I personally saw and heard with respect to the organizational meeting in Chicago.

The question relative to the holding of a meeting the purpose of which was to achieve the cooperation and union of Christians, regardless of by what names they were called, was first raised in the independent Tabernacle (the Swedish Mission Tabernacle) on the South Side of Chicago.

Some time after the question was raised, the board of the church was convened. This was on October 18, 1884. The purpose of the meeting was to discuss further the matter under consideration, together with some other brethren who had been invited.

At this meeting C.A. Björk and F.M. Johnson were appointed as a committee to query the preaching brethren of the Mission and Ansgar Synods if they were in favor of a united meeting when occasion would be provided, fraternally to deliberate on and decided about cooperation and union among those pastors and congregations who would like and be able to participate in [*vara med om*] an ordered activity of this type.

The committee carried out its task and published a circular which was sent to the brethren in question, and, as the matter was accepted with general interest, the brethren felt that the time was ripe for a meeting to be held. In this way the organizational meeting in question came about.

As evident in the announcement of the meeting, not only the pastors of the synods, but also delegates from the independent congregations were invited to take part in the meeting and its deliberations. This invitation was received with gladness, evidenced by the large group of representatives attending the meeting.

The reason for not including the independent pastors in the same way as those from the synods is not hard to understand. If the independent pastors, as a whole, had been recognized and recommended by the brethren, they would, without doubt, have been invited to the meeting on the same conditions as the pastors of the synods.

I know some independent pastors who in all things honor their vocation; on the other hand, I know some who in word and deed dishonor their calling and whose work has brought lamentable consequences for the precious children of God. Many can with me affirm the truth of these claims. Should these have been invited to the meeting? No! Paul's words may be applied here, "To be among those which are valued and dedicated, a thing of use to the Master of the house, a man must cleanse himself from all those evil things [persons]; then he will be fit for any honourable purpose" (2 Timothy 2:21, NEB).

Because of this diversity among the independent pastors, the committee turned to the independent congregations who were in favor of such organized work with the request that they be represented by delegates at the meeting.

This arrangement for the meeting has been subjected to harsh and unbrotherly criticism to the effect that the meeting was called "only on behalf of partisan interest under the guise of a most transparent hypocrisy." Furthermore, the evil distinction that was made in that the pastors of the synods were invited and the independent ones were not, has been sketched.

In the same issue of *Chicagobladet* (where the criticism occurs) in the section devoted to letters, a direct warning is given about the meeting as an evil; this has deeply wounded the sensible Christians throughout the land. This, together with some other matters, formed the basis of the meeting's action with respect to Brother Princell. The warning in "The Mailbox" (referred to above) and published in *Chicagobladet*, February 10, 1885, was as follows, "We do not understand what congregations and individuals, who want to act in accordance with God's Word and maintain their rights, can have to do with a meeting of this kind.

"Some brethren have considered that the independent congregations should take the invitation to the meeting literally and send enough delegates to overwhelm the self-invited with numbers and evidence; but when the whole meeting is arranged in such a warped manner as it is, it is best and most proper to leave entirely alone what one cannot support and to resort to other ways of presenting oneself and of witnessing against it."

That Brother Princell, after painting the arrangements for the meeting in such unattractive colors for the public and sounding warnings against it, nevertheless comes and asks for the right of membership in the meeting—this seems very peculiar and has given rise to many strange thoughts.

This unequivocal manner of acting as well as the attacks upon individuals and the principle of organization appearing in a series of articles printed at the time that the meeting was announced in *Missions-Wännen*—this led to the following thought: Brother Princell intends indirectly to undermine our planned meeting in Chicago. This thought was given support for many by the appearance of the statement in "The Mailbox" which presented the meeting in the most unfavorable light; without doubt there existed a secret wish that the whole meeting would go up in smoke; what was published in *Chicagobladet* gave substance to such a thought [suspicion]. This was the basis for the action of the meeting. It would probably have been better if the meeting could have overlooked the wounding comments against the brethren and the arrangements for the meeting which had been thrown out before the general public, and, in spite of all this, extended the right hand of fellowship to Brother Princell; but it usually turns out that what one sows one harvests even when one is dealing with brothers.

In any event, the meeting progressed in a brotherly and sincere spirit and reached a result far beyond our expectations, which totally buries the notion that the meeting was arranged "by and for factional interests." All were willing to sacrifice their old symbola [creeds] and their priestly status that had existed in the synods. All was sacrificed for a biblical foundation; thus a Covenant was erected which justifies the congregations to assume exclusive leadership of the Mission Covenant.

And despite the harsh criticism to which the organizational meeting and its deliberations were subjected, not a single element of the constitution has been attacked as unbiblical or impracticable, but rather recognized; for example, Brother Princell has published the suggestions [for a constitution] submitted to him at the meeting in Galesburg, 1884, to demonstrate the similarity between his proposal [for a constitution] and the proposal adopted by the organizational meeting in Chicago, as if to say: the platform adopted by the meeting in Chicago incorporates the very idea that *Chicagobladet* and I have worked for. Which means that even the Covenant and its constitution are fully recognized by these brethren.

And now that the Covenant is established and has passed through general and individual judgment, or criticism, and no legitimate complaint has been lodged against the Covenant as "covenant" or over its constitution, I feel most grateful to God for his wonderful guidance at our organizational meeting in Chicago. And what was this other than an answer from our God to the many cries that resounded in his ears both day and night regarding this matter. . . .

With reference to the two proposals for [a membership clause] in the constitution, one made by Brother Princell in Galesburg and another adopted by the meeting in Chicago, I would like to make a few comments:

Article IV in Brother Princell's proposal calls for three classes: 1) preachers, 2) individuals, and 3) one or two delegates from every Christian congregation; whereas Article IV in the proposal adopted in Chicago . . . only allows [credentialed] delegates from the congregations to assume leadership of the Covenant. As early as the meeting in Galesburg in 1884, the meeting voted down the proposal for three estates, and proposed in addition to the negative vote that only congregational delegates should have leadership responsibilities in the Covenant then under consideration. For even then we wished to remove the self-appointed estates, even though Brother Princell could not at that time embrace the idea.

However, many of the brethren were afraid of the iron scepter of despotism and gave their fear expression at the meeting in Galesburg. For that reason I rejoice to see that our present Covenant does not justify any other leadership of itself than that exercised by the congregations through their credentialed delegates.

In an appended paragraph Nils Peterson defends the secretaries appointed by the organizational meeting against the charges leveled by Princell that they (the secretaries) had no right to include in the minutes the report by the committee of five. This committee tried to extract an apology from Princell for his negative, sometimes opprobrious, writings in Chicagobladet *directed toward those involved in the organizational effort. Princell refused to admit any fault and was not given speaking rights at the meeting. There was no real question of giving him voting rights, for he did not represent an organized congregation committed to the unifying of the churches, a condition for participation.*

Peterson then continued his article.

Since the time of the meeting several individuals, especially those not present at the meeting, have submitted writings which have been printed in *Chicagobladet*. These brethren have adjudged both the meeting and the Covenant as an evil and have claimed that it (the Covenant) suffers from an illness which will soon bring it to its grave. Another writer has likened the meeting to the gathering of 400 prophets who prophesied lies to King Ahab. The treatment of Brother Princell has been likened to the dismissal of the prophet Micah because he prophesied the truth in the name of the Lord.

Are these Christian and brotherly paintings? Is there anyone with the mind of Jesus who in a watchful moment will thus tramp his brothers and their endeavors under his feet without sooner or later being brought under God's discipline? . . . But I must close. Soon the king will scrutinize his guests. Blessed is he who then has God's approval on his words and deeds!

This statement, as Nils Peterson himself explains, was addressed originally to the readers of Chicagobladet. *When that paper would not print it, the article was published in* Missions-Wännen *and hence to a different group of readers.*

The piece is clearly rhetorical, that is, it is written to persuade people who opposed the organizational meeting and the resulting Covenant that "Free" and Covenant are much closer than they realize. In trying to achieve this result, Peterson casts a shimmer over the organizational proceedings that tends to distort some of the facts.

I shall adduce only one of several possible examples. Peterson says in connection with the organizational meeting, "The meeting reached a result far beyond our expectations. . . . All were willing to sacrifice their old symbola and their priestly status that had existed in the synods. All was sacrificed for a biblical foundation. . . . "

Some of what Peterson claims was true. The meeting did achieve an unexpected unity, but the pastoral and creedal problems were not solved; they were merely passed over, and have remained with us for a century. It may be well to point out that the Mission Synod and the Ansgar Synod never did achieve any "priestly status" for their clergy, and that the symbola were not easily jettisoned. In fact, it could be persuasively argued that one of the lacks of the Mission Synod—less noticeable in the Ansgar Synod—was the lack of training and discipline in the clergy. A better educated and more secure pastoral group would have been able to deal more effectively with the Martenson-Princell intrusions. In the face of these disturbances the leadership of the Mission Synod, with some exceptions, tended to withdraw.

The creedal cleansing was no simpler. Björk remained staunchly Lutheran all his life, and in the first decade of the Covenant's history there were several pastoral defections to the Augustana Synod. Some of the pastors who stayed in the Covenant felt drawn in the same direction but had no opportunity to move.

APPENDIX E

Skogsbergh's Ecclesiology

In *A Precious Heritage,* a recent historical volume about Covenant life in the Northwest Conference, Philip J. Anderson gives us an important insight not only into the early life of the Minneapolis Tabernacle (the First Covenant Church), but also into the temperament of its renowned pastor, the Rev. E. August Skogsbergh.

Skogsbergh came to the Tabernacle in 1884 and served it for a quarter of a century. In 1909 he moved west to the Covenant parish in Seattle. By that time, writes Anderson, "Skogsbergh's health had suffered; he was tired and overworked; and between 1900 and 1905 the Tabernacle had lost over 250 members (down to 734). By 1910 it was at a low of 660" (p.73).

Anderson goes on to comment on this situation in a note:

> In his memoirs (*Minnen och upplevelser*) Skogsbergh wrote of his con-
> flict between pastoral work and itinerant preaching missions. More and
> more the church chafed because of his absences. He left in January,
> 1909, exactly twenty-five years after he came with the thought: "Why
> should I let myself be tied with a calf rope any longer? No, I want to get
> out. I want to get out!" (*Minnen*, p.264). Skogsbergh thought pastoral
> work to be far more demanding than evangelism, and he was extremely
> critical of the large number of evangelists who were in it for their own
> gain. In fact, Skogsbergh thought that they comprised the majority. But
> his own love for the lost could not be contained. It is well expressed in
> the Swedish ditty he loved to quote:
> I must go, I must go!
> While the day is aglow.
> I must be at my fishing again (n.28, p.140).

There can be no doubt that Skogsbergh's temperament made pastoral work a chore. These negative predilections affected his work as a builder and shepherd of an established congregation.

Of course, other factors also served to erode the large membership of the Minneapolis church in this period. Among these factors were the extension of the periphery of the city itself by the growth of the suburbs and the increase in popularity and use of the automobile. But apart from demography, Skogsbergh was not ever a dedicated churchman in the sense that he could work happily for the day-to-day development of the structured church. He was a fisherman and neither shepherd nor farmer.

This does not mean that he failed to see the value of organization and accountability. He tells in his memoirs (*Minnen*, p.157) of the sad state of affairs he found in the North Side (Chicago) Mission Church in the late 1870s. There was virtually no organization of the membership or the ministry before Skogsbergh's arrival. Hence he set to work to give the congregation some order. He manifested the same administrative abilities in organizing the South Side (Chicago) Mission Tabernacle in 1877 and in getting a building erected; he was also involved in the construction of the Minneapolis Tabernacle a few years later. Organizationally he helped with the founding of the Northwest Conference in 1884 and with the establishment of the Covenant in 1885.

But his passion was evangelism, and he admits that his frequent and extended absences from the churches he served did impact their corporate life (*Minnen*, p.182). That this was not just a subjective impression is indicated by the Tabernacle (Chicago) church records available in the Covenant Archives.

Skogsbergh came to Chicago in October, 1876. He had been invited to the North Side Mission congregation to assist its ailing pastor, J.M. Sanngren, and especially to work among the growing numbers of Swedish immigrants who were beginning to flood the Midwest. From the very start Skogsbergh became deeply involved in preaching the Gospel to these newcomers. He tells of extending his preaching ministry to a group of Swedes meeting on Chicago's South Side; he also started with a regular Sunday afternoon preaching assignment at Moody Church.

While still in Sweden and even before he reached his twenty-fifth birthday, Skogsbergh had begun his career as a folk evangelist, especially in the area around Lake Vätter. He drew large crowds, even if we may wonder at his statistics (he reports crowds of 10,000 at some of his outdoor meetings), but there is no reason to doubt his reputation as a proclaimer of the Gospel. This reputation preceded him to North America with the result that within a few months of his arrival here, he was being invited to preach in the immigrant settlements in St. Paul and Minneapolis as well as those developing in Illinois.

In the meantime he continued his flourishing work on Chicago's South Side, especially to a group of believers and seekers temporarily accommodated at the meeting hall of the Svithiod Society at 29th and State Streets. Here his ministry was an instant and phenomenal success, extending even to the blasé habitués of the society. In February, 1877, Skogsbergh's converts were ready to form a congregation, and on November 18 the same year they dedicated an imposing red brick building at 30th and LaSalle Streets, an edifice seating some 1,200.

An enterprise so auspiciously begun would seem to augur well for the future, but its rapid start was due to the popularity of its young pastor and within the next seven years this popularity was almost its undoing. Because of the frequent and extended absences of Skogsbergh, who earned the reputation of the "Swedish Moody," the church began to suffer not only from faulty administration but from its lack of a doctrine of the church and of church life. This circumstance was further exacerbated by the church's refusal to continue as an integral part of the larger denominational scene. Thus in 1881, under the influence of some "free" spirits, the congregation withdrew from the Mission Synod and not much later it had to suffer the pain of a division, with a significant number of members joining a layperson named Andrew Lantz and departing for a new identity as a "Free" church.

Some of this lack of an effective church doctrine was no doubt due to Skogsbergh's absenteeism, as he himself admits, but some of it must be attributed to his own labile ecclesiology. In 1876 he made contact with a young man named John Martenson. Martenson was converted through Skogsbergh's preaching, and because he was a printer and something of a projector, he soon set to work to publish a Swedish religious and political newspaper which he called *Chicagobladet*. In this enterprise he sought for and got the moral support of Skogsbergh. Within the next decade the Skogsbergh-Martenson friendship was to have serious consequences for the work among the Lutheran Mission Friends. Partly through the influence of Martenson, Skogsbergh's ideas about denominational life took on a freer cast and, although he remained personally loyal to the Mission Synod which had called him into ministry, given him a significant role among the immigrant people, and ordained him to his pastoral calling, his lack of clarity in ecclesiological matters complicated developments at the time of the organization of the Covenant.

Meanwhile, as we have indicated, the Chicago Tabernacle's infrastructure was giving way. The Covenant Archives, although enriched by an increasing number of microfilms of church records, lacks the Tabernacle minutes for the period 1877-1883. But from other sources, it is obvious that the congregation was floundering.

The entries in the church registry (which *are* available for this period) are so scanty as to be of doubtful value. When compared with those of subsequent periods, these early entries reveal the absence of a firm congregational fabric.

Skogsbergh served the church until December 31, 1883. In 1882 he added a further activity to his already large extracongregational program; he began to publish a Christmas annual which he called *Christlig Chrönika (Christian Chronicle)*.* Some of the contents of this publication were fillers, clipped from Swedish or Swedish-American publications or from American ones and furnished with a Swedish translation. There were many such annuals published at this time among the immigrants and most of them borrowed widely without concern for copyright. What strikes us in the contents of *Christlig Chrönika* hence is not its originality but its fairly strong emphasis on materials from the millenarian circle. This circle dominated much of evangelical life in the last decades of the last and the first decades of the present century. Its ultimate theological source was unquestionably the ideology of Darby, but on the American scene and under the softening influence of D.L. Moody it changed character somewhat and is hence difficult to define precisely. But it is possible to identify some of its modes and adherents.

Put simply, this milieu was characterized by a dispensational eschatology and by an ecclesiology that was both minimal and other-worldly. Under Moody's influence this ecclesiology tended to become more optimistic than in the hands of Darby and often found its optimal form in mass evangelism and intense missionary activity.

In any event, Skogsbergh's fairly frequent sympathetic references to persons from this milieu would suggest that the Swedish-American evangelist was not unaffected by it. Many of these references are found in the *Christlig Chrönika*, and although we cannot claim that the milieu was solely responsible for his ecclesiological bias, we can certainly note its impact.

*Sigurd Westberg, Covenant archivist, has helpfully investigated available date about *Christlig Chrönika*. The following years and numbers of copies are available in Covenant Archives:

1883	7 copies	1887	6 copies
1884	4 copies	1888	5 copies
1885	2 copies	1889	0 copies
1886	0 copies	1890	4 copies

Almost no specific data about this publication exist. Hence we do not know what the zero tallies for 1886 and 1889 mean. It seems probable that since not a single copy is available, no annuals were published for those years. Skogsbergh research is complicated by the fact that relatively little in the way of personal papers has survived.

In the pages of the *Christlig Chrönika,* published 1883-1890, the following people or subjects are given a prominent place in the materials. They point to the Moody milieu as it was influenced by the thinking of J.N. Darby. No effort has been made to classify or analyze these references, but they include, among others: Harry Moorhouse; J.G. Princell; Mrs. Grattan Guiness; Major D.W. Whittle; Leander W. Munhall; the D.L. Moody schools in Northfield; the Northfield Conference lectures featuring William E. Blackstone and Arthur Tappan Pierson, both millenarian stalwarts; the Prophetic Conference in Chicago in 1886, at which Princell served as a lecturer; and some Northfield Conference notes from the year 1880.

The attraction of this milieu for Skogsbergh is at least suggested by these facts. This attraction did not erode his loyalty toward the Mission Synod or later toward the Covenant and their people, but it probably affected his ecclesiology. If the English language had not been a barrier for him, it is possible that his ministry may have included a much larger dependence on the methodology and spirit of this group than was, in fact, the case.

APPENDIX F

Doughty's Questions

In his study of the Doughty case, Don Robinson includes a refer-ence to questions with which Doughty confronted Earl Dahl-strom and Henry Gustafson at the Annual Meeting in Rockford, Illinois in 1954 (p.333). Robinson writes:

The first correspondence that occurred between Pastor Doughty and Bethany Covenant Church and North Park concerning the theological integrity of the seminary's faculty occurred in 1954. The letter, dated June 8, 1954, and signed by both Pastor Doughty and the church chair-man, Robert Elde, was written to Harold A. Anderson, chairman of the Board of Education for the schools. The letter is very direct in its intent, stating:

> This letter is not intended in any way to create ill will or schism. Nor is it our intention to in any way embarrass these men. We feel that it is merely the exercise of our rights as Covenant people to make inquiry concerning the men who are to occupy teaching positions in our semi-nary. We as a church have no desire to arouse or engage in controversy on these matters. Nor do we question the right of these men to their own viewpoints. We only desire a forthright declaration by these men as to what they believe.

The inquiry was prompted by the proposed additions to the seminary teaching staff. The proposed additions to the staff were Dr. Earl Dahl-strom and Henry Gustafson. The church was requesting clarification

478

from Harold A. Anderson as to "where these men stand relative to the historic evangelical position of the Covenant." The letter then goes on to ask the following:

1. What do they believe concerning the literary nature of the first three chapters of Genesis? Do they hold that these are history in the same sense that chapters 4 through 50 are history, or do they hold that these are myth in the sense that they are pictorial representations of religious truth?
2. Do they believe that the Genesis cosmology is a purification of pre-Babylonian and Babylonian mythology, or do they believe that these are corruptions of the Genesis account?
3. With regard to the creation of living creatures in the Genesis account, do they believe that God created finished products within each species, or do they hold to some form of evolutionary development?
4. Do they hold to the miracles of the Old Testament or do they question some of these? For instance, do they believe the ax head really floated as recorded in 2 Kings 6:1-7 or do they have some doubts about this?
5. Do they hold that the inspiration of the Hebrew-Christian Scriptures differs in degree only, or in kind, as compared with all other religious and secular writings?
6. With regard to Jesus Christ, do they hold to an Incarnation which necessitates a Virgin Birth, or does their viewpoint allow room for a normal biological conception?
7. With regard to one aspect of the atonement: Do they believe that the entrance of sin erected a barrier to forgiveness within the Godhead, which barrier was effectively removed by God at the Cross, or do they believe that sin erected a barrier in man only and that the work of the Cross was directed toward removal of the same?
8. In regard to the resurrection of Jesus Christ, do they believe that the dead body placed in the tomb was the object of resurrection, or do they believe that no one knows what became of the body, and the Christ in his subsequent appearances was, in reality, only a spirit presence to the disciples?
9. With regard to a specific aspect of eschatology, do they hold to a post-millennial, pre-millennial, or a-millennial position?

APPENDIX G

The Stewards

At the Covenant Annual Meeting in Worcester, Massachusetts, in June, 1955, I was invited to preach a sermon on "stewardship." I was to consider the topic, not from the perspective of contemporary church usage (that is, as the management of money), but from that of the New Testament community. I found that in the early Church, as in 1 Corinthians 4:1, stewardship referred to taking care of "the mysteries of God," that is, the Gospel. Three Greek words carry this meaning in the New Testament: *oikonomos* (our word "economist," that is, "household," "manager"); *epitropos* (our word "overseer"); and *episkopos* (our word "bishop," "overviewer").

Although I am not a Greek scholar, I found the little word study around "stewardship" intriguing, and during the past thirty years it has helped me understand the historical development of the Church somewhat better.

Because, for good reasons, the Church began to professionalize itself and handed more and more responsibilities to people in fixed roles, overseeing soon became the province of the "religious." The sticky problem of the relation to Church and State largely concerns how far the stewardship of the two bodies should extend. The Reformation found a partial solution by giving the task of stewardship to the State. In America, by contrast, the stewardship of the Church became the province of the clergy and the laity. Here gradually a further division of responsibilities took place: the clergy devoted itself to matters spiritual; the laity concerned itself with indispensable fiscal concerns. In that shift "stewardship" came to mean less and less caring for, that is, taking care of, "the mysteries of God," and more and more being responsible for raising money and handling real property, bricks and mortar, investments and temporal securities.

Fortunately the distinction between the two kinds of stewardship is in the process of eroding. The robust concern for the temporalities that characterize the New Testament is becoming more and more the province of both clergy and laity in the Covenant, and the mysteries of faith, the meaning of the Gospel for the everyday existence of all believers, are seen as the responsibility of the whole Church.

It is in this spirit that the names of those who have served on the Executive and Administrative Boards of the Covenant during the past decade are presented in this appendix. But I confess to a real difficulty in making this selection.

After walking through twelve decades of Covenant prehistory and history and being in touch with literally thousands of names, the conviction grows that there is no way of encompassing these massed legions of Christian saints within meaningful classifications. I know no categories that would give them identity except that of "friends of Jesus" and then all would have to be included.

The writer of Hebrews set out to select Israelites who might fit into his particular category of "faith," and the poor man, though gifted with special inspiration, was forced to yield graciously to the enormity of his task in words that would continue to be the solace of chroniclers. "And what shall I more say? For the time would fail me to tell of Gideon and of Barak and of Samuel and of Jephthah; of David also, and of Samuel and of the prophets" (Hebrews 11:32).

Not enough time, not enough ink or pens or computers or energy. All fails before this heaving, foaming sea of people, wave upon wave, crash upon crash, almost but not quite forever since we are reminded by St. Anselm that the number of created souls is finite and not infinite. Confronted, nonetheless, with this flood of believers we must present "representative" people, as once Emerson. We must deal with the few in order to convey how significant the many have been.

This is the reason why our thousand pastors are given more attention than our 100,000 laypersons, and why we now recognize a few hundred board members rather than chronicling the myriads of those who have served with fidelity on regional and local committees and boards, and on choirs and Sunday school staffs from Hudson Bay to Ecuador and from Zaire to Nova Zembla.

From the first intimations of dawn among the North American Mission Friends 120 years ago there have been lay workers like Henry Palmblad, A.V. Julin, S.W. Youngquist, C.G. Swanson, Swan Peterson, C.A. Bygel, Alfred Winholst, Nicholas Nelson, Aaron Carlson, John Isaacson, C.R. Carlson, Carolina Sahlstrom, Josephine Princell, Emilie Johnson, and thousands more who have symbolized the Covenant *demos*, the essential citizenry.

They are now represented by the members of the various boards listed in these pages. We owe them all an incredible debt. They have been the volunteers who have filled the ranks, performed distinguished service for Christ and his kingdom, and symbolized the faithful thousands both living and dead who now fill the stands surrounding the active arena.

Executive Board

	Class of		Class of
A. Harold Anderson	1980, 83, 87	John H. Lindberg	1977
Quintin A. Applequist	1986	Wallace N. Lindskoog	1979, 82
Gordon A. Bengtson	1979, 82	Eugene D. Lundberg	1981, 84
Adaline Bjorkman	1980	Bruce R. Magnuson	1987
Paul W. Brandel	1977	DeForest W. Metcalf	1981, 84
Elizabeth M. Carlson	1986	Elom L. Nelson	1978
Ray H. Carlson	1977	Robert W. Nelson	1978
David S. Dahlberg	1978, 81	Samuel D. Paravonian	1986
Malcolm H. Erickson	1981, 84	Elmer B. Pearson	1979, 82
Jack R. Hall	1983	Marilyn J. Peterson	1983
Stanley L. Holme	1980	Robert H. Peterson	1978
Robert A. Honnette	1979	Sheldon W. Peterson	1985, 88
Burton C. Johnson	1987	William L. Peterson, Jr.	1977
Jerome K. Johnson	1986	Wayne L. Stark	1988
Norbert E. Johnson	1979, 82	Burton E. Swardstrom	1985
Paul A. Johnson	1984, 87	Donald E. Wahlquist	1985, 88
Paul E. Larsen	1980, 83	Glen V. Wiberg	1985, 88
Chester E. Larson	1986		

Board of Christian Education

	Class of		Class of
Charles C. Anderson	1983	Sandra C. Lund	1985
Myrtle A. Erickson	1980	Ruth I. Nelson	1989
Alan R. Forsman	1988	Marilyn Nixon	1979
Daniel E. Fullerton	1984	Mark S. Olson	1989
Edwin A. Hallsten, Jr.	1982	Timothy P. Olson	1978
William R. Hausman	1977	Mark T. Pattie III	1990
Alayne Johnson	1982	Kathleen Pearson	1980
Barton F. Johnson	1978	John C. Pearson	1990
Constance Johnson	1977	Dale W. Peterson	1981
Daniel N. Johnson	1983	Judy B. Peterson	1988
Nancy R. Johnson	1985	Richard P. Rabine	1981
Georgia C. Kindall	1984	Jo Ann Sterling	1987
Carl J. King	1979	Paul R. Swanson	1987
Ronald F. Lagerstrom	1981, 86	Pamela J. Wilkins	1986

The Board of Church Growth and Evangelism

The traditional Board of Home Mission was phased out in 1983 together with the Board of Evangelism to make way for a newly created board, that of Church Growth and Evangelism. The functions of both boards were subsumed under the new board, which also provided the opportunity for integration of activity and novel initiatives.

The following persons served on the Board of Home Mission from 1976 to 1983:

	Class of		Class of
James A. Anderson	1985	Harold A. Larson	1984
Marion Anderson	1979	Earl R. Lindgren	1979
Harold V. Carlson	1984	Lee O. Lownsberry	1987
Richard W. Carlson	1978	Kurt A. Miericke	1985
Eleanor N. Claus	1986	Sally L. Mortenson	1983
David A. Elowson	1980	John R. Person	1986
Keith C. Fullerton	1982	Sheldon W. Peterson	1981
Carlos Guzman	1987	Stanley M. Rottrup	1977
Ernest L. Hanson	1980	Helen Samuel	1982
George L. Hedstrom	1982	Ben A. Schellenberg	1977
Jerome K. Johnson	1983	J. Robert Strandmark	1981
Lois Johnson	1978		

The Board of Evangelism was phased out in 1983. The functions of that board were subsumed under those of the newly created Board of Church Growth and Evangelism. The following persons served on the Board of Evangelism from 1976 to 1983:

	Class of		Class of
Stanley W. Anderson	1984	Willie B. Jemison	1979
Marvin Bjorlin	1980	Eldon H. Johnson	1982
Herbert S. Carlson	1985	Darryl L. Larson	1984
Marjorie S. Dean	1977, 83	Albert C. Magnuson	1981
Evangeline Dennis	1982	Wesley W. Nelson	1977
Donald N. Eiken	1987	William R. Notehelfer	1983
Mary Ann Frizen	1986	Burdette R. Palmberg	1978, 86
Dawn L. Fullerton	1985	Marilyn Peterson	1980
Jean Haley	1981	Burton E. Swardstrom	1978
Dean R. Honnette	1987	Don Alan Thomas	1979

The new board, which has members drawn from the rosters of the Boards of Home Mission and Evangelism has had the following membership:

	Class of		Class of
Stanley W. Anderson	1985	Gordon Halverson	1990
Steven W. Armfield	1990	Dean R. Honnette	1987
Harold V. Carlson	1984	Darryl L. Larson	1984, 89
Eleanor N. Claus	1987	Harold A. Larson	1985
Gladys Fryhling	1989	Lee O. Lownsberry	1988
Dawn L. Fullerton	1986	Burdette R. Palmberg	1986
Carlos Guzman	1988		

Board of Covenant Women

	Class of		Class of
Dorothy L. Almquist	1984	Elaine Johnson	1982
Isolde K. Anderson	1987	Lois M. Johnson	1989
Betty M. Carlson	1982	Verna Mae Larson	1981, 86
Margaret D. Carlson	1984	Bonnie Nelson	1983
Ruth H. Cederberg	1981, 86	David A. Peterson	1990
Bonnie A. Eng	1988	Mary Lou Sather	1983
Beth L. Fredrickson	1988	Carol Shimmin Nordstrom	1983
Christine Groppe	1989	Betty E. Vetvick	1980, 85
Shirley M. Hacker	1990	Marva Watts	1987
Marilyn L. Hjelm	1980, 85		

Board of the Ministry

	Class of		Class of
Lloyd F. Alex	1981	Jean C. Lambert	1990
Arthur W. Anderson	1977	Edward Larson	1985
Craig E. Anderson	1986	Robert E. Liljegren	1983
Vernon A. Anderson	1980	Arthur A.R. Nelson	1988
Robert V. Bergquist	1985	Roger J. Nelson	1979
George B. Elia	1990	John C. Notehelfer	1981
Luther M. Englund	1988	William R. Notehelfer	1989
Paul H. Erickson	1989	K. Wesley Olson	1983
Robert L. Erickson	1978	Kent D. Palmquist	1987
Michael A. Halleen	1982	Alton W. Peterson, Jr.	1982
Stanley R. Henderson	1984	William L. Peterson, Jr.	1987
Allan C. Johnson	1985	Paul E. Sparrman	1980
Clifford H. Johnson	1986	Wayne L. Stark	1978
Paul A. Johnson	1979	Gerald V. Stenberg	1984
S. Jerome Johnson	1979	Orville C. Sustad	1984
Albert R. Josephson	1984	Roger W. Wiganosky	1977

Board of Pensions

	Class of		Class of
Russell A. Bankson	1979	Glenn R. Mars	1986
Charles G. Beckstrom	1984	Arnold S. Nelson	1990
David G. Brewick	1986	Mark W. Nelson	1989
Donald A. Carlson	1985	Robert E. Peckenpaugh	1977
James R. Ecklund	1986	William Dean Robertson	1984
M. Gordon Gaddy	1987	Paul T. Stone	1985
Jonathan R. Heintzelman	1982, 87	C. William Storm	1979
Teddy Hogle	1982	E. Marvin Strom	1983
Gordon W. Holmen	1981	Robert V. Thonander	1982
Robert T. Jackson	1988	L. Clayton Tissell	1977
Fred M. Johnson, Jr.	1983	Kenneth R. Wahlberg	1990
Rodney K. Johnson	1978	Donald E. Wahlquist	1981
Lynwood J. Larson	1980	Everett L. Wilson	1980
James R. Lundell	1989	Warren R. Wise	1988
J. Arnold Lundgren	1978		

Board of Publications

	Class of		Class of
Gerald E. Baker	1977	Charles W. Keysor	1990
John S. Benson	1980	Jean C. Lambert	1982
J. David Cassell	1990	David A. Larson	1982
Robert C. Dvorak	1985	Richard M. Lindman	1985
Rose Edin	1979	Janet R. Lundblad	1988
Clifford G. Erickson	1981	Dean A. Nyquist	1984
Grant D. Erickson	1979	Harry A. Nicholls	1989
Alan F. Hearl	1978	George H. Schermer	1980
Mary M. Helfrich	1977	Sharon A. Seeberger	1987
Walter G. Hodgkinson	1978	Melissa Smith-Strongman	1986
Roy M. Hoffman	1983	Joyce Sturdy	1981
William A. Horner	1989	Byron A. Turnquist	1986
Alva M. Johanson	1984	John Wiens	1988
Allan F. Johnson	1983	Albert J. Wollen, Jr.	1987

Board of Benevolence

	Class of		Class of
William R. Ahlem, Jr.	1982, 88	J. Eldon Johnson	1977
Lawrence P. Anderson	1980, 86	S. Jerome Johnson	1990
Gordon A. Bengtson	1989	Thomas S. Johnson	1987
Kenneth L. Block	1983	Bengt Junvik	1977
Paul W. Brandel	1982	Donald E. Lindman	1984
Charles R. Brobst, Sr.	1988	Bruce R. Magnuson	1978
Robert B. Carlson	1977, 84	Donald C. Michealsen	1979
Rolland S. Carlson	1987	Mary V. Miller	1987
Adele Cole	1982	Bruce A. Metcalf	1989
Darryl L. Crow	1982	Lester E. Munson, Sr.	1983
Russell A. Dahlstrom	1979, 86	Norman W. Nelson	1980
Philip E. Danielson	1985	Donald S. Ohannes	1990
Carl D. Elving	1980	Robert H. Peterson	1984, 90
Fred W. Englund	1978	Wallace H. Pratt	1982
Grant D. Erickson	1988	K. Ejnar Rask	1979
James W. Erickson	1977	Wesley H. Ryd	1985
L. Daniel Ericson	1981	William M. Sandstrom	1987
Franklin D. Ferris	1986	Lois M. Satterberg	1988
Walter W. Filkin	1981, 89	Margaret L. Sebastian	1983
Kenneth E. Gundersen	1983	Robert W. Sundeen	1985
Dorothy Harper	1978	Robert A. Swanson	1979, 89
Carl E. Hawkinson	1981	Richard L. Swedberg	1986
Mary M. Helfrich	1990	L. Clayton Tissell	1981
Walter G. Hodgkinson	1984	Glen W. Wilson	1978
Myron E. Isaacson	1981	Vincent E. Young	1977
Alden S. Johnson	1980	Russell P. Zetterlund	1985

Board of World Mission

	Class of		Class of
Craig E. Anderson	1978	Lloyd J. Larson	1984
Delmar L. Anderson	1978	Quentin D. Larson	1979
Philip D. Anderson	1980	Wanda Lemons	1980
Naida H. Aschenbrenner	1989	John H. Lindberg	1985
John S. Bray	1987	Donald E. Logue	1990
Carol L. Bringerud	1987	Betty J. Nelson	1977, 82
Rodney L. Brodin	1989	Melvin H. Nelson	1990
Timothy C. Ek	1977	Quentin D. Nelson	1988
Paul H. Erickson	1981	Philip N. Stenberg	1983
Richard L. Erickson	1978	Robert P. Stromberg, Sr.	1981
Kathleen Fretheim	1985	Wesley C. Swanson	1986
Gladys Fryhling	1979	Donald E. Thorpe	1984
Warren E. Hedstrom	1988	Melsie M. Waldner	1986
Burton C. Johnson	1983	Clarence G. Winstedt	1977
Chester E. Larson	1982		

Board of Directors, North Park College and Theological Seminary

	Class of		Class of
Gordon E. Anderson	1984	Richard L. Joutras	1989
Leonard O. Anderson	1982	Jay A. Kershaw	1988
Lorraine Anderson	1979	Gordon E. Kirk	1990
Quintin A. Applequist	1981	Haddon E. Klingberg, Jr.	1984, 89
Robert W. Ash	1986	Ann Elise Lindgren	1985
W. Reece Bader	1989	Eugene D. Lundberg	1978
Robert A. Berghoff	1983	Dean A. Lundgren	1983, 90
Ruth E. Brewick	1985	Albert C. Magnuson	1990
Robert M. Blomgren	1986	George P. Magnuson	1986
Mary Lou R. Bonander	1989	Donald A. MacPhee	1984
J. Frank Cassell	1977	DeForest W. Metcalf	1977
Margaret J. Cucci	1987	Arthur A.R. Nelson	1981
Stanley A. Edin	1981	John E. Nilson	1979
Timothy C. Ek	1985	Virginia M. Ohlson	1977
C. Milton Ekberg	1977, 81	Leonard A. Olson	1987
Roger E. Erickson	1985	Samuel D. Paravonian	1981
Carolyn P. Fylling	1983	Carlton D. Peterson	1985
Mary Helen Haas	1988	Stuart F. Peterson	1982
Jack R. Hall	1979	Ralph L. Sager	1979
Carl E. Hawkinson	1987	Richard O. Sandquist	1980
Stanley F. Helwig	1983, 89	Leland P. Solie	1987
James E. Holst	1984	Ralph W. Sturdy	1984
Joyce Jackson	1990	Victor A. Sundholm	1978
Arnold W. Johnson, Jr.	1980	Donald A. Sveen	1987
Gordon S. Johnson	1988	Edgar E. Swanson, Jr.	1982
G. Timothy Johnson	1978	Richard J. Swanson	1980
Ivan M. Johnson	1982	John A. Tyler	1982
Marianne Johnson	1978	Richard B. Walbert	1984
Sherry Johnson	1988	Marilyn Whisler	1980
John E. Jones	1986	Paul L. Ziemer	1986

References Cited

Åberg, Göran. 1972. *Enhet och frihet (Unity and Freedom)*. Lund.

Abraham, William J. 1984. *The Coming Great Revival*. San Francisco.

Anderson, Axel T. 1928-29. *Svenska missionsförbundet inre missionen*. Stockholm.

Anderson, Glenn P., ed. 1980. *Covenant Roots: Sources and Affirmations*. Chicago.

Anderson, Philip J. 1984. *A Precious Heritage*. Minneapolis

Anderson, Robert H. 1960. "Analysis of Congregational Aid to Scandinavian Churches." B.D. research paper, North Park Theological Seminary, Chicago.

Bass, Clarence B. 1960. *Backgrounds to Dispensationalism*. Grand Rapids.

Booth, William. 1880. *In Darkest England*. London.

BOS. *By One Spirit*. See Olsson, Karl A. 1962.

Bowman, C.V. 1907. *Missionsvännerna i Amerika*. Minneapolis.

Bredberg, William. 1937. "Bibeltrogna vänner." *Svenska folkrörelser*, vol. 2. Gunnar Westin, editor. Stockholm.

-----. 1937b. "Ungerth, Lars." *Svenska folkrörelser*, vol. 2. Gunnar Westin, editor. Stockholm.

-----. 1948. *P.P. Waldenströms verksamhet till 1878*. Stockholm.

Bredberg, William, and Oscar Lövgren, 1953. *Genom Guds nåd*. Stockholm.

Brolund, Eric. 1938. *Missionsvännerna*, Chicago.

"Bryan, William Jennings." *The Encyclopaedia Britannica*, 14th ed., 4:298,299.

Carlson, Leland H. 1941. *A History of North Park College*. Chicago.

Darby, John Nelson. 1867-83. *The Collected Writings of John Nelson Darby*, 34 vols. William Kelley, editor. London.

Dayton, Donald W. 1976. *Discovering an Evangelical Heritage*. New York.

Edman, Irwin. ed. 1928. *The Works of Plato*. New York.

Elmen, Paul H. 1935. "The Swedeless Covenant." *Covenant Conference Review*.

Evangelii basun I. 1881. E. August Skogsbergh and A.L. Skoog, editors. Chicago.

FF. *A Family of Faith*. See Olsson, Karl A. 1975.

Fleming H. Revel, publ. 1886. *Prophetic Studies of the International Prophetic Conference, Chicago, November, 1886*. Chicago.

Franson, Fredrik. 1897. *Himlauret (The Heavenly Clock)*. Stockholm.

Franson, Fredrik, ed. 1882. *Utförligt Referat öfwer förhandlingarna wid den för de profetsika ämnenas studier afsedde konferensen i Chicago, Amerika den 13-18 April 1881 (Detailed Report of the Proceedings at the Study of Prophetic Subjects Which Took Place at the Conference in Chicago, America, 13-18 April, 1881)*. Kristinehamn.

GGN. *Genom Guds nåd*. See Bredberg, William and Oscar Lövgren. 1953.

GNAFS. *Genom norra Amerikas Förenta stater*. See Waldenström, P. 1890.

Hale, Frederick. 1981. "The Swedish Department of the Chicago Theological Seminary." *Bulletin of the Congregational Library*. 33 (Winter).

Hillerdahl, Gunnar. N.d. *History of Swedish Darbyism*. Unpublished manuscript.

Kinder, Herman, and Werner Hilgemann. 1978. *The Anchor Atlas of World History, Vol. 2*. New York.

Kraus, Norman. 1958. *Dispensationalism in America*. Richmond.

Latourette, K.S. 1929. *A History of Christian Missions in China*. New York.

-----. 1958-62. *Christianity in a Revolutionary Age*, 5 vols. New York.

Linderholm, Emanuel. 1925. *Pingströrelsen i Sverige (The Pentecostal Movement in Sweden)*. Stockholm.

Lindorm, Erik. 1937. *Oscar II och hans tid, en bokfilm*. Stockholm.

Lindsell, Harold. 1979. *The Bible in Balance.* Grand Rapids.

Linge, Carl. 1951. *Fredrik Franson.* Uppsala.

Lionstone, A. Alf. 1933. *Stars in the Night.* Minneapolis.

Lövgren, Oscar. 1964 *Psalm och sånglexikon.* Falköping.

Lund, Nils. 1935. *Outline Studies in the Book of Revelations.* Chicago.

-----. 1942. *Chiasmus in the New Testament, a Study in Form-geschichte.* Chapel Hill, North Carolina.

Miller, Perry. 1933. *Orthodoxy in Massachusetts.* Cambridge.

McPherson, Dave. 1975. *The Incredible Cover-up.* Plainfield, N.J.

Nelson, A.P. 1901. *The History of Puritans and Pilgrims.* Boston.

-----. 1906. *History of the Swedish Mission Friends in America.* Minneapolis.

Nelson, Wesley W. 1975. *Crying for My Mother.* Chicago.

NO. See Nyvall, David, and Karl A. Olsson.

Nyvall, C.J. 1959. *Travel Memories of America 1876,* Translated by E. Gustav Johnson. Chicago.

Nyvall, David, and Karl A. Olsson. 1954. *The Evangelical Covenant Church.* Chicago.

Nyvall, David. 1974. *My Father's Testament.* Translated by Eric G. Hawkinson. Chicago.

Olsson, Karl A. 1953. "Covenant Beginnings: Mystical," *The Covenant Quarterly* 13(May); "Covenant Beginnings: Communal," *The Covenant Quarterly* 13(August); "Covenant Beginnings: Doctrinal,"
Our Covenant, An Illustration Annual of the Evangelical Covenant Church of America. 1927-1964.
The Covenant Quarterly 13(November).

-----. 1962. *By One Spirit.* Chicago.

-----. 1966. "Controversy on Inspiration in the Covenant of Sweden." *The Covenant Quarterly* 24(February).

-----. 1975. *A Family of Faith.* Chicago.

Pethrus, Lewi. 1953. *Den anständiga sannigen,* vol. 1. Stockholm.

Princell, Josephine. 1916. *J.G. Princells levnadsminnen.* Chicago.

Rhoden, Nils. 1937. "Hans J. Lundborg." *Svenska folkrörelser,* vol. 2. Gunnar Westin, ed. Stockholm.

Robinson, Donald T. 1978. "William C. Doughty: One Man's Cause for Concern in the Covenant." Unpublished, Covenant Archives.

Sandeen, Ernest R. 1970. *The Roots of Fundamentalism.* Chicago.

Sandstrom, David H. 1985. *Landmarks of the Spirit.* New York.

Sånger till lammets lov. 1875. Compiled and translated by Erik Nyström. Chicago.

Soneson, Jöns. 1937. "Hall, Nellie." *Svenska folkrörelser,* vol. 2. Gunnar Westin, editor. Stockholm.

Stephenson, George M. *Religious Aspects of Swedish Immigration.* New York.

Sweet, William Warren. 1950. *The Story of Religion in America,* rev. ed. New York.

Tabernacle Church in Chicago. 1883-84. *Minutes, Svenska Tabernakelförsamlingen i Chicago, 1883-84.* Microfilm in the Covenant Archives.

Torjesen, Edvard T. N.d. *Fredrik Franson after 100 years.* Chicago.

-----. 1977. *The Doctrine of the Church in the Life and Work of Fredrik Franson.* Chicago.

Walan, Bror. 1964. *Församlingstanken i Svenska Missionsförbundet.* Stockholm.

Waldenström, P. 1873. *Om försoningens betydelse (On the Meaning of the Atonement).* Stockholm.

-----. 1881 *Handlingar rörande svenskarnas andliga och sociala förhållande på vissa platser i Amerikas Förenta stater.* Microfilm in the Covenant Archives.

-----. 1890. *Genom norra Amerikas Förenta stater.* Gävle.

-----. 1901. *Låt oss behålla vår gamla Bibel.* Stockholm.

Weber, Timothy P. 1983. *Living in the Shadow of the Second Coming: American Premillennialism 1875-1982.* Grand Rapids.

Westin, Gunnar. 1932. *Emigranterna och kyrkan.* Stockholm.

-----. 1937. "De religiosä folkrörelsernas uppkomnst i vårt land" (The Origin of Religious Folk Movements in Our Land). *Svenska folkrörelser,* vol. 2. Gunnar Westin, ed. Stockholm.

Covenant Yearbook.

Youngqvist, C.M. 1892-93. "Review of the Free Evangelical Mission among the Swedes in America," 19 chapters. *Hem-Missionären.*

Index